SOUL FOOD

SOUL FOOD

CLASSIC CUISINE
FROM THE DEEP SOUTH

Sheila Ferguson

GROVE PRESS
NEW YORK

To the three most precious gifts ever bestowed upon me,

my husband, Chris, and my twin daughters, Alicia and

Alexandria Robinson, I dedicate this book.

For without their love, support, patience, sacrifice, and

inexhaustible tastebuds, this book could never have been

written.

Text and black-and-white photographs copyright © 1989 by Sheila Ferguson

First published in Great Britain in 1989 by
George Weidenfeld & Nicolson Limited, London

Published simultaneously in Canada
Printed in the United States of America

Library of Congress Cataloging-in-Publication Data

Ferguson, Sheila.
  Soul Food/by Sheila Ferguson.
      p.   cm.
  Bibliography: p.
  Includes index.
  ISBN-10: 0-8021-3283-9
  ISBN-13: 978-0-8021-3283-3
  1. Cookery, Afro-American. I. Title.
TX715.F337   1989
  641.59'296073 – dc20   89-9028

Designed by Harry Green

Grove Press
an imprint of Grove/Atlantic, Inc.
841 Broadway
New York, NY 10003

07 08 09 10   20 19 18 17 16 15 14 13 12

CONTENTS

*S*PECIAL THANKS

*F*irst, I would like to thank the players, the people who fought so hard to make this book the very best they knew how: Mandy Little and Sheila Watson, my literary agents, whose initial belief in my writing ability startled me; Vicky Hayward, editor and friend *extraordinaire*, whose artistry in editing is clearly visible throughout these pages and without whose knowledge, experience, and strength of character I might have collapsed towards the end (well, I did collapse, but she sat me back up at the word processor, assuaged my tears, and sent me straight back to work); Ralph Hancock, for his nocturnal wizardry at interpreting the two languages in question—American and English!; Peggy and Lewis Robinson, my wonderful in-laws, who upon seeing me almost in traction pounding away at the typewriter gave me a word processor; Felicity Luard of Weidenfeld and Nicolson for her belief in the concept of soul food and her ability to liaise with all parties with dignity and charm; and Michael Dover, who came, saw, tasted, and decided to publish in the first place.

Next we have the soul food cooks, family members and dear friends who contributed so very much: in Philadelphia, Ms Linda Ferguson, Mrs Odessa Greene, Mrs Evelyn Battle (Aunt Peacie), Mrs Beverly Yancy, Mr Walter Ferguson, Mrs Ann Chambers, and Kenny Stovall and everybody at Sonny's Barbecue Restaurant; in New Jersey, Mrs Clarice Johnson (Cousin C.J.), Miss Renata Johnson, Mrs Alice Johnson, Mrs Lilli-Mae Johnson, Mrs Hester Scott, Mrs Claudette Moore, Mrs Geri Stowers, Mrs Bobbi-Jean Jackson, Mrs Daisy Smith, and Mr Aredias (Ollie) Oliver.

Finally to all those writers who have, quite unknowingly, given me hours of pleasurable reading. No one person ever writes a book. So I would like to thank all those authors whose knowledge and creative insight showed me just how much there always is to be learnt and helped me to shape my ideas. They have elicited argument and controversy within me and I have tried to use their knowledge to the best of my ability—but they are not responsible for any mistakes, you understand.

My deepest feelings of gratitude go out especially to two writers with whom I have corresponded and who have given me greatly valued moral support: Mr John Martin Taylor of Charleston and Mr John Thorne of Boston.

Special thanks to Mr André Jacquemin of Redwood Recording Studios for allowing us to film the cover shot there, and to anyone whom I might inadvertently have overlooked.

SO WHAT IS SOUL FOOD?

Ah, soul food. Soul food is just what the name implies. It is soulfully cooked food or richly flavored foods good for your ever-loving soul. But soul food is much more than a clever name penned by some unknown author. It is a legacy clearly steeped in tradition; a way of life that has been handed down from generation to generation, from one black family to another, by word of mouth and sleight of hand. It is rich in both history and variety of flavor.

To cook soul food you must use all of your senses. You cook by instinct but you also use smell, taste, touch, sight, and, particularly, sound. You learn to hear by the crackling sound when it's time to turn over the fried chicken, to smell when a pan of biscuits is just about to finish baking, and to feel when a pastry's just right to the touch. You taste, rather than measure, the seasonings you treasure; and you use your eyes, not a clock, to judge when that cherry pie has bubbled sweet and nice. These skills are hard to teach quickly. They must be felt, loving, and come straight from the heart and soul.

Ah, but when you taste good soul food then it'll take ahold of your soul and hang your unsuspecting innards out to dry. It's that shur-'nuf everlovin' down-home stick-to-your-ribs kinda food that keeps you glued to your seat long after the meal is over and done with, enabling you to sit back, relax, and savor the gentle purrings of a well satisfied stomach, feeling that all's right with the world. Yes suh! As the good Baptist minister says every Sunday morning, Yes suh!

Let me give you a for instance. Say you fry up a batch of fresh chicken to a golden-brown crispness, but you keep the insides so moist, so tender, that all that good juice just bursts forth with the first crunchy bite. Then maybe you bake up some cornbread and buttermilk biscuits, ready to smother with freshly churned butter, and you cook up a big pot of collard greens and pot likka seasoned with ham hocks, onion, vinegar, red pepper flakes, and just enough hot sauce to set fire to your palate. Just a little fire though! Now you pile on a mound of slightly chilled home-made potato salad and fill a pitcher full of ice-cold lemonade ready to cool out that fire. And when you've eaten your way through all of that, you finish it off with a big healthy hunk of pecan pie topped with a scoop of home-made vanilla ice cream. Now, tell me the truth – do you think you could move after a meal like that? Only for second helpings, of course!

But that's just the fun-loving, toe-tapping, belly-busting, knee-slapping, thirst-quenching, foot-stomping side of a cuisine that has its more serious side too. For the basic framework of this style of cooking was carved out in the deep South by the black slaves, in part for their white masters and in part for their own survival in the slave quarters. As such, it is, like the blues or jazz, an inextricable part of the African-Americans' struggle to survive and to express themselves. In this sense it is a *true* American cuisine, because it wasn't imported into America by immigrants like so many other ethnic offerings. It is the cuisine of the American dream, if you like. Because what can't be cured must be endured. As John Egerton so aptly puts it in *Southern Food*,

> In the most desolate and hopeless of circumstances, blacks caught in the grip of slavery often exhibited uncommon wisdom, beauty, strength, and creativity. The kitchen was one of the few places where their imagination and skill could have free rein and full expression, and there they often excelled. From the elegant breads and meats and sweets of plantation cookery to the inventive genius of Creole cuisine, from beaten biscuits to bouillabaisse, their legacy of culinary excellence is all the more impressive, considering the extremely adverse conditions under which it was compiled.

A slave's rations were supposed to consist of a peck of corn and three pounds of bacon or salt pork a week, along with molasses, clabber, and small rations of seasonal fruit and vegetables. Yet with just these meager rations, the slaves managed to find a measure of variety. Around those two basic staples, corn and pork, many of the soul food dishes evolved. The pork was highly seasoned and the fat cut with a combination of red hot peppers, vinegar, and onion to cook up the likes of fatback, chit'lin's, sow belly, trotters, cracklin's, sausages, and head cheese. The corn was sometimes thrown into the fire and roasted as whole hominies, often wrapped in old cabbage leaves; or otherwise ground, either finely into meal to make pones or more coarsely into hominy grits eaten rather like a porridge or like Italian polenta. Many of these techniques had been learnt by the first settlers from the American Indians. Sometimes a dish used both, as in cracklin' bread flavored with bacon bits, or a simple dish of fatback rolled in cornmeal and fried up just as it was.

The slaves continued to look to their own resourcefulness to supplement their meat rations. They drew upon skills remembered from their native lands to hunt. Since they were rarely allowed to bear arms of any kind, they became expert at designing and building traps. If it ran on the ground they could surely catch it; if it flew in the air they could surely devise a slingshot for it. Their most common quarry was raccoons – from which the derogatory name of coon came – squirrels, rabbits, an abundance of wild fowl like turkeys, geese, and guinea hens. Occasionally they might catch larger game like a groundhog or a bear.

But the most noted and controversial of all their game fare was the 'possum. As Eugene D. Genovese noted in *Roll, Jordan, Roll*, it was a favorite meat of African-Americans. 'The flesh of the coon,' wrote Solomon Northup, who had lived as a free man in the North before being kidnaped into slavery (a fate, I might add, which befell many a free black) and who did not suffer from nostalgia for the old plantation in Louisiana, 'is palatable, but verily there is nothing in all butcherdom so delicious as a roasted 'possum.' Today there is a stigma attached to eating 'possum. I find that ironic, considering all the other things we are prepared to eat. Why should a li'l ole itty-bitty 'possum evoke such emotion?

Sometimes the slaves were allowed to own a few chickens, and they would plant seeds that they had brought with them out of Africa – we can never know how these were carried. In this humble way many precious foods were introduced to the South: the tender collard green, which produced the tasty and nutritious juice called pot likka on which slave children were fed to keep them strong and healthy; the ever wonderful black-eyed pea, which records show arrived in the year 1674; watermelon; yam; okra; sesame, which in the Carolinas is still called by its African name of benne, and is supposed to bring good luck. Nor is it difficult to see how our taste for hotter and hotter foods was honed: to chilli peppers from the Caribbean was added malaguetta pepper from West Africa, which was used heavily throughout the slave trade because it was thought to prevent dysentery. As seasonings, they gave poor cuts of meat more zest. Both in North America and in the Caribbean blacks used near-lethal doses of hefty spices, and that taste was quickly appreciated and taken up by their white masters.

Rations were usually issued once a week, on Saturday nights, and then the righteous jubilation would commence in the slave quarters. The slaves pretty much insisted on having Sundays as their day to worship. Of course, no alcohol was allowed. Don't be ridiculous! It was alright for white folk, but bad for African and American Indian blood. However, that didn't matter. The slaves had their own way to lift up their souls. They would pray, they would sing, and they would eat! They would throw pork skins into the fire until they crackled, bake up some cornpones nice and brown using bacon fat, and cook up any game or eggs that had been found and hadn't been confiscated.

Then they would sing and dance. The most vivid account of this comes from a book entitled *Black Magic*, written by Milton Meltzer and the amazing Langston Hughes, a writer who first came into prominence during the time of the early twentieth-century Black Renaissance. Patting juba, as it was called – creating rhythms for dancing by using the heartbeat as an inner metronome and striking the hands first on the knees, then on the shoulders, while keeping time with the feet and singing – soon became an accompaniment for all kinds of new dance steps. There were the wonderful jubas and jigs created by the black field hands; the cakewalks done by house servants; and, most popular of all, the plantation stick dance, which was soon imitated by white minstrels and performed as a comedy routine.

The songs were unsophisticated, but they fulfilled their purpose: the slaves could let go of their souls and find solace in the little they had. In Congo Square, an area down in New Orleans, slaves would often gather on Sundays and holidays, much to the delight of crowds of local whites and Northern tourists who would congregate to watch and listen to the mystifying magic of Africans playing drums and dancing wildly. Sometimes a dozen drums would be playing simultaneously, together with all other forms of home-made percussion, creating a magnificent array of complex rhythms, pulses, and beats. Some musicologists believe that it was in that old dusty place that jazz was born. Certainly a primal beat was displayed in its finest form.

Later it became an object of fascination to the white world, including such notable people as Edgar Allen Poe and the poet and musician Sidney Lanier:

'Here's music in its rudest form, consisting of rhythm alone ... the most curious noise, yet, in such perfect order it furnishes music to dance by ... I have never seen it equalled in my life.' Sounds just like soul music to me! Unfortunately, few of the early slave or coon songs, religious or secular, were written down; just as little effort was made to record the genuine cooking of the slave quarters.

Slaves who were taken into the plantation owner's house as cooks and other servants soon learned to combine their own soul food style with the cuisine of their masters. Their repertoire stretched through biscuits, deep-dish fruit pies and pecan muffins made with refined white flour, grandiose hunt breakfasts with fine smoked hams, amazing picnics with barbecued meats and refreshing mint juleps. In New Orleans they also learned the cuisines of French and Spanish masters who came and went, leaving behind the mingled influences and greater sophistication of Creole food: bisques and jambalayas, mousses, and brandied sauces. But alongside all of those they were also making their own soulful gravies and cornpones, frying up a mess of chicken and savoring yams cooked in any number of ways. And soul food was on the move at every social level, especially where racial divides were less sharp.

As the poorer Africans lived alongside the Indians, in both freedom and slavery, and intermarried – one of my great-great-grandmothers, Vashti, was a Shawnee and another, named Sally Ferguson, a Choctaw – they gained from them their knowledge of native vegetables, roots, and herbs. The most famous result of this cultural blending is gumbo. The word itself comes from an African name for okra; but the ground sassafras that flavors it, called gumbo filé, is an herb first used by the Choctaw Indians.

The poorer whites, or po' white trash as they were called, who either owned no slaves or worked alongside them on small farms, also began to adopt soul dishes. When I was a child, Aunt Ella always used to tell me that little white girls and boys were really skinny until they started soppin' up the pot likka along with us – no doubt her way of enticing me to go on eating it. Soon, she said, they too were tuckin' into more and more soul food. Genovese says, 'What the slaves did, they taught themselves to do, and they contributed more to the diet of the poorer whites than the poorer whites ever had the chance to contribute to theirs.' It was often said that all blacks were born cooks, perhaps because slave children learned to cook before they were old enough to go out into the fields to work.

On a professional level too, 'colored food,' as it was called, won itself a reputation. Among the free blacks who lived in both the North and the South, working in a wide variety of occupations, those who worked as cooks or with food in some other way earned great renown. The black-owned and -operated Fraunce's Tavern in New York City was one of George Washington's favorite restaurants. Later our third president Thomas Jefferson chose to bring back with him from France a black servant, James Hemmings, who had qualified there as a first-class chef of the French school. Leonard E. Roberts described his contribution in *The Negro Chef Cookbook*:

He and Jefferson concocted the great continental cuisine of France and made some of our most glamorous American dishes. At Monticello and the White

House, they introduced ice cream, macaroni, spaghetti, savoye [savoy cabbage], cornbread stuffing, waffles, almonds, raisins, vanilla, and many more dishes and foods to America. James Hemming and other of Jefferson's servants from those two great houses handed down to generations of Negro and white families alike the repertory of the American table.

Later, too, it was black cooks and waiters who established the tradition of fine dining and elegant service in the Pullman cars of the old railroads.

But life remained difficult for free blacks, especially in the South. There were state laws limiting their educational and economic development, others forbidding them from buying or selling alcoholic beverages, yet others forbidding the marriage of blacks and whites. This is the reason that I know so little about my great-great-grandfather Dennison Harrell, a free black who had arrived in America as a child with his mother, a runaway slave from England. His first wife was a

ABOVE LEFT *Three of my great-great-grandfather Dennison Harrell's daughters, Pearlie, Minnie and Jenny, the children from his first marriage to Virginia, a white woman from the North who has never been traced. The little girl in the picture is unknown.*

ABOVE RIGHT *Jenny Harrell, one of Dennison's daughters, my great-grandmother.*

OVER *My great-grandfather John Lynch, Grandma Maggie Ferguson's father, on the left in the white overalls, and his brother Harold and his wife Rosa. They were sharecroppers in South Carolina and scraped through the worst of the Depression years trying to beat the boll weevils. They stuck it out and remained in the South for their entire lives rather than migrate to the North.*

white Northern woman named Virginia, who was disowned by her family after marrying Dennison. To protect her, even after her early death, he never spoke of their marriage and sent all their family photographs and papers to be locked away in a lawyer's vault, where they have remained to this day so that no one can ever get to them.

Even after the Civil War and the formal abolition of slavery, conditions remained bad or frequently worsened. Many of the huge plantations were split up into small plots and sold off cheaply to white farmers. They, in turn, allowed destitute blacks to move onto their land, advancing them enough money to buy tools, seed and food in exchange for a share of their profits. As farmers they had access to foods that we today consider a treasure – freshly churned butter and buttermilk, wild berries and fruits, greens like poke sallet, fish, wild game, free-range fowl, and other farm animals living off what the land provided. Of course,

sharecroppers like my great-grandfather, John Lynch, always seemed to owe more money than their crops could bring in and their debt grew larger from year to year. They were dirt poor. When yields were shallow, these families were filled with hunger and despair. The conditions on plantations often deteriorated too, and there is evidence to suggest that malnutrition among these 'free' people became severe at this time.

One solution was migration to the North. From the early days of the Underground Railroad in the 1830s through the massive exodus that resulted from the Great Northern Drive and on into the twentieth century, blacks moved North in ever increasing numbers. My Granddaddy Battle fled North in the early 1900s, changing his name for a little extra insurance. He would never have his photograph taken. In the forties, my Dad came up to Philadelphia from Charlotte, North Carolina, when he got fed up earning 45 cents an hour as a boilermaker while his white counterparts were getting $10.00 an hour standing around watching him do all the work. Granddaddy and Daddy and millions like them came up through what became known as the Freedom Belt to settle in the key cities of Philadelphia, Chicago, Detroit, and New York. They brought with them into the ghettos their religion, music, dancing, and last but by no means least, their fabulous food.

Slowly the white world began to discover the richness of that heritage. The Harlem Renaissance was a turning point. At the beginning of the century Harlem, which had been a swanky white part of town with big houses and flash harness horse races, did a full turnabout and became black. But it still stood for the best: the best in entertainment, the best in bootlegging, and the best in food. Black writers, artists, singers, dancers, actors, and musicians all flocked there because they had a chance for self-expression, to be seen and heard. Soon white people began flocking there too, to see the great black revues. The most famous venue of all was the Cotton Club, the launching pad for so many black entertainers: Lena Horne, Duke Ellington, Josephine Baker, Louis Armstrong, Bessie Smith, and countless others. Every single performer who ever worked there was black; but the audiences were always lily-white.

But the white world also flocked there for the barbecue and soul food joints to be found up and down every block. A certain place would quickly develop a reputation for doing – oh, say, the best ribs or down-home biscuits or potato salad or sweet potato pie in town, and then the crowds would start flocking there. When you remember that the food was good enough to drag the rich whites down to the gutbucket world, then you'll realize that we are talking some serious cookin'.

I remember vividly riding through the streets of Harlem for the first time as a teenager, for my first-ever solo performance, at the legendary Apollo Theater on 125th Street. That night my entire world consisted of one dream, meeting Marvin Gaye, who was topping the bill; but I was also amazed by the number of soul food restaurants there.

Anything and everything seemed to be available, and twenty-four hours a day. Word of mouth, the finest marketing technique known to man, told you exactly where to go for whatever your li'l ole stomach desired. The restaurateurs themselves would even advise me. They didn't seem to be competing with one another. In a brotherly spirit each would gladly head me towards the best rib joint, fried chicken house, or whatever fit my bill. All I had to do was stand at the back stage entrance of the Apollo and ask and I would be steered in the right direction. If I wanted the hottest, or Alabama-style, or Mississippi-fried, someone would know where to send me. If it was black-eyed peas I was after, I had to be more specific. Which kind? Soul or West Indian? Hot or mild? Dry or juicy? Eating establishments flourished or went under depending on their reputation for cleanliness, where their cook came from, and how well he or she could bake biscuits. Other cities had their conglomerate of soul food joints, but there was no place that came close to The Big Apple.

The fame of the soul food cook spread. It speaks worlds that when Hattie McDaniels became the first black actor to win an Academy Award, she did so for her portrayal of a robust and whiplashed-tongued mammy in *Gone With the Wind*. After coming under heavy scrutiny from the black community for playing such stereotyped roles, Miss McDaniels once said, comfortably ensconced in her fashionable Beverly Hills mansion, that she'd rather earn one thousand dollars a week playing a cook than ten dollars a week actually having to be one in a white person's home.

Speaking of Hollywood characterizations of the soul food cook, have you ever given any thought to the big black mammy in the Tom and Jerry cartoons? We don't really know a lot about her. We don't even see her face. We only know that she's one big fat mamma, that she's got a Southern drawl, and that she's got heavy-duty arms from a lifetime of doing the 'three C's' — cleaning, cuddling, and cooking. But what do we *presume* about her? We presume that she can cook up one mighty fine storm and that the blackberry pies she puts out on the ledge to cool will taste some kinda good. We can feel her strength and we can almost smell the aromas coming from her kitchen. Now that's one helluva strong faceless image! Why does everyone love those Tom and Jerry cartoons with her in them? I think it is because she typifies all that we hold dear about the wealth of spirit and strength of character of the black soul food cook.

When I look back at my childhood on the streets of Philadelphia in the sixties, I am filled with memories of that wealth of spirit. All my life I'd been conditioned to being called a Negro, a word which in itself conjured up an aura of inferiority; a second-class citizen. Now, all of a sudden, I was Black! And didn't all the cowboys with black hats get done in? Those years were full of a new black awareness. With the growing strength of the Civil Rights movement, James Brown lifted us up high by daring us to sing, 'Say it loud, I'm black and I'm proud.' Almost overnight, black became beautiful. Sometimes I remember those days, and I think that the song is so true. The skies were so much bluer then. Or were the harsh realities of the world outside my own little community just farther away? We did not have material wealth but life was oh so rich in so many other ways. The general feeling in our house was that, no matter how hard the times, you could bargain on clothes, furniture, cars, and the like, but never, ever cheat on your stomach!

We all shared in one another's problems, a habit dating back to the days when black families took in anyone who had come up from the South or was in need of a roof over their head or of a meal. In crisis, everyone charged to the rescue of neighbors, family, and friends. This is how the rent party first sprang up and flourished during the Depression years. Rent parties were still in existence when I was a child and they probably still are. If a family needed to raise the funds to pay the landlord, notice would be sent out that they were hosting a rent party. Then, they would cook up and sell the best darn soul food dinners you can imagine. There'd be trotters, potato salad, sweet potato pie, fried chicken, or baked ham – the choice of meat set by the cost of the dinner you were purchasing. A platter also always had to have some very serious greens. You could spice up your own plate before you left their house with the handy little bottle of hot sauce sitting near by. Paper plates and later Styrofoam were used, so you wouldn't lose any of that good pot likka onto your lap.

Everyone on the block or from the general neighborhood would save up their pennies to help out. Rent parties served many purposes. Everybody who dropped in to this open house affair got a good down-home cooked meal because the platters had to offer good value for money. The family in question saved face while earning enough money to pay the rent. And 'the man' got paid (for that month anyway). So everyone came out a winner! Most often these parties were just too hot to trot and an astounding hit.

Oftentimes, a rent party would turn into an unofficial block party. When it was too hot to hold one indoors, the community would preset a specific date for one. The local police department would be contacted and asked to cordon off the block from traffic for the day with those big wooden horses. Everybody would cook their specialties, turn up their hi-fis and stereos, and decorate the block with streamers; then the dancing would begin. This was the true meaning of dancing in the streets, honey! Some folks (like my daddy) would immediately set up their card tables and the marathon games of pinochle and bid whist, blackjack and tonk would begin. Dad would brag, 'I sho' nuf put the P in pinochle, so everybody better watch out when they play with big bad Fergy.' Oh, nothing gave me greater pleasure in those games than giving my dad a headrub, the ultimate insult and defeat for any pinochle player.

All that glorious food was displayed right outside on fold-away tables, just like an old-fashioned country picnic. Barbecue grills would blaze with ribs, chicken, and hot dogs, big old drums were filled with lemonade, and you could just walk along from one person's food set-up to another, sharing with each the food, music, jokes, and life! If you happened to taste one family's spread and the ribs weren't really smoking (hot and delicious, that is), the word would quickly spread and they would undoubtedly have a mess of leftovers.

Other memories are not so grand. I remember the fear I felt when my Daddy was stopped on our way down to Charlotte, North Carolina, by the state troopers. And he was stopped every single time we made that trip south, not for speeding, no suh, but just for being black. I remember all of the drinking fountain signs that clearly stated which dirty fountain I was permitted to drink from and which to avoid at all costs. I think of my Granddaddy Bert Ferguson trying not to alarm me in the back of the old pickup truck when rowdy teenagers started poking fun at my kinky hair and how he would gently nudge me off the sidewalk if a white person ever walked close by. Even now, I can still feel the shame he, who was no cowardly man, must have felt at being so utterly and completely helpless.

But I hold sweet memories of the South too, thank goodness! Picking berries and playing Huck Finn with my cousins; spending long hot lazy days searching for the crawdads that we kids called mudbugs; crankin' away at the ice cream churner; trying in vain to catch a moving chicken; always being on the lookout for those dastardly snakes that made my young life a constant misery. Sitting in church all day long and circulating the heat with a paper fan while the preacher was shoutin', 'Do not sin' – but I must've been doin' some powerful sinning, because most of the time, my mind was focused on all the delicious food just waitin' outside. These were happy and carefree times. And as my stepmother Dot always used to say, 'Happiness is not having what you want, but surely wanting what you have.' Well, I knew I had all that food out there and I was certainly happy when the minister was headin' towards the rousing finish, so I could get to it!

It was down South too, that I went to my first family reunion. Now, I know I should be telling you that the highlight of this affair was the prayers that one member was chosen to deliver. But if I were to tell the gospel truth, and I think I'm a-gonna, it was definitely the dishes that everybody turned out. Oh, dear, I'm making myself sound like some kinda pagan, but all that food, spread out majestically, on a long banquet-sized picnic table, sure was one sight for a small girl to behold. The table at the farm on Blanton Street in Charlotte kinda sloped with the terrain, but that didn't stop us from keeping the food well balanced and from swatting the flies away from the pecan pies, stacked a mile high, I might add. With one long and narrow slice you had a hunk of pie big enough to last you for quite a spell.

I should explain, though, that an African-American family reunion stands for a great deal more than just the sharing of a really fine meal. It is a testimonial both to the past and to what the future holds in store for the entire family. We gather to share all that is most precious to us, especially with those family members we don't get to see that often. We eat, we drink, and we pray, but also we encourage each other and lift our heads in praise of what our offspring have accomplished. We share in each other's joys and good fortunes and offer solace when the chips are down. We comfort each other and this enables us to retain a special kind of closeness, even when we're hundreds of miles apart.

Everytime our family gets together we try to pay some humble tribute to the accomplishments of our race in one way or another. My family, for example, after discovering the existence of my great-great-grandfather Dennison Harrell, now meets annually for a grand family reunion expressly in his honor. We come together from all over the States – and in my case from across the Atlantic each time – tracing new family members we have never met before, as we continue to pay homage to the man who founded our family in America. Everyone who attends gives in the best of spirit and puts all of their personality into the dishes they concoct. At the same time, we are remembering all of our forebears and all that they gave, often against apparently insurmountable odds.

This is precisely why we feel we must get down to some real serious cookin' at the time of a family reunion. It represents sharing the very best with those we love the very most and that love is best conveyed in the pride we take in preparing our food. By now, it has become a family tradition. And believe you me, can we burn when we cook. Everyone is asked to bring a dish, usually their specialty, and each cook has to maintain an exceedingly high standard of cooking, baking, and innovation. One dish just walks all over and surpasses another, and we always delight in sharing and comparing recipes. Once Aunt Peacie brought along her 'Jesse Jackson Sweet Potato Pie.' Well, it was gone before you had a chance to take a good look. Man, that pie was 'the T' – the talk of the day. But another thing is for dang sure: if your cooking isn't quite up to scratch, you sure as shootin' won't be asked to bring a dish next time round! You'll be nicely passed over with, 'Oh, honey, that's OK, why don't you just sit this one out.'

Even if it's not a big family reunion, it is still considered an extreme insult if you don't put yourself out and cook a fine and exquisite meal. I wouldn't dream of presenting my family and friends with a meal consisting of frozen fried chicken, frozen collard greens, store-bought cartons of buttermilk sausage biscuits and gravy made out of some sorry old box of granules. Oh, they'd eat it all right. But they would just feel so put down and outright insulted that they would commence telling me off, royally, right on the spot. Then, they would continue to talk about me for fifteen more years! My folks pull no punches when it comes to telling you off and they don't necessarily wait until they're politely out of earshot either. I can just hear them signifying now: 'Well, she sure didn't sweat long over that sad plate of stuff.' 'Do you call that food? Sure was pathetic.' 'I don't care how busy the girl is, she could certainly take a little time to think about her family once in a while, humph!' That is the spirit through which soul food traditions continually evolve – *pressure!*

Howessenever, as the old folks say, I would never have dreamed of writing a cook book had I remained in America. Oh for sure, I always cooked (when I wasn't on tour, that is), but with a family like mine, full of passionate and creative soul food cooks, one simply had no need for the use of cookbooks. When I wanted to cook something new I telephoned a relative and, believe you me, I would be told exactly how to do a thing with very graphic blow-by-blow directions when necessary. But when I moved to England it wasn't quite that simple. Could you imagine my phone bill to acquire the recipe for, shall we say, a Black Bottom Pie? After living in England I realized just how much I'd taken my American soul food roots for granted, having had so many great cooks at my disposal. I began collecting recipes from each of them.

I was also acutely aware that, because of my absences, my twin daughters Alicia and Alexandria were growing up estranged from their heritage. Their meals frequently consisted of fish sticks and French fries (fish fingers and chips to the British) prepared by their definitely non-soul food cooking nanny. Then, as if that wasn't enough, to my total and utter amazement they thought that fish came out of the sea already breaded and in the shape of a rectangle. This most certainly did not please me, so I decided to rearrange my priorities and set my work schedule so that I could do all of the cooking. I cooked grits, sweet potato and apple casserole with a marshmallow topping, pancakes with maple syrup, corn fritters, greens with ham hocks, and American biscuits with butter and jelly (jam). It was so delightful to watch my lovely daughters, who are growing up to be proper little English ladies indeed, dunking their biscuits into gravy and dousing their sausages with maple syrup.

Mind you, my gorgeous British husband was especially grateful for this change of heart, because he'd also missed those soulful foods that he'd developed a love for when we first got married and lived in Valley Forge, Pennsylvania. I am proud to say that my darling Chris can put a serious hurting on a bowl of collards! After an extensive tour, recording session, or television project the first thing I always do is to cook up a big (and I do mean big) soulful dinner, and we all sit down and catch up on each other.

My aim has been to write an everyday cookbook that anyone, from beginner to experienced cook, could enjoy using. Since I have made just about every mistake possible in the field of cookery during my experimentation in England, I have tried to write the recipes down with as much clarity, accuracy, and detail as possible, especially after realizing how many differences and pitfalls there are in ingredients and measurements. And in addition I wanted to give a little bit more, a glimpse into the people who were responsible for my interest in soul food, along with a vivid idea of just how it came into being.

To me, my kitchen is the core of my home. Just show me a kitchen full of bright robust laughter with busy bustling hands creating wonderfully tempting meals and I'll show you one big happy family. Here in my English home, I always prepare a big American Sunday breakfast. It pleases me to see my little girls craving apple pancakes and other American foods. Just like my Dad, they insist on their newly acquired favorites like their Aunt Linda's French toast, sprinkled with cinnamon, butter, and maple syrup, and a scrambled egg with cheddar cheese melted in it — the way their American relatives have been eating eggs for generations. It assures me that wherever they go in life or whatever they do, they will always maintain a close tie with at least part of their black American heritage. Although we reside in England, they will never lose touch with the soul foods of their ethnic background. Well, I just won't let 'em.

IT DON'T MEAN A THING IF IT AIN'T GOT THAT SWING!

THE AFRICAN-AMERICAN WAY OF TALKING

*B*lack folks have always had a natural rhythm in the way they walk and in the way they talk. So perhaps it would be more appro-po if I were to say, it don't mean a thang if it ain't got that swang! We shimmy when we dance and we sway when we pray. We talk when we sing and we sing when we talk. That distinctive rising of our voices, coupled with our God-given body language, lends itself to colorful inflections, mood, and innuendo, and there's even a unique way to express ourselves when we eat. Praise the Lord and can I get an Amen!

To put these words in the right mouths, let me take you to my Aunt Peacie's house in Philadelphia. It's dinner time with eight or nine people around the table and the food's being laid on.

Uncle Thomas opens, 'Mama, these greens is mean, oooo weeee, they make me wanna slap my grandmamma.' To accompany this robust remark, Uncle Thomas rhythmically pats his foot under the table and clasps his hands together to show his true appreciation, love and admiration for the meal Aunt Peacie has turned out. This is, of course, followed by rip-roaring laughter, exclamations of delight and Amens all round.

Cousin Beverly continues, 'Hey, ma, you sure stepped in those sweet potatoes, umph umph umph!' Cousin Junior interjects, 'Yes, ma'am, Mom sure knows how to burn a mean pot, don't she now?' By now Uncle Frankie will jump in with, 'Will y'all, all, stop talking that trash and pass me the black-eyed peas before there ain't none left.' 'Yeah,' agrees Cousin Lawrence. 'Quit talkin', get down and greeze!'

I do hope you realize that never once in this scenario is a grandmother slapped, a sweet potato mashed by a foot, a pan burnt, or grease thrown around. Everyone has simply been complimenting the chef. And I don't, by any means, wish to imply that all black families, including Aunt Peacie and Uncle Thomas, use jargon such as this all the time. Let's be real! Nobody goes in for what used to be called jive-talkin' all the time. But I'd be very surprised to find an African-American family who is not, at the least, aware of these expressions and one that doesn't use some of them somewhere, somehow.

Let me further illustrate my point by a comparison. Let's say there's a white person with a posh accent — we'll call him Reginald — and he's sitting down with his very upper-crust British family to exactly the same meal, and they're really enjoying it. What would they say? Of course, they have their own speech rhythms and inflections, and they have their own body language – that's to say, practically none at all.

Reginald says to his wife – let's call her Lavinia – 'I say, old girl, those vegetables were *rather* good.'

And she replies, 'Thank you, Reggie darling. Cook went down to that West Indian market place and got them. I think she said they were called colored greens. It's called soul food, don't you know, and absolutely everyone's eating it.' 'I must say, those darkies know a thing or two. What do you think, Torquil?' (That's their chinless son.) 'Yes, simply super. And those other thingies, yams do you call them? were pretty decent.'

Reginald is so ecstatic that he takes out his monocle and polishes it on his linen table napkin. He turns to the butler. 'I say, Briggs, would you tell Cook, you know, jolly good show and all that?'

Now, folks, you've got to admit that it ain't quite the same thing, now is it?

We think that African-Americans developed their expressive speech and gesture out of necessity. Sometimes they couldn't understand each other, having been thrown together into bondage from so many different tribes, so they needed a way of communicating. Sometimes, on the other hand, they didn't want to let the white man in on what dey was talkin' 'bout either. In both cases body language had to play a major part. Given also that it was against the law in many of the slave states for a black person to learn to read or write during the days of slavery, the snippin' off or slurrin' of the ends of certain words isn't all that surprising. And anyway the blacks, sure as shootin', weren't about to give in to the white man's English all that readily.

Nowadays, though, we blacks have fun using language for the pleasure of it, or perhaps even as a weapon! Now that gives me food for thought. We rap today, as much as ever, but to display pride, not disdain, for our heritage. The slang changes, but it keeps that natural lilt and swing. And, just as with the minstrels or coon singers years ago, the white folks still try to emulate that rhythm and body language in their own slang and the dance crazes that just keep on coming out of the black community.

Take 'bad' as an example – as in that downright 'bad' meal Aunt Peacie cooked, meaning it was a really tasty treat. It is one of our oldest slang words, but only recently become a household word through the great Mr Michael Jackson himself. Today, everyone understands that, like a lot of black slang, it simply employs the trick of opposite usage. If I say, 'He's one bad lookin' dude,' I mean he's a stunning creature and I wish I had a piece of him. Or if a plate of home fries are some 'bad boys,' then you can bet your bottom dollar that they are some kinda good and I'll be tastin' a few directly.

Some expressions can be used while dining, dancing or … well, just about anything that we like to do. In musical terms, the bridge is the middle eight, but when you're cooking chit'lin's you might 'take it to the bridge' – meaning go even further – with the hot sauce. A big mammy jammy could be the description of a beautiful and statuesque woman, but in talking food, it definitely describes the volume and glory (that's ga-low-rie, in three syllables please) of a magnificent cake. Or if a man really wants to please the woman of his dreams, he might tauntingly say, 'Honey, just wrap your chops around this.' Well, I'd be the first to admit that he could be trying to get the cold parts of his anatomy warmed up, but for my purposes, he is definitely asking her to taste one of his prized dishes, like a hunk of pie or a piece of fried chicken. And that's only the beginning!

Another important aspect of language is in the food related nicknames we give people. Honey, suga', dumpling, sweetmeat, sherry, hambone, cookie, cupcake, sweet thang, puddin', tart (oh, well, perhaps we'll leave that one out), and so forth.

Now, I am not an advocate of the excessive use of bad grammar or the misspelling of words to express the tones in which we speak. I think it condescends. On the other hand, I see no reason to deny or be in any way embarrassed by a way of speaking that comes as a direct result of the expressions derived from a mirrored reflection of our roots and is as much our language as our religion, our music and our food. I am continually elated by what the African American has given and is still giving to America. Today, more than ever, we can strut tall and proud and say, 'Hey y'all, this is the way we talk and yes sir, this is the way we eat.' I know that I certainly could not have written this book without the use of this very intimate style of language.

So here it is. Everything you could possibly need to clue you in! What it is — what it was — and what it shall be! If you ain't singing you ain't swinging, if you ain't moving you ain't grooving, and if you ain't eatin' soul, then perhaps you ain't been told.

GLOSSARY

Ashcake A simple cornpone roasted or baked in or under the ashes or coals of an open fire.

Biscuit A soft, unyeasted bread dough usually baked in small rounds and very similar in texture to an English scone. Not to be confused with an English biscuit, which is an American cookie.

Big mammy jammy Describes anything lumberjack-size and delicious. Could be a woman, a Cadillac or Rolls Royce, or a stack of buckwheat cakes.

Black Bottom A wonderful and lively 1920s dance. I thought break-dancing was hard work until my Mom showed me the Black Bottom. It is also the name of a serious Southern pie.

Bobwhite In the Eastern United States, another name for a quail. In the South, a bobwhite is called a partridge.

Buckwheat cake A griddle cake or pancake, slightly heavier and a touch more bitter than buttermilk or other pancakes because of the use of buckwheat flour. You can get this flour at British health food shops.

Burn Means to dance up a storm or to drive extremely fast (as in burning rubber) or to cook well, as in, 'She sure burns a mean pot.' 'Man, can that dude burn.'

Butter Freshly churned butter, creamy, warm, and lightly salted was so much a part of soulful eating in the past that people still talk and dream about it. Unfortunately, almost nobody makes it these days.

Buttermilk (or clabber) See Milk.

Chit'lin's (or properly chitterlings) These little babies are the epitome of soul food at its finest. Some folks squeal at the thought of eating parts of the pig's small intestines. Tut … tut … don't knock 'em unless you've tried 'em.

Cobbler One big bad deevine mammy jammy of a fruit-filled dessert with one crunchy pastry top, or sometimes a pastry top and bottom, or once in a while with the pastry baked inside too.

Collards Perhaps the most popular of all the greens in Soulville USA. Strictly speaking, collards are a form of kale, but you wouldn't know it to taste them. When you boil their fleshy leaves down with a slab of fatback, hog jowl, or ham hock, then oooo weeee, baby, you're gonna think you've just entered greens paradise. British cooks may be able to get these at West Indian greengrocers. Chinese shops often have kale which is quite like them (as well as sharper-tasting mustard greens which look confusingly similar). Ordinary kale and spring greens are too dull in flavor to be used as substitutes.

Cookie Strictly speaking, an American word, probably derived from *koekje*, the name given to a little cake by the Dutch, who were one of the prime time players in the settlement of colonial America. So now you know, they're the culprits for all this transatlantic confusion about cookies and biscuits. Thanks heaps - or should I say *alstublieft*?

Cornmeal Yellow or white grainy meal ground down from dried corn (maize). There's just no end to the wonders of it. Originally it was an American Indian specialty, but then they passed it on to us. Soul food cooks have been using it to dredge meat or fish or bake up all those cornbreads and pones so near and dear to our little old pea-pickin' hearts. And Lawd knows, there's enough of them. There are corn cakes, flat cakes made with a simple batter; corn dodgers, small cornbreads baked, fried, or boiled and still very popular at Kentucky Derby time, I hear tell; corn sticks (also called corn dogs); and, of course, cornpones, the first simple corn breads made without any milk or eggs (see pone). In the South, white cornmeal is preferred for baking pones, but I'm a Yankee and grew up on the yellow variety. Both can be got in Britain from serious food stores or health food shops.

Corn oyster Just a li'l ole itty-bitty fried fritter thang made out of corn kernels. It's called an oyster because that's what it looks like after you fry it. The kernels give it a ragged texture but you can try other leftover cooked vegetables as well, like okra or eggplant.

Corn syrup A syrup made from cornstarch, used in many Southern pies and desserts. Available at a few British delicatessens; otherwise use golden syrup.

Cracklin' bread Delicious cornbread made with crisply fried hog's fat cracklin's (the crisp part left after all the lard has been fried out of the skin) baked into the batter.

Crawdad A crawfish in the United States, or crayfish in Britain.

Crocus sack A wonderful old burlap (hessian) sack used to catch frogs, snakes, and other living creatures. Compulsory farm stuff. Also used by hunters for lugging home game.

Crumb crusher Not to be confused with a rolling pin! This is an affectionate name for a child who is acting up and my favorite! Linoleum lizard or curtain climber are my other favored alternatives.

Fatback One of the key seasonings in soul food. Salt pork from the upper part of the side of the pig, fatback is used to season greens, sweet potatoes, and just about every other vegetable. Sometimes it is fried up crisp, maybe rolled in cornmeal first, and eaten just as is. Substitute unsmoked streaky bacon.

Flapjack Another name for a pancake.

Fritters Tiny, delicious cake-like critters. A great way to use leftovers – bacon bits, ham, sweet potatoes, eggplant, or fruit (see page 177). You name it, I'll fritter it! Kids love 'em because they're little. I love 'em because they're mean.

Grapes American grapes include native species as well as European varieties. One of these is the musky-scented muscadine or fox grape, of which one yellowish-green variety grown in the South is Scuppernong, named after a river in North Carolina; wines – like C. J.'s Fox Grape Wine – are sometimes made from it. The popular deep-purple Concord, used for juice and jelly, is a hybrid of fox and another native species, catawba.

Greeze 'Let's greeze' means 'C'mon everybody, let's eat!'

Griddle A heavy, flat plate of metal or soapstone on which to cook pancakes, bacon, or hamburgers. And so griddlecake, another name for pancake.

Grits (or hominy grits) A mainstream staple for soul food lovers. Coarsely ground hulled corn meal, usually bleached white and eaten boiled, fried, or baked, either as cereal or as a starch with butter or luscious gravy. If you can't find this, polenta, from Italian delicatessens, is a reasonable substitute, so I'm told.

Gumbo A thick soup; a luscious stew; a Louisiana specialty – and a direct gift from the African slave culture to the Southern States. In some recipes gumbos are thickened with okra pods; in others, they are thickened with gumbo filé (ground sassafras), one of the spices used by the Choctaw tribes. The word comes from *ngombo*, the name for okra in Angola. Gumbo is also the name of a dialect spoken by blacks and Creoles of the French West Indies and Louisiana.

Hash browns Fried potatoes mashed into the skillet and crisped up on both sides.

Hoecake A kind of bread made with cornmeal that used to be baked right on the blades of the hoes of the slaves in an open fire.

Hog jowl A cheeky bit of pork. Hog jowls were another cut of the pig given out in the slave quarters. Used for seasoning greens or other vegetables along with ham hocks or fatback.

Hog maw The mouth, throat, or gullet of the hog. Yes, soul food cooks use it, too, to season our food.

Home fries Sliced or cubed potatoes fried up in bacon fat. Not mashed like hash browns, these retain their shape.

Hominy (from the Indian word *rockahominy*) Corn kernels either soaked or boiled in a weak solution of lye until their hulls drop off, then washed until the lye is off completely. Hominy used to be boiled with meat scraps or bits of vegetables. Nowadays it is usually eaten as a side dish or starch. Difficult to find in Britain, though if you were really determined you could make it yourself.

Hush puppies Small balls of cornmeal fried in deep fat and thrown to the hounds in the past. I love 'em with fried catfish. Let the hounds fend for themselves.

Jambalaya Favorite Louisiana dish made from rice, ham, shrimp, tomatoes, and other vegetables and spices. Creole food at its creolest.

Jelly A fruit preserve or jam, not to be confused with a gelatin-set dessert, which in the States is called Jell-o (they also use it in salads). On trips down South as a child, we'd always bring back home pots of Grandma's delicious Scuppernong grape jelly.

Jodies Little mammy jammies (see page 22); used to describe smaller versions of monstrous things (see page 26), like cookies, biscuits, or anything petite.

Johnnycake A cornbread, often baked flat on a board in an open oven or on a griddle. Food writers and historians seem to agree that the name is probably a variant of journey cake, a sturdy cake made for travelling that could be wrapped in a hankie and carried around, perhaps in a pocket, from place to place. Practical for bumpy trips in buckboard wagons!

Julep Plantation drink made from mint leaves pounded and infused in bourbon. More popular with the white folks who drank it than the black folks who made it.

Kissin' cousin Someone or something with whom you share such a closeness that you could almost be related. Say Lucy-Mae is always hanging around your house, or she's a distant niece of a fourth cousin twice removed, she's a kissin' cousin. So a jambalaya is a kissin' cousin to a gumbo just as Creole cookin' is to soul food.

Likka Pot liquor, the juice resulting from the simmering of a big fat pot of greens. Highly seasoned and rich in vitamins and minerals; sometimes sopped up with cornbread or biscuits.

Mean Bad, unreal, beautiful, outrageous, superb, too delicious to swallow so you just keep swilling it around in your mouth.

Milk The term sweet milk is still used by country folk to distinguish regular milk from all the other milks they use. Sour milk is sweet milk which has turned sour on its own – but pasteurized milk probably won't go sour in the right way, and it's better to simulate it by adding 1 tablespoon of white vinegar to 1 cup (250 ml) of fresh milk. Buttermilk (or clabber, which is left after the buttermilk is made) isn't to my taste but is still considered the drink of champions by Southerners like my Daddy. He fills up a tall glass with clabber, crumbles up a hunk of cornbread in it and enjoys every thick lump. Evaporated milk and sweetened condensed milk are also frequently used in soul food.

Molasses Sweet brown syrup made from sugar cane or sorghum. Sorghum molasses is the real deal and the one I kindly favor for soul food cooking and eating. It is now often very costly and difficult to find.

Monstrous Absolutely the apex! Awesome.

Muddler Small rod-shaped implement used to bruise the mint leaves or stir the ice in a drink like a mint julep. Also a person who's a pain in the neck.

Mustard greens Tangy greens from the same family of vegetables as cabbage. Cooked in much the same way as collards. If there are no West Indian greengrocers near you, try Indian or Chinese shops (but see also Collards).

Niggertoe Another name for a Brazil nut. Someone somewhere with poor eyesight and no brain thought that the dark, rough shell resembled the toe of a Negro.

Pancake A small, thick, slightly heavy fried breakfast cake, awesomely tempting doused with maple syrup. Outrageous!

Pilau Rice dish. The word, originally Persian, is known under many different spellings, like pilaf or purloo. In *Southern Food*, John Egerton says he came across sixteen different forms.

Pone Any basic bread made with cornmeal, salt, and water comes under the heading of pone. Originally called *appone* when the Indians gave it over to us. Pones include ashcake, hoecake, and johnnycake.

Pound cake Old-fashioned cake, so called because you use a pound of everything to make it.

Prawleen Let us not have any high falutin' fancy pronunciation here, please. A prawleen, or praline, is a neat, sweet, delightful treat from down Louisiana way made from nuts, usually pecans.

Red-eye gravy Gravy made from the drippings of a big fat slab of country ham with a small piece of bone in it. The residue in the pan after you pour off the excess fat leaves a slightly reddish hue, which is how this old Southern specialty derived its name.

Salt pork The fatty back or middle of the pig, salt cured or hickory smoked. It is used in all soul cooking to season greens or other vegetables as well as to eat it on its wonderful own. As a seasoning, you can substitute unsmoked or smoked streaky bacon.

Scratch cake Just that – a cake made from scratch, using a recipe, not a box of cake mix.

Sheet cake A sheet cake is a large single-layer cake, popular for get-togethers like church socials, bridal or baby showers and birthdays – or good if you just wanna pick 'n' greeze all week long.

Shirt-tail relative Country expression for someone who is just barely in the family – just hangin' on by his or her shirt-tails. Also a hanger-on.

Signify When a soulful person gets a roll going, they don't avow or state or proclaim; they just tell it like it is and that's called signifying.

Skillet Cast-iron frying pan with a long handle to use on an open fire or a stove top, or in a closed oven. Skillets feature greatly in soul food cooking. The older and more seasoned they are, the better. They fry up the best chicken and turn out the most exquisite corn bread you can make. A necessary implement for a soul food cook.

Smidgen A smidgen is less than a dash and a lot less than a pinch. It's so small that you have to write it with a little dash – like that, or you'll miss it.

Smoking As in 'That pie was smoking.' Nothing to do with a cigarette or hot fat. 'She smokes' means she burns a mean pot, she's a real hot mamma. So a smoking pie is one mean dream of a smoking machine.

Soda biscuit Another name for a buttermilk biscuit, made with baking soda and sometimes sour milk instead of buttermilk. Some folks call these sodie biscuits.

Sorghum A cereal like millet, also called Guinea corn. There is also a sweet variety. The juice from this sweet sorghum is the basis of the best molasses.

Spoonbread The richest kind of cornbread. Should be just as light as a feather and soft enough to be served with a spoon.

Stepping in it To cook a thing exceedingly well. For example, 'She sure stepped in that pot of greens.'

Succotash Mixture of corn and beans given to the first American foreign settlers by the Powhatan tribe of the Algonkian Indians. Usually made with lima beans and corn as a base, it can be cooked very soulfully.

Sweet potato An important part of slaves' rations that has become a soul food specialty, partly because George Washington Carver devised more ways of cooking a sweet potato than you can shake a stick at.

Trotter Pronounced trodder in some parts. Another name for the foot of a pig. A hot plate of trotters can make a big man weep. And by hot I do mean hot. You oughta see how much hot sauce and vinegar some folks pour on their trotters!

Tube pan A large round pan with a funnel in the center. Also known as a funnel pan, angel cake pan, or bundt pan. Don't try and improvise with foil. It leaks. Trust me – I know!

Vinegar An essential part of soul food flavoring along with hot peppers and onions. Used especially in pork dishes, where it helps to cut the fat. I remember my soul cookin' aunties using cider vinegar, and that is the ideal type, but it should be a dry one without too much apple flavour.

Yam In soul food cooking this means a red type of sweet potato, not the Old World tubers which are properly called yams. British West Indian shops have a confusing variety of roots, so be sure to ask for sweet potato.

ON MEASURING

If someone were to ask me what had been the most difficult aspect of writing a cookbook, the answer would be, without a shadow of doubt, getting my folks to write down recipes. It has, indeed, been my divine challenge. Oh, they will gladly show me how to make anything, but the general attitude is 'Got no time to waste writin', let's get on with the makin'.'

This reasoning is really quite simple. Down-home cooks never measure. They just scrunch up the palm of their hands to dole out a tablespoon or a teaspoon and feel the difference right then and there in their hand. They know how much liquid to add to a batter or dough by the consistency and feel of it. No doubt this reflects soul food's evolution outside a well equipped kitchen. There are very few soul recipes where a touch more baking soda or a hint less salt could spoil the dish. Practice soon irons out mistakes and adds each cook's personal touch.

In this book I opted for the way I was taught to cook at school, with the American system of teaspoons, tablespoons, and cups. I don't use any special kind of measuring cup, just a plain old everyday, run-of-the mill stoneware teacup. Take one from your cupboard, and an ordinary, not too large tablespoon. If you can measure 16 tablespoons of water into the cup, you've cracked the basic 'cup' concept: 1 cup (of either solids or liquids) = 8 fl oz = 16 tablespoons. If you keep this underlying principle in mind, it will be a very easy system to use.

Having travelled extensively, I am more than aware that some people feel the cup system is not as rational or accurate as a weight system, like British pounds and ounces or Continental grams. I can see their point when making complicated French pâtisserie or sauces spoiled by the slightest change in a fixed formula, but for me, those little varmints are just too far away from the spirit of soulful cooking.

Nevertheless, for those who feel unhappy without their scales, I'm putting approximate weight equivalents – both grams and ounces – into my recipes, or number equivalents for things you don't weigh, like eggs or onions. And here are a few specific guidelines to help when cooking with my cup system of measurement.

FLOUR   Always sift before measuring, because unsifted flour is downright heavy and tends to pack itself into the measuring cup. Unsifted flour will yield more flour than called for in the recipe and will make a denser cake. After sifting, pile flour into a measuring cup with a tablespoon; never shake or tap the cup because that will surely pack it down. This is especially important when using cake flour. It is better to have a little less flour than a little more. Nobody minds a lighter cake, but who wants a heavy, hard-to-digest-without-a-heaping-glass-of-milk one. (Incidentally, in the States three grades of flour are commonly used: bread flour, which is equivalent to British strong flour; all-purpose flour; and cake flour. British plain white flour is more or less the same as all-purpose flour, though it can be used for cakes too. There is a note on flour for cakes in the introduction to 'Cakes and Cookies', page 180.)

SOLID FATS   Use my water displacement method to learn to measure any awkward weights of solid shortening. For example, if you want to measure one-third of a cup of butter from a solid chunk, fill a measuring cup two-thirds full with cold water, then add butter until the water level reaches the one cup line. Drain off the water and there you'll have it. Keep it up and you'll soon be able to judge, by eye, where to slice your butter.

*E*ASY EQUIVALENTS

Although equivalents are given in all the recipes, you may find these rough guidelines useful. They are all approximate, and the metric equivalents are on the high side to give round numbers. If you multiply up the small quantities, you'll see that they don't quite tally with the larger ones. But don't worry: none of that will make any real difference in the recipes.

SPOONS AND CUPS

3 teaspoons	1 tablespoon
4 tablespoons	$\frac{1}{4}$ cup
8 tablespoons	$\frac{1}{2}$ cup
16 tablespoons	1 cup
5 tablespoons + 1 teaspoon	$\frac{1}{3}$ cup

For water, and approximately for watery liquids like soup or gravy, or for cooking oils or fats, 1 fl oz weighs 1 oz and 1 ml weighs 1 g. Note the difference between American and British pints: a US pint is 16 fl oz, a UK pint 20 fl oz. The equivalents given in brackets in the recipes include UK pints.

SPOONS OR CUPS	US FLUID MEASURE	UK FLUID MEASURE	METRIC FLUID MEASURE
1 teaspoon	$\frac{1}{6}$ fl oz	$\frac{1}{6}$ fl oz	5 ml
1 tablespoon	$\frac{1}{2}$ fl oz	$\frac{1}{2}$ fl oz	15 ml
$\frac{1}{4}$ cup	2 fl oz	2 fl oz	60 ml
$\frac{1}{3}$ cup	$2\frac{1}{2}$ fl oz	$2\frac{1}{2}$ fl oz	75 ml
$\frac{1}{2}$ cup	4 fl oz	4 fl oz	120 ml
$\frac{2}{3}$ cup	5 fl oz	5 fl oz	150 ml
$\frac{3}{4}$ cup	6 fl oz	6 fl oz	175 ml
1 cup	8 fl oz	8 fl oz	250 ml
2 cups	1 pint	16 fl oz	500 ml
$2\frac{1}{2}$ cups	$1\frac{1}{4}$ pints	1 pint	600 ml
3 cups	$1\frac{1}{2}$ pints	$1\frac{1}{4}$ pints	750 ml
4 cups	1 quart	$1\frac{3}{4}$ pints	1 l
5 cups	$1\frac{1}{4}$ quarts	1 quart	1.2 l

Ounces and pounds	Grams and kilograms	Ounces and pounds	Grams and kilograms
$\frac{1}{4}$ oz	7 g	8 oz	250 g
$\frac{1}{2}$ oz	15 g	12 oz	375 g
$\frac{3}{4}$ oz	25 g	14 oz	430 g
1 oz	30 g	1 lb	500 g
$1\frac{1}{2}$ oz	45 g	$1\frac{1}{2}$ lb	750 g
2 oz	60 g	2 lb	1 kg
4 oz	120 g	3 lb	1.5 kg
6 oz	175 g	4 lb	2 kg

Apples 2 medium apples = 2 cups sliced

Bacon 8 slices crisp cooked bacon = $\frac{1}{2}$ cup crumbled-up bits

Bananas 3 medium bananas = $2\frac{1}{2}$ cups sliced, or 2 cups mashed

Breadcrumbs 2 slices fresh bread = 1 cup soft breadcrumbs

Cabbage 1 lb solid white cabbage = $4\frac{1}{2}$ cups shredded

Carrots 1 lb carrots = 3 cups shredded

Cheese 4 oz hard cheese = 1 cup shredded

Chocolate 6 oz chocolate chips = 1 cup

Coconut 4 oz shredded or flaked coconut = $1\frac{1}{3}$ cups

Corn 2 ears corn = 1 cup whole kernels

Cornmeal 1 cup uncooked cornmeal = $3\frac{1}{2}$ cups cooked

Crab 1 lb fresh crab in the shell = $\frac{3}{4}$ to 1 cup flaked crab meat

Cream 1 cup heavy (double) cream = 2 cups whipped

Dates 1 lb pitted dates = $\frac{2}{3}$ cup chopped

Eggs 5 large eggs = 1 cup whole eggs

   7 large eggs = 1 cup egg whites

   12 large eggs = 1 cup egg yolks

Fat (butter, lard or other solid shortenings) 1 lb = 2 cups

Flour 1 lb flour = $3\frac{1}{2}$ cups packed or unsifted, or 4 cups sifted

Lemons 1 medium lemon = 2 to 3 tablespoons juice

   1 grated lemon rind = $1\frac{1}{2}$ to 3 teaspoons rind

Lettuce 1 lb lettuce = 6 cups shredded or torn

Limes 1 medium lime = $1\frac{1}{2}$ tablespoons juice

Marshmallow 11 large marshmallows = 110 miniatures = 1 cup

   1 large marshmallow = 10 miniatures

Meat 1 lb = 2 cups chopped or diced cubes

Mushrooms 8 oz raw mushrooms = 1 cup sliced and cooked

Nuts 1 lb shelled nuts = 4 cups chopped

Onions 1 medium onion = $\frac{1}{2}$ cup chopped

Pasta 4 oz uncooked macaroni = $2\frac{1}{4}$ cups cooked

   4 oz uncooked noodles = 2 cups cooked

   7 oz uncooked spaghetti = 4 cups cooked

Peaches 4 medium peaches = 2 cups sliced

Pears 4 medium pears = 2 cups sliced

Pepper 1 large green bell pepper = 1 cup diced or cubed

Potatoes 3 medium white potatoes = 2 cups cooked and cubed or $1\frac{3}{4}$ cups mashed

Raisins 1 lb raisins = 3 cups

Rice 1 cup raw long grain rice = 3 to 4 cups cooked
  1 cup precooked rice = 2 cups cooked

Shrimps (or prawns) $1\frac{1}{2}$ lb fresh, unpeeled shrimps = 2 cups cooked, peeled and deveined
  1 lb fresh jumbo shrimps (or prawns) = 18 to 20 shrimps

Strawberries 1 quart strawberries = 4 cups sliced

Sugar 1 lb granulated sugar = 2 cups
  1 lb brown sugar = $2\frac{1}{4}$ cups firmly packed (throughout this book the quantities given for light and dark brown sugar assume that it is firmly packed in the cup)
  1 lb confectioner's (icing) sugar = $3\frac{3}{4}$ to 4 cups

Sweet potatoes 3 medium sweet potatoes = 3 cups sliced

Tomatoes 1 lb tomatoes = 5 medium tomatoes = $1\frac{2}{3}$ to 2 cups chopped

SOUL FOOD

THE HIGH AND MIGHTY BREAKFAST

*J*ust imagine how important breakfast was for folks who worked from dawn to dusk, picking the cotton and plowing the fields, churning the butter and making the sausage, feeding the chickens and planting the rice . . . and on and on and on. It's easy to see why the soul food breakfast is about as mighty as they come.

Happily, it has survived even though we no longer need all that fuel for a long day's toil. One reason is that our breakfast foods are so very diversified. How could anyone tire of so many varieties of pancakes and breads or pass up down-home sausage and grits? Some Southerners, like my dad, have to start the day with freshly pan-fried fish, hash browns, stewed tomatoes, and clabber. The possibilities are endless, as you will see.

Another reason soul breakfasts are still popular is the Southern institution of brunch, which started out in New Orleans as a late breakfast for the merchants of the French quarter who began their work day long before dawn. A true New Orleans brunch would include elaborate dishes like stuffed omelettes and crawfish bisque, but alongside would be all the old soul favorites.

Now I'm not suggesting that one should devour a soul food breakfast every single morning, as that certainly would not fit into most modern lifestyles. Nor did I write this book just to try and make y'all get fat! But on a slow, lazy day of relaxation, like a Sunday or a holiday, a big family breakfast with a good range of dishes can still be savored and enjoyed. When I was a kid we sure as shootin' used to need one to hold us through Uncle Frank shouting from the pulpit for several hours. The custom's stuck with me, but these days more as a way of starting the day with a late brunch, which fits magnificently into the scheme and purpose of a day of rest!

PANCAKE MAKING

Every culture seems to have its own version of the awesome pancake: the Russian blini, the French crêpe, the Jewish blintz are just a few. Since America is so vast, it stands to reason that we have many versions of and different names for pancakes: griddlecakes, flapjacks, buckwheat and cornmeal cakes, hoecakes and johnnycakes to name but a few. The same basic rules hold true for all of them.

Grease a good heavy griddle with vegetable oil – not butter as it makes them stick – and heat it to the right temperature. Use this simple water test to determine the 'right' temperature. Flick on a few drops of water. If it evaporates immediately and goes up in smoke, then your griddle is too hot. If it just sits there and lazes around, then your griddle is too cold. But if those drops skedaddle around, then you know you're dead on target. Get those pancakes burning!

The batter should be about the same consistency, or a wee bit thinner, than that for a cake. Determine this by the amount of milk you use, adding more for thinner pancakes, less for heavier ones. You'll soon know which you prefer. Ignore any lumps existing in the batter, as you should never over-beat pancakes. Batter containing fruit will do better if allowed to stand for a few hours. Overnight is OK, too. This is called a resting period and produces a superior result.

Pour the batter from the mouth of a pitcher to control the flow. If you don't have one, a large spoon will do. Allow ample space between each cake on the griddle, because when the batter hits the heat, it will expand a bit. Wait until bubbles appear and the edges look slightly browned underneath, about 2 or 3 minutes. Then flip the pancake before all the bubbles break. Only flip once, and never flatten with a spatula, it will toughen them. The second side will take less time to cook, no more than 2 minutes, and never browns quite as evenly as the first side, so don't think you're doing anything wrong at this stage.

Real connoisseurs throw the first pancake away. Their word has it that once you've cooked that first pancake your pan is seasoned and the heat will be just right. I do this myself, although I never throw the first one very far away.

When making big fat stacks of pancakes, you'll be wanting to keep them warm. Do this by placing them on an ovenproof plate lined with a kitchen towel (linen is good) and folding the towel over the pancakes, one by one, as you go along. Put them in a low oven (around 150°F or at most 200°F [70–95°C, gas low–$\frac{1}{4}$]). Use more than one towel if you need to. If you don't keep the cakes separate, the steam will seep from one to the other and they will be soggy. Don't use a paper towel for this as the paper will allow the steam to seep through.

Follow these rules and all your pancakes will be truly awesome.

THE AWESOME PANCAKE

MAKES ABOUT 20 PANCAKES

These delicious plain pancakes, like small fat airy crêpes, are eaten for breakfast along with crisp bacon or sausages or fluffy scrambled eggs. There are several good variations and I have given them below.

2 large eggs, well beaten

2 cups (16 fl oz, 500 ml) milk

2 tablespoons melted butter (or bacon grease)

2 cups (8 oz, 250 g) sifted all-purpose flour

4 teaspoons baking powder

3 tablespoons sugar

1 teaspoon salt

vegetable oil to grease griddle

$\frac{1}{2}$ cup (4 oz, 120 g) melted butter

2 cups (16 fl oz, 500 ml) pure maple syrup or honey

Combine your eggs, milk, and melted butter.

Sift together all of your dry ingredients; then whisk them into the egg mixture. Whisk until almost smooth but do not over-beat.

Pour your batter onto the prepared griddle. About $\frac{1}{4}$ cup (2 fl oz, 60 ml) of batter per pancake works well for me. When your pancakes begin to bubble and air pockets form, flip them over. Brown the other side and serve at once with melted butter, maple syrup, or honey.

VARIATIONS For each cup of batter:

Apple Pancakes Add $\frac{1}{2}$ cup peeled, cored, and finely chopped apple (1 small apple) and $\frac{1}{2}$ teaspoon ground cinnamon. Allow your batter to stand for 1 hour before cooking.

Blueberry Pancakes Add $\frac{1}{2}$ cup (3 oz, 90 g) fresh, frozen, or canned blueberries. If using frozen or canned blueberries, be certain to drain them well before adding to the batter.

Bacon Pancakes Add 4 slices of crisply fried bacon, crumbled.

Spicy Raisin Pancakes Add $\frac{1}{3}$ cup (2 oz, 60 g) raisins and $\frac{1}{2}$ teaspoon ground cinnamon. (These are my children's favorites.)

Buttermilk Pancakes Using my Awesome Pancake recipe, substitute buttermilk (or rich sour milk or yoghurt) for the milk; add 1 teaspoon baking soda and separate the eggs, beating the whites until stiff. Fold in the beaten egg whites just before cooking.

CORNMEAL GRIDDLECAKES

SERVES 4

Cornmeal griddlecakes are a country cross between cornbread and pancakes. They are oh so fine smothered with jelly – my choice – or any syrup of your choosing.

1$\frac{1}{2}$ cups (6 oz, 175 g) sifted all-purpose flour	1 tablespoon sugar
	2 large eggs, separated
$\frac{1}{2}$ cup (2$\frac{1}{2}$ oz, 75 g) yellow cornmeal	2 cups (16 fl oz, 500 ml) milk
4 teaspoons baking powder	$\frac{1}{4}$ cup (2 oz, 60 g) bacon or sausage grease
1$\frac{1}{2}$ teaspoons salt	(or oil)

After first sifting your flour, sift again along with all of your other dry ingredients.

Beat your yolks, then add the milk and bacon or sausage grease and whisk to blend. (Or you can use any type of oil; it's just that I think bacon and sausage grease make a griddlecake with a much nicer flavour. Also, you can make use of the grease from the meat you've fried for breakfast.) Add it to the dry ingredients and stir only until just smooth. Don't over-beat. Just ignore the lumps!

Beat your egg whites until they form stiff peaks, then fold them into the batter. Cook as directed on page 32. Serve hot with butter and warm maple or blueberry syrup, honey, or jelly (jam).

VARIATION To make *Wholewheat Griddlecakes* substitute 1 cup (4$\frac{1}{2}$ oz, 130 g) wholewheat flour and 1 cup (4 oz, 120 g) sifted all-purpose flour for the flour and cornmeal. To further enhance the flavor, substitute honey or molasses for the sugar.

BUCKWHEAT GRIDDLECAKES

SERVES 6

Some folks prefer buckwheat pancakes because of the tiny little bits of crushed buckwheat seed and the dark sweetness of the molasses. Whiskin' up the egg whites keeps these pancakes light.

$1\frac{1}{2}$ cups (7 oz, 200 g) buckwheat flour
$\frac{1}{2}$ cup (2 oz, 60 g) sifted all-purpose flour
$1\frac{1}{2}$ teaspoons salt
$\frac{1}{3}$ cup butter (or margarine or vegetable shortening)

2 large eggs, separated
$2\frac{1}{4}$ cups (18 fl oz, 550 ml) milk
1 tablespoon molasses

First you sift all your flour, then you sift again along with the salt. With your fingertips or a fork, cut in the shortening.

Beat your egg yolks slightly and stir into the milk. Add the molasses and mix well. Pour your egg mixture into dry ingredients and blend your batter only enough to moisten. Don't beat it to death!

Beat your egg whites until they form stiff peaks, then fold them into the batter. Cook as directed on page 32.

Serve 'em up by the stackful smothered with butter and warm maple syrup.

AUNT GUSSIE'S ONION FLAPJACKS

MAKES ABOUT 20 FLAPJACKS

My Aunt Gussie from Jamaica, Long Island, New York, used to make up a big batch of these bad boys to smother with creamed sweetbreads or to accompany Uncle Boykin's wonderful gumbo (see pages 44 and 113). We would use them to sop up all the gumbo bits. Since then I've adapted Gussie's idea to add a little soul to all kinds of other food. Try them on for size with a yoghurt, cucumber, and garlic dip and you won't look back.

1 recipe The Awesome Pancake (see page 33)
2 tablespoons butter

2 cups finely diced onion (4 medium onions)

Make up your pancake batter and allow it to stand for at least 1 hour.

Melt the butter in a heavy sauté pan over medium heat. Add your onions. Lower the heat and sauté for 5 minutes or until the onions are soft and transparent. Let the onions cool down a bit, say for 10 minutes, then scrape them into your batter and stir to blend.

Prepare your griddle and cook as directed on page 32. Serve hot.

POTATO PANCAKES

SERVES 8

So *vhat* are Jewish latkes doing in a soul food book already? They are here because my dad makes them to eat with fried porgies and creamed corn and my Aunt Peacie makes them to go with her roast pork Sunday dinners – and they sure ain't Jewish. I never even knew they were called latkes until a friend of mine informed me of such. So here they are with the soulful touch.

6 medium potatoes (about 2 lb, 1 kg)
1 medium onion
1 large egg, beaten
2 tablespoons all-purpose flour
1 teaspoon salt

$\frac{1}{4}$ teaspoon white pepper
1 tablespoon cream
$\frac{1}{2}$ teaspoon baking soda
$\frac{1}{4}$ cup (2 oz, 60 g) butter (or bacon fat)

Peel and grate your potatoes, submerging them totally in ice water to prevent them from going brown. Allow them to soak for at least 2 hours (or overnight if you've a mind to).

Drain the potatoes, lay them out on kitchen towels or paper towels. Squeeze out as much of the excess moisture as you possibly can.

Put your potatoes in a bowl and grate in the onion. Pour in your beaten egg, flour, salt, pepper, cream, and baking soda. Mix thoroughly.

Heat your butter to just about the sizzling stage (I prefer butter to bacon fat in this recipe) in a large skillet over high heat. Using about 2 tablespoons of potato mixture for each pancake, drop your mixture in by the spoonful. Lower the heat, press each pancake flat with a spatula and brown. You mustn't allow your butter to burn; it destroys the taste. Turn only once, after about 5 minutes, and brown the other side. Serve hot.

WAFFLES

MAKES 6

Aunt Odessa makes the best waffles in the world, maybe because her waffle iron is seasoned just right after so much use. Your batter must be lighter than that of a pancake, which is why your eggs should always be separated and the whites beaten before being added. Don't forget that the golden-brown holes are only there to be filled with melted butter and warm syrup, so no waitin' around politely, eat quickly and enjoy!

2 cups (8 oz, 250 g) sifted all-purpose
   flour
1 teaspoon salt
4 teaspoons baking powder
2 tablespoons sugar

3 large eggs, separated
1$\frac{1}{2}$ cups (12 fl oz, 375 ml) milk
about 1 cup (8 oz, 250 g) melted butter
   (or vegetable oil or other fat)

Sift all your dry ingredients together. Beat the egg yolks and add the milk and $\frac{1}{3}$ cup (2$\frac{1}{2}$ oz, 75 g) of the melted butter.

Beat the liquid into your dry ingredients until thoroughly blended.

Beat the egg whites until stiff and fold into the batter.

Preheat your waffle iron according to the manufacturer's instructions. Pour about 1 tablespoon melted butter into each waffle section. Pour the amount of batter specified in the manufacturer's instructions onto the iron and bake until golden brown, which is usually when the steaming stops – about 4 or 5 minutes. Take care not to overfill the waffle iron because this will make for a real messy affair.

Serve hot with melted butter and warm maple syrup or honey.

NOTES I sometimes whip up $\frac{1}{2}$ cup (4 oz, 120 g) butter with $\frac{1}{2}$ cup (4 oz, 120 g) honey to make up a honey butter. It's real mean!

Or I make what I call *Nutty Waffles*: stir $\frac{1}{4}$ cup (1 oz, 30 g) finely chopped pecans or hazelnuts into the waffle batter.

If your family really loves waffles, bake a large batch. Individually wrap each waffle in aluminum foil or clear plastic wrap and freeze. Then, whenever you want a waffle, remove one from the freezer and place straight into a toaster on light setting. Toast twice and serve as above.

LITTLE LINDA'S CRISP FRENCH TOAST

SERVES 3

This is my sister Linda's recipe for French toast. It is the one that we all grew up on while living on Girard Avenue in West Philadelphia. Boy, Anthony and Linda and I could really down some French toast in those days. I can remember many a time knocking off an entire loaf of bread in one sitting. So you'll have no problem imagining my size as a budding teenager. I was a beast! – while Linda, who ate double quantities, was a rake.

On my first trip to gay Paree, I had a big shock waiting for me. No, it wasn't a man. It was diabolical French toast! The bread was so thick and soggy that it must have been soaking in the mixture for two days. And it had no flavor whatsoever. I never did work out whether they just needed to fire the chef, or whether that was the real thing.

I'll take Linda's recipe over the Paris variety any time. I can visualize the French reaction, 'Zees craazy Américains, now zey 'ave evon bastardized zee Freench toast.' Well, my reply to that would be, Linda's version is the real deal, lightly coated and deliciously crisp. So remember folks, don't soak that bread. Just coat it lightly.

2 large eggs	$\frac{1}{4}$ teaspoon ground nutmeg
1 cup (8 fl oz, 250 ml) milk	6 slices white bread (as thin or thick as
1 teaspoon pure vanilla extract	you like)
1 teaspoon ground cinnamon	butter for frying

Whisk together your eggs, milk, vanilla, and spices in a shallow bowl until nice and foamy. Dip your bread slices in, one by one, on both sides just as you are ready to fry. Whatever you do, don't let them get too soggy. They quickly soak up all of the egg mixture.

My little sister Linda, always just as skinny as a rake although she could put away a pile of French toast, a panful of fried apples, and a heap of sausage patties even when she was this size.

Heat a cast-iron skillet or griddle over medium heat. When hot, coat with the butter and gently fry the bread until golden brown on both sides. Add more butter during cooking if necessary.

If you like, you can melt just a small dollop of butter on each slice just before smothering them with maple syrup or fruit jelly (jam). Serve hot with crispy bacon, grits, fried or scrambled eggs, or fried apples (see page 44) on the side.

French toast is an excellent way to get a little bit of egg into the diet of kids who might normally refuse eggs.

*H*ASH BROWNS

SERVES 4

The thing I like best about hash browns is the crunchy crispness that comes from the potatoes being mashed down into the pan.

4 cups (1¾ lb, 850 g) cubed cooked
   potatoes
2 teaspoons all-purpose flour
salt and black pepper

6 tablespoons bacon fat (or oil)
2 teaspoons chopped fresh parsley
1 small onion, finely chopped
Worcestershire sauce

Put your potatoes in a bowl and sprinkle with flour and about 1 teaspoon each of salt and black pepper. Using a fork, gently toss the potatoes until they are nicely coated.

Heat your bacon fat (I prefer bacon fat for the flavor it gives to the potatoes) in a large skillet over high heat. When the fat is hot, throw in the potatoes. Sprinkle on your parsley and chopped onion. Toss around with a spatula, mixing well to coat your potatoes nice and evenly. Give them several shakes of Worcestershire sauce and sprinkle with a little more salt and pepper. Press the potatoes down with a spatula to pack them firmly into the skillet. Lower the heat and continue cooking for about 15 minutes, pressing with a spatula from time to time. Do not stir.

When the potatoes are crisp and brown on the underside, break the panful in half with the spatula and flip each half over as you would an omelette. Cook on the other side for 10 minutes or until nice and brown. If the potatoes begin to stick to the pan, add a bit more fat. Season with more salt, pepper, and Worcestershire sauce if you so desire. Serve hot.

NOTE If for some reason you choose to use raw potatoes, just add one more step to the cooking process. Cover the skillet with a tight-fitting lid for a portion of the cooking time to allow the potatoes to steam and cook through. Turn up your heat for the final browning on each side.

SCRAMBLED BRAINS 'N' EGGS

SERVES 4

Now listen, folks, I have got to admit that I have never put a single brain into my mouth. I am extremely open-minded about food but I figure this way: I've gone this long without eating anybody's brains, so I can certainly go a little while longer.

But this is a most typical dish from the deeeep deeeep South and lots of people like it. So, here's how it's made.

1 lb (500 g) pork brains (about 2 sets, I'm told)	$\frac{1}{3}$ cup (5 oz, 150 g) butter or bacon grease
1 tablespoon vinegar	salt and pepper
	4 large eggs, well beaten

Soak your brains for 3 hours in a quart of cold water to which you have added 1 tablespoon vinegar. Now what do you think you do with the poor things? You place them in a colander and pour boiling water over them to rid any traces of blood and membrane which remain. (You want to sort of clear the mind, so to speak.)

Next you melt your butter or bacon fat in a skillet over high heat. When the fat is hot, but not smoking, you just throw your old brains right on in there. Lower the heat but don't stop stirring them around, oh no, or they might decide to clump up or stick to the pan. Well, now that your brains have been nicely browned, oh about 10 minutes in all, pour in your already beaten-up eggs and scramble it all up there together. Serve hot.

THE HARRELLS' BREAKFAST
OF SCRAMBLED CHEESE 'N' EGGS

This was a favorite dish of my great-great-grandfather, Dennison Harrell, or so I have been told by the only living person to have actually known him, my aunt Cleo Hunter, who lives in Brooklyn, New York. This is my Aunt Odessa's recipe and I have loved them her way all my life. She says it's the dash of water that keeps the eggs creamy while milk or cream would just toughen them up. (In England, I've found that Red Leicester or Double Gloucester are excellent cheeses for this recipe.)

For each egg:

dash of water

2 tablespoons grated sharp cheddar (or other) cheese

salt and pepper

1 teaspoon butter

My great-great-grandfather Dennison Harrell, the son of a wealthy Englishman and a black slave girl, who stowed away aboard a ship, perhaps from Liverpool. Sometime later he arrived at Charleston Harbor, finally settling in Scotland Neck, South Carolina. He is the American root of my maternal family tree. Dennison worked as a skilled carpenter and was a preacher. He was an extremely quiet and secretive man, largely to protect his first wife, Virginia, a Northern white woman. This is the only photograph we have of him.

Beat your eggs for several minutes. Add a dash of water (no more than $\frac{1}{2}$ teaspoon per egg), cheese, and salt and pepper to taste.

Melt the butter in a skillet over low heat. Pour in your egg mixture and stir gently as it begins to set, making sure all of the cheese melts. Just before the eggs are completely set, remove from the heat and finish cooking off the heat.

Serve immediately with home fries, buttery grits, and crispy bacon, and of course, hot buttered biscuits with jelly (jam) spread on them.

ROLAND'S HOME FRIES

SERVES 6

Home fries are rather like sauté potatoes, but not quite as thick and with an onion and bacon flavor. Now Roland, my sister Linda's better half, cooks up one mean pan of home fries. He begins with cold cooked potatoes and adds green pepper and celery to further enhance the flavor, although they are just as good without the green pepper and celery and sometimes I do mine like that, but always with onion. I make these with raw potatoes to ensure they retain their shape, and by allowing them to steam and cook through as for hash browns (see page 38), but feel free to use cold boiled or baked potatoes if you wish.

2 tablespoons bacon grease
2 tablespoons butter
6 medium-sized peeled, cooked potatoes (about 2 lb, 1 kg), diced or sliced
1 medium onion, diced or sliced
1 cup (5 oz, 150 g) finely chopped celery

$\frac{1}{2}$ cup chopped green pepper (1 small pepper)
salt and black pepper
dash of seasoning salt, onion salt or powder, to taste

Heat up your bacon grease and butter in a large skillet over high heat. When the fat is hot, add your potatoes and any other vegetables you choose to use. Lower the heat to medium and cook, stirring often, until the potatoes are nicely browned on all sides. Season them with about $\frac{1}{4}$ teaspoon each of salt and pepper to start.

Cover with a tight-fitting lid and cook for 15 to 20 minutes or until well browned. Stir, taste, and add your chosen seasonings as the potatoes cook. Add more grease if necessary, but don't add too much. Home fries should never be swimming in fat.

When the potatoes are brown and crisp, remove them from the heat. Drain on paper towels, and enjoy.

LINDA'S FRIED APPLES

SERVES 4

My sister Linda would make fried apples as long as there was an apple in the house to fry, and usually she would eat them all too with French toast. But sometimes, Dad would find enough left over to cook at dinner time with smothered fried pork chops, ham, or duck. I love them on their own, too, as a quick snack. If you make them for any meal other than breakfast (when you want them nice and soft), you can leave the skins on for color and crunch.

4 firm tart apples
4 tablespoons butter or bacon fat
$\frac{1}{3}-\frac{1}{2}$ cup (3–4 oz, 90–120 g) sugar, white
   or light brown

dash of ground cinnamon
1–2 tablespoons cold water

Peel and core your apples. Slice into circles about $\frac{1}{2}$ in (1.5 cm) thick.
Heat up your butter or bacon fat in a heavy skillet over low heat. Cook your apples, placing them in the pan one layer at a time. Sprinkle them with sugar, cinnamon, and a little water and cook over a low heat until your apples become nice and syrupy, about 6 minutes. Serve warm.

You can also cook them without any water by tightly covering the pan to allow the apples to steam through nicely. They will take on a glazed look.

CREAMED SWEETBREADS WITH

MUSHROOMS

SERVES 6

3 pairs sweetbreads
1 tablespoon cider vinegar
3 tablespoons butter
$\frac{3}{4}$ lb (375 g) mushrooms, sliced
1 tablespoon chopped onion
2 tablespoons all-purpose flour

1 large egg yolk
$1\frac{1}{2}$ cups (12 fl oz, 375 ml) light (single)
   cream
salt and paprika
sprinkling of freshly ground black pepper
$\frac{1}{2}$ cup (4 fl oz, 120 ml) dry white wine

There is a ritual that sweetbreads must undergo before they can be cooked and this is it. Soak them for 1 hour in cold water. Drain, then blanch them by putting them in cold water to cover, to which you add 1 tablespoon cider vinegar. Bring them slowly to the boil. Simmer for about 5 minutes. Drain and plunge the sweetbreads into iced water. When cool, remove any connecting, covering tissue. Cut your drowned, boiled, drained, plunged, and manicured sweetbreads into bite-sized pieces. Well, there's not much more you could do to the poor creatures, is there?

Ah, but there is. Melt the butter in a skillet over medium heat. Add your sweetbreads, mushrooms, and onion, and sauté until nicely browned, about 5 minutes. Toss the flour into the mixture. Beat your egg yolk into the cream then pour it into the skillet. Now throw in your seasonings and dry white wine. Cook until it thickens, about 3 minutes, stirring often.

Serve with new potatoes and fresh green peas or just as it is on toast.

CORN OYSTERS

SERVES 3

As a child, I always looked forward to having these on Sunday mornings alongside scrambled cheese and eggs, crisply fried bacon, and biscuits smothered with butter and Concord grape jelly. They replaced the grits and were some kinda good.

1 cup (8 oz, 250 g) crushed canned corn
3 tablespoons all-purpose flour
wisp of pepper

1 large egg, beaten
$\frac{1}{4}$ teaspoon salt
about 1 tablespoon butter

Drain your corn and crush, if necessary, then add the other ingredients and stir to blend. Drop by spoonfuls onto a hot griddle or frying pan to which a small amount of butter has been added. Cook for about 3 minutes over medium heat or until the bottom is brown. Turn and brown the other side. Serve immediately.

DOWN-HOME BREADS

*D*own-home breads have been a part of soul food since the earliest days of slavery. One of the very first was a simple pone or cornbread, made out of cornmeal and water and thrust into an open fire on the blade of a hoe, and called, for obvious reasons, a hoecake. Other versions, like ashcakes and johnnycakes, were born in slave quarters, out of the need to find variety within the monotonous ration of cornmeal.

We also have the hot, rich buttermilk, soda, or baking-powder biscuits baked in the plantation kitchens and back cabins of early colonial days, or the sweet muffins which probably arrived in America via the first French settlers. I love to eat them for breakfast, lunch, brunch, or dinner, piping hot and oozing with butter. Today in America these breads are just as popular as they were long ago, and perhaps the most wonderful thing about them is that they can adapt easily to any meal or menu.

You will no doubt notice that there is no recipe for a basic yeast bread or for dinner rolls in this chapter. There's a very good reason for this omission. At home, we simply buy rolls from a favorite baker. Last time I visited Philly, everybody I spoke to agreed that the best dinner rolls in the Delaware Valley came from Mom's Bakery, a couple of blocks down from Sonny's Soul Food Rib Restaurant on Stenton Avenue.

So, being a responsible author, I went straight down there to check out this rumor. I bought a roll, slipped outside, and ate it on the spot. Boy, was it good, something like a light, airy, buttery croissant and a scrumptious yeast bread rolled into one. No stopping me now. I made a bee-line for Mom and asked for her recipe. She told me in no uncertain terms that I could hold her down and pull out each of her teeth, one by one, but she'd never divulge her famous recipe. You can see Mom's rolls on pages 138–9 – but you'll just have to go to Philly to try them.

Never mind. Who needs to fiddle around with yeast? It's better left to a good baker, and then you'll have more time to experiment with the recipes here. I have given precise measurements, but real soul cooks like Aunt Peacie and Aunt Ella wouldn't bother with these trivialities. They just scrunch up the palm of their hands to measure and then, working quickly, adjust the dough by feel. Even if you do rely on measurements – as I do, I might add – try to notice and feel how the dough alters with each batch of flour, the weather and so on.

SPIDER CORNBREAD

SERVES 8

Way back, cornbreads were baked in a spider, an iron pan or skillet, supported by a metal frame with three short spidery legs. The spider was placed on an open hearth over hot coals and filled with batter. My Dad assures me that the modern conventional ovens bake much more evenly and efficiently, but it just doesn't sound as much fun as cooking on a spider — even if that is romanticizing the good old days. Anyway, here's Dad's recipe. It uses the delicate, light white cornmeal that Southerners prefer and is excellent, spider or no spider.

1⅓ cups (6 oz, 175 g) white cornmeal
⅓ cup (1½ oz, 45 g) all-purpose flour
1 teaspoon salt
1 teaspoon baking soda
2 tablespoons sugar
2 cups (16 fl oz, 500 ml) buttermilk or
    sour milk (see page 23)

¼ cup (2 fl oz, 60 ml) milk
2 large eggs, well beaten
1½ tablespoons melted butter
2 tablespoons bacon grease

Preheat your oven to 400°F (200°C, gas 6).

Sift your cornmeal, flour, salt, baking soda, and sugar together. Blend in the milks, eggs, and melted butter until smooth. Warm the bacon grease in a heavy cast-iron skillet in the oven. Turn your skillet to coat it evenly.

Pour your batter into the warmed skillet and bake for about 30 or 40 minutes or until golden brown. Slice into wedges or squares, butter, and serve hot.

GOLDEN CORNBREAD

SERVES 8

Here's a recipe for today's basic cornbread, richer and cake-like. I call it golden because that's the way it looks when it comes out of the oven. It goes dry very quickly once it's cut, so wrap foil around the edges to keep it moist.

If you've a mind to, you can really be creative with cornbread by adding chopped-up cracklin's, diced ham, or bacon bits to the batter. This makes a nice change, so get down to some real soulful eatin'.

¼ cup plus 2 tablespoons (3 oz, 90 g)
    melted bacon grease (or butter or
    vegetable shortening)
1 cup (4 oz, 120 g) sifted all-purpose flour
4 teaspoons baking powder

½ teaspoon salt
2 tablespoons sugar (optional)
1 cup (4½ oz, 130 g) yellow cornmeal
1 large egg
1 cup (8 fl oz, 250 ml) milk

Set your oven to 425°F (220°C, gas 7). Put 2 tablespoons of the bacon grease into an 8 in (20 cm) square pan or round cast-iron skillet. Sit it in the oven until it sizzles, being sure to tilt the pan so that it's coated evenly all over. Work fast or take care that the pan doesn't get too hot and start to smoke. If it does, take it out or lower the oven heat until just before your batter goes in.

Sift together your flour, baking powder, salt, and sugar, until well combined, two or three times if necessary. (You can add a touch more sugar if you find you like it sweeter). Then stir in your cornmeal.

Using a separate bowl, beat your egg lightly with a fork. Now make a well in the center of your dry ingredients and pour in your egg, milk, and the rest of the bacon grease. Beat vigorously for about 1 minute. (If you're adding cracklin's or the like, stir in $\frac{1}{4}$ to $\frac{1}{2}$ cup [$1\frac{1}{2}$–3 oz, 45–90 g] now.)

Pour your batter into the hot pan and bake, at 425°F (220°C, gas 7), for 20 to 25 minutes or until golden brown.

Serve piping hot and dripping with butter. Most folks will automatically add on a dap of jelly (jam) or honey when eating cornbread at breakfast time and use it to sop up their gravy if it's dinner time.

VARIATION   To make *Buttermilk Cornmeal Muffins*, substitute buttermilk for milk and pour the batter into well greased muffin tins instead of a skillet. Fill each tin two-thirds full and bake at 425°F (220°C, gas 7) for 15 to 20 minutes or until golden brown.

HUSH PUPPIES
6 HEALTHY SERVINGS

There are all kinds of tales attached to the way in which hush puppies came by their name. The most common one is that the hillbillies of Kentucky used to throw them to their hounds to keep them from howling when they smelled the aroma of fresh food cooking. Craig Claiborne writes in his book *Southern Cooking* that they were tossed to the dogs by the Confederate soldiers to keep the Yankees from knowing their precise whereabouts. But Aunt Odessa has a quite different version. She tells me that it was from the old black Southern cooks who used to pick out the bits of fried cornmeal batter which floated to the top of the pot of frying lard, so that the lard would be clean for the next batch. They threw these bits out of the back door of the kitchens, yelling at the yapping dogs, 'Hush, puppies!'

There are two things that are for dang sure – one, somebody was definitely talking to a dog; and two, everybody agrees that hush puppies should be served with fried fish, especially catfish (see page 69).

2 cups (9 oz, 275 g) cornmeal, preferably white

2 tablespoons all-purpose flour

$\frac{1}{2}$ teaspoon salt

1 teaspoon baking powder

dash of cayenne pepper (optional)

$\frac{1}{4}$ cup ($1\frac{1}{2}$ oz, 45 g) finely chopped onion

1 small clove of garlic, minced (optional)

1 large egg

1 cup milk

about 2 cups (1 lb, 500 g) lard or vegetable shortening

Mix together all your dry ingredients, onion included, and any other optional ingredient. Make a well in the center, drop in your egg, stir in your milk, and blend well to make a nice smooth batter. Let it sit for 2 minutes and then form it into teaspoon-sized balls.

Heat the lard to 350°F (175°C) – use a cooking thermometer – in a deep-fat fryer (or in a deep, heavy skillet). Drop your batter into the hot fat and fry until your hush puppies are golden brown. Drain them on paper towels and serve at once.

If you have any old hounds around, you can always try them out on them first if you like!

SPOONBREAD

SERVES 6

Spoonbread is to my mind a gourmet's delight. You should be able to spoon it out onto your plate and eat it with a fork. To ensure this, I treat spoonbread with the respect it deserves and separate the eggs and beat the whites. Some people don't and it comes out just fine, but I like that extra little bit of fluffiness that beaten egg whites give.

1 cup (4½ oz, 130 g) yellow or white
  cornmeal
2 cups (16 fl oz, 500 ml) water
1 teaspoon salt
1 cup (8 fl oz, 250 ml) milk or buttermilk

2 tablespoons melted butter
1 teaspoon baking powder
3 egg yolks
3 egg whites, stiffly beaten

Preheat your oven to 375°F (190°C, gas 5).

Pour your cornmeal into boiling salted water. Cook, over medium heat, for 5 minutes or until thick, stirring constantly.

When the consistency is just about right, remove the pan from the heat and slowly stir in the milk. Let it cool down a bit before beating in your butter, baking powder, and egg yolks. Beat vigorously for a couple of minutes then fold in the stiffly beaten egg whites (stiff but not dry, that is).

Pour the batter into a well buttered 2 quart (1¾ UK quart, 1 l) baking dish and bake for 35 to 40 minutes or until golden brown. It's done when a toothpick inserted into the center comes out clean.

You can serve spoonbread with just about any kind of meat – ham, pork loin or chops, spareribs, roast chicken or seafood dishes. It is also terrific for breakfast!

DOT'S ASHCAKE
SERVES 4

One of the most pleasant surprises I had while writing this book was discovering just who among my family members were closet soul food cooks. When I went to Philly to visit and to chew the fat with family about old recipes and yarns as long as a piece of string, my beautiful stepmother Dot – Dorothy Preston Ferguson – came out and walloped me, bang, with this remarkable recipe. My mouth dropped open as I listened to this college graduate describe how she used to make bread baked in ashes in the open fireplace down on her family's farm in Martinsville, Virginia.

My Daddy's face dropped too, 'cause he's always done all the cooking and grocery shopping. Dot's no fool, heh? Well, he said no way was he gonna eat

My stepmother Dot, a graduate in psychology from Howard University in Washington, DC, whose country specialties, like ashcake and creamy fried corn, are just too gull-dern magnificent for words.

anybody's bread baked in dirty ashes. But that night he ate his words. Dot made a fire and baked up a loaf which was so good he just couldn't resist it.

So here is Dot's amazing recipe, taught to her and her sisters by their mother, Grandma Rose. Next time you have an open fire, instead of roasting chestnuts, try Dot's Ashcake.

1½ cups (7 oz, 200 g) white cornmeal	½ teaspoon salt
¼ cup (2 fl oz, 60 ml) water	⅛ teaspoon black pepper

Make a blazing fire in an open fireplace.

Mix your cornmeal, water, salt, and black pepper thoroughly. Make one big oval-shaped ball.

Make a clean space in the fireplace but leave a few very hot coals as a bed to put your corn ball on. Cook on the opened bed until the ball gets a little hard and stays together.

After the ball is hard, cover with very hot coals and cook for 15 to 20 minutes, perhaps more or less. You must use your own judgment here. Dot says they used to insert a long piece of straw to check for doneness. But if you don't have one of those, stick in a knife. If it comes out hot and clean, the ashcake is done. Then remove it from the fireplace and clean by brushing with a clean kitchen towel.

CRACKLIN' BREAD

SERVES 8

Cracklin' breads were often made in the slave quarters when the only rations left were pork skins. They would throw them into the fire until they crackled and then they just threw them in with a basic cornbread batter – no egg, wheat flour, milk, or sugar then – just before baking. Today cracklin' bread is still a delight enjoyed by lots of Southern folk, black and white alike.

½ cup (4 oz, 120 g) chopped salt pork or bacon	1 teaspoon salt
	1 teaspoon baking powder
2 cups (9 oz, 275 g) cornmeal, yellow or white	1 cup (8 fl oz, 250 ml) water

Preheat your oven to 450°F (230°C, gas 8).

In a heavy skillet, over medium heat, sauté your salt pork for about 10 minutes or until it's crisp and brown. Drain off and reserve the fat. You now have cracklin's.

Sift together your corn meal, salt, and baking powder into a small mixing bowl. Pour in the water along with 1 to 2 tablespoons of your reserved fat. Stir in your cracklin's.

Mold your dough into a preheated and well greased 1 quart (1¾ UK pint, 1 l) pan or a skillet. Bake for 30 minutes or until golden. If you prefer, you can shape the dough into little mounds and bake them on a well greased baking sheet at 450°F (230°C, gas 8) for 20 minutes or until golden.

BUTTERMILK BISCUITS

MAKES ABOUT 16–20 BISCUITS

2 cups (1 lb, 500 g) sifted all-purpose flour
2 teaspoons baking powder
1 tablespoon sugar
1 teaspoon salt
½ teaspoon baking soda

½ cup (4 oz, 120 g) lard or vegetable shortening
⅔–¾ cup (5–6 fl oz, 150–175 ml) buttermilk or sour milk (see page 23)

Preheat your oven to 450°F (230°C, gas 8).

Sift together all your dry ingredients. Cut in the shortening, using a fork, pastry blender, or two knives. When your mixture takes on the consistency of coarse cornmeal, slowly add buttermilk, just enough to hold it all together.

Turn your dough out onto a lightly floured board and knead for about 30 seconds. Pat it out ½ in (1.5 cm) thick and cut into rounds, using a 2 in (5 cm) biscuit cutter or the floured rim of a glass.

Place your biscuits, just touching, in two well greased 8 in (20 cm) round cake pans and bake for 15 to 20 minutes until golden brown. Serve immediately.

GRANDMA BATTLE'S BISCUITS

MAKES 12–16 BISCUITS

To most people, the American biscuit conjures up a picture of the old pioneer days in the wild, wild West, with cowpokes eating beans and biscuits out of a tin pan way out on the range after a long cattle drive. But in my mind's eye a very different picture comes into focus. I see Grandma Battle at our old family home on Woodstock Street, in North Philadelphia, sweeping through the kitchen with her full apron on, taking a swipe at Gerald, my cousin, and I as we were making a bee-line for the back door, her freshly baked biscuits in hand.

You see, the smell of her hot fresh biscuits baking could drive any sane person into wanting to steal some as soon as they came out of the oven. It never occurred to us that Grandma Battle actually counted out the number of biscuits she'd baked for the family. We thought we could just take one or two, move the rest around a little, and no one would ever be the wiser. Wrong! But it was sure worth a swat or two to get one of those bad boys.

American biscuits aren't so different from English scones, but you eat them for breakfast, lunch, or dinner. Whether you like them plain, oozing with butter and jelly (jam) or honey, or with butter and gravy, they are best served piping hot.

2 cups (8 oz, 250 g) sifted all-purpose flour
4 teaspoons baking powder
1 tablespoon sugar (optional)

1 teaspoon salt
3 tablespoons butter
2 tablespoons vegetable shortening
⅔–¾ cup (5–6 fl oz, 150–175 ml milk)

Preheat your oven to 450°F (230°C, gas 8).

Sift your flour, baking powder, sugar, and salt together. Using a fork, pastry blender or two knives, cut in your butter and shortening. When the consistency is like that of coarse cornmeal, add your milk, very slowly so as not to make the dough sticky or gooey. You want a firm dough that you can handle, but remember that too much handling makes dough tough.

Turn dough out onto a lightly floured board or flat surface and knead gently for about 30 seconds. Using a lightly floured rolling pin, roll the dough to a thickness of about $\frac{1}{4}$ to $\frac{1}{2}$ in (or roughly 1 cm). Cut out circles with a 2 to 3 in (5–8 cm) cookie cutter. (I tend to use a floured glass – that works just as well as a biscuit cutter for me.)

Place your biscuits on an ungreased baking sheet and bake in the oven for about 12 to 15 minutes or until golden brown.

Serve hot in any way you like – but don't be surprised if you have fewer than you thought when you began baking.

Martha Virginia Bullock Battle, otherwise known as Grandma Battle, was half Indian. She was educated as a schoolteacher but her qualifications weren't recognized when she moved North, so she settled into being a full-time housewife, mother (to my mother and six other children), and brilliant cook. She had a flick of the wrist that helped her bake with great speed and accuracy – and without measuring.

SWEET POTATO BISCUITS

MAKES ABOUT 16–20 BISCUITS

Our family has always made up these biscuits when some sweet potato casserole (see page 153) happens to be left over from the night before. This means the potatoes are already seasoned with cinnamon, nutmeg, orange or lemon juice, and any other spices in the casserole. So, if you want to make them up from scratch – and boy, is it worth it when you have a honey-roast ham in the house – don't forget to add the seasonings you like.

½ cup (4 oz, 120 g) melted butter
1 cup (8 oz, 250 g) cooked mashed
  seasoned sweet potatoes
⅔ cup (5 fl oz, 150 ml) milk, at room
  temperature

2 cups (8 oz, 250 g) sifted all-purpose
  flour
2 tablespoons brown sugar
1 teaspoon salt
4 teaspoons baking powder

Preheat your oven to 400°F (200°C, gas 6).

Beat your melted butter into the mashed sweet potatoes. If they aren't already seasoned and spiced, add what you want. Then stir in your milk.

Sift together the flour, brown sugar, salt, and baking powder. Slowly stir all your dry ingredients into the sweet potato mixture. When a nice ball forms, turn out your dough onto a well-floured board.

You will need a considerable amount of flour on your hands for patting out the dough because it is a bit sticky. Pat it out ½ in (1.5 cm) thick and cut into circles with a 2 in (5 cm) cookie cutter or the rim of a floured glass.

Lay your biscuits with the sides just touching in two greased 8 inch (20 cm) round cake pans and bake for about 20 minutes or until golden. Serve immediately.

SAUSAGE BISCUITS

MAKES ABOUT 18–20 BISCUITS

These jodies are simply out of this world. John and Ann Egerton explain in *Southern Food* that they were invented by an unknown Southerner who simply loved sausages and biscuits. Well, I take my hat off to whoever invented this mouth-watering combination! Now, of course, it has spread far and wide: every American supermarket seems to carry frozen sausage biscuits of some variety. But none of them can come close to the real McCoy. Until you've tried a sausage biscuit made with down-home sausage and freshly mixed dough, then in my book you haven't lived.

1 recipe biscuit, either Grandma Battle's
  or Buttermilk (see page 54)

8–12 oz (250–375 g) uncooked ready-
  made sausage meat

Make up your biscuit dough. Separate it into two individual balls then roll each out to a thickness of about ¼ in (6 mm) on a lightly floured board.

Spread an even layer of sausage meat on each layer of dough, then roll up each just like you would a jelly roll. Pat down each end to tidy it up. Wrap the rolls in waxed paper and refrigerate for about 30 minutes. Now your sausage rolls will be much easier to slice.

Preheat your oven to 425°F (220°C, gas 7).

Slice each roll into ½ in (1.5 cm) thick pieces. Place on a lightly greased baking sheet and bake for 15 to 20 minutes or until the sausage is done and your biscuit dough is nicely browned. Drain on paper towels and let 'er rip!

Eat them on their own, or broken up in a bowl and doused with warm maple syrup, which is the way my twin daughters love them. Sausage biscuits can also be served with a down-home breakfast of eggs, home fries, and grits.

MUFFIN MAKING

Here are three favorite soul muffins – blueberry, pecan, and apple. The origin of the word muffin may be the old French for a soft bread, *pain moufflet*. But while a muffin on that side of the Atlantic is made with yeast and is more like a teacake or bread, the American version is crumbly and cake-like, and is made with butter and baking powder.

A practical word or two or three. Never, never over-beat muffin batter; it only serves to make them tough. If any muffin cups are left unfilled, before baking fill these one-third full of water to prevent them from scorching. It also helps to keep the muffins moist. Remove your muffins to a cooling rack as soon as they come from the oven. You can put them back into the oven for about 5 minutes to warm them through. If you want to keep them hot, without the bottoms sweating, lift them up and set them sideways in the cups while warming. You can freeze muffins in foil for later use. But don't let them thaw out naturally. Just throw them in the oven, still wrapped in the foil, and bake at 350°F (180°C, gas 4) for about 45 minutes. They'll taste just as if they were freshly baked.

BLUEBERRY MUFFINS

MAKES ABOUT 12 MUFFINS

2 cups (8 oz, 250 g) sifted all-purpose flour
¼ cup (2 oz, 60 g) sugar
3 teaspoons baking powder
¾ teaspoon salt
¼ cup (2 oz, 60 g) melted butter

¾ cup (6 fl oz, 175 g) milk
2 large eggs, lightly beaten
1 cup (6 oz, 175 g) fresh blueberries (or canned or frozen, washed and well drained)

Preheat your oven to 400°F (200°C, gas 6).

Sift all the dry ingredients together, twice. Combine your butter, milk, and eggs, and add to the dry ingredients. Stir lightly but do not beat. Fold in the blueberries, stirring just enough to distribute them through your batter, which should look lumpy.

Generously grease muffin cups and fill them two-thirds full. Bake for about 25 minutes or until golden brown. Serve hot, smothered with butter.

PECAN MUFFINS

MAKES ABOUT 12 MUFFINS

2 cups (8 oz, 250 g) sifted all-purpose
 flour
3 teaspoons baking powder
$\frac{1}{4}$ cup (2 oz, 60 g) sugar
$\frac{1}{2}$ teaspoon salt

1 large egg, lightly beaten
1 cup (8 fl oz, 250 ml) milk
$\frac{1}{4}$ cup (2 oz, 60 g) melted butter
$\frac{1}{2}$ cup (2 oz, 60 g) chopped pecans

Preheat your oven to 400°F (200°C, gas 6).

After sifting your flour, sift it again with the baking powder, sugar, and salt twice – yes, three times in all. Add your lightly beaten egg, milk, and butter. Stir until just moist, remembering that your batter should *not* be smooth. Stir in your chopped pecans.

Spoon your batter into well greased muffin cups, filling them two-thirds full. Bake for 20 to 25 minutes or until golden brown.

APPLE BROWN MUFFINS

MAKES ABOUT 12 MUFFINS

2 cups (8 oz, 250 g) sifted all-purpose
 flour
$\frac{1}{3}$ cup (2$\frac{1}{2}$ oz, 75 g) light brown sugar
2 teaspoons baking powder
$\frac{1}{2}$ teaspoon salt
$\frac{1}{4}$ teaspoon ground allspice
$\frac{1}{2}$ teaspoon ground cinnamon

1 cup (8 fl oz, 250 ml) milk
$\frac{1}{3}$ cup (6 oz, 175 g) melted butter
1 tablespoon fresh lemon juice
1 large egg, well beaten
1 cup grated or finely diced, peeled and
 cored sweet apple (1 medium apple)

Preheat your oven to 400°F (200°C, gas 6).

Sift all the dry ingredients together, twice. Combine the milk, butter, and lemon juice with the beaten egg. Pour into your dry ingredients, stirring just enough to moisten. Do not over-beat. Fold in the grated apple.

Generously grease muffin cups and fill them two-thirds full. Bake for 20 minutes or until golden and delicious.

NOTE If you want to make an extra-special treat, mix together about $\frac{1}{2}$ cup (2 oz, 60 g) chopped mixed nuts, $\frac{1}{2}$ teaspoon ground cinnamon, and $\frac{1}{2}$ cup (3$\frac{1}{2}$ oz, 100 g) brown sugar. Sprinkle on top of each muffin just before baking.

GRITS, GRITS, GRITS

What are grits? I can't begin to tell you just how many times I've been asked this question, nor how long it takes to answer it. When I reply that grits are broken-up or coarsely ground grains from a hominy, the other person inevitably asks, 'Well, what on earth is a hominy?'

The answer is that a hominy is a dried corn which has had its hull and germ removed by a soaking in wood ash, lye, or baking soda. This is why grits, which come in a box – dry and ready to be boiled – are white. Grits are bleached cornmeal, if you like. They used to be associated with the poor (or po') factions of American society and so, of course, with the African-American population, particularly in the South. But just as many white as black folks eat grits, and they have now reached across the length and breadth of the United States, carried along by Southerners who just cannot live without them.

I can hear you coming out with the next question. 'What exactly do grits taste like?' Well, folks, this is the hardest one of all to answer, simply because there's no other food with which you can easily compare them. They have a somewhat bland flavor, so they vary a great deal according to the way they are seasoned.

The most common way to serve them is smothered with butter and sprinkled with salt and a dash of pepper alongside an eggs, bacon, and buttermilk biscuit breakfast. Most down-home country folk, like my dad, wind up mixing together everything on the plate and using the biscuits to mop it all up.

Grits are also served with lots of sugar and cream or milk as a breakfast cereal; smothered with rich pan gravy, highly seasoned with cayenne pepper, with fried chicken, cornbread, and collard greens. They can also be baked with various cheeses, butter, cream, and garlic, or made into a soufflé with raisins, nuts, and cinnamon. They are so versatile that it's easy to see how they became a mainstream staple throughout the South.

But I must also say, very emphatically, that if you haven't grown up with grits, they are an acquired taste. I once cooked them for a broad-shouldered Italian boyfriend from Rhode Island who was heavily into meatballs, linguine, and antipasto, but insisted on trying them. As long as I live, I will never forget the look on his face after the first mouthful, when I said, 'Sure is better than your mamma's pasta, isn't it?' He looked like he might take out a contract on me.

Believe you me, I am in no way trying to put you off grits. It's just that these particular recipes are designed for the grits connoisseur. So, before you take the plunge, make sure you first test the water. Buy a box of grits, boil them in salted water until they reach the consistency of hot porridge, season them with butter, salt, and pepper — and just see whether or not your taste buds can handle them. That is the only way for you to discover for yourself just what grits really are.

GRITS AND CHEESE BAKE
SERVES 8

For this recipe you'll be cooking your grits in milk instead of water, to give them a creamier consistency and taste.

4 cups (1¾ pints, 1 l) milk
1 cup (7 oz, 200g) uncooked grits
1 cup (8 oz, 250 g) butter
1 large egg
2 cups (8 oz, 250 g) grated sharp cheddar cheese

salt
dash of cayenne or black pepper
paprika
2 tablespoons grated parmesan cheese

Preheat your oven to 350°F (180°C, gas 4).

Warm your milk in a saucepan almost to boiling point. Slowly pour in your grits and stir. Continue to stir while you add half of your butter. Allow the grits to boil down and thicken up, stirring frequently, until they have the consistency of hot porridge, about 20 minutes. Now remove the pan from the heat and allow it to stand, covered, for a couple of minutes.

Beat in your egg and the rest of the butter. Stir in the grated cheddar cheese and season with salt, cayenne or black pepper and a sprinkling of paprika. Mix well. Taste and adjust your seasonings.

Pour into a well buttered 2 quart (1¾ UK quart, 2 l) soufflé dish and sprinkle with your parmesan cheese and some more paprika. Bake in the oven for 30 to 40 minutes or until the top is nice and brown. Serve immediately.

SWEET GRITS SOUFFLÉ
SERVES 8

If your taste for grits has come this far, then let me be the first to congratulate you. You are a true gritser! This is my adaptation of a prize-winning recipe for Southern Indian Pudding that I found printed on a box of grits years ago.

½ cup (3½ oz, 100g) uncooked grits
¼ teaspoon salt
2 cups (16 fl oz, 500 ml) water
½ cup (4 oz, 120 g) sugar
3 large eggs, separated
1 tablespoon butter
2 teaspoons pure vanilla extract

1⅓ cups (11 fl oz, 340 ml) milk (or light [single] cream)
1 teaspoon ground cinnamon
dash of ground nutmeg
¼ cup (1½ oz, 45 g) seedless raisins
¼ cup (1 oz, 30 g) slivered almonds
1 teaspoon confectioner's (icing) sugar

Cook your grits in lightly salted water according to the instructions on the package. When thick, remove them from the heat and let stand, covered, for about 3 minutes.

Now beat in your sugar, egg yolks, butter, milk, vanilla, cinnamon, and nutmeg.

Beat your egg whites until they form stiff but not dry peaks, and fold in.

Pour your mixture into a well buttered 2 quart (1 ¾ UK quart, 2 l) baking dish. Toss your raisins and almonds with the confectioner's sugar then throw them on top. Place in a cold oven and bake at 325°F (160°C, gas 3) for about 1 hour or until the edges are light brown and top is golden.

Serve either hot or cold with generous helpings of whipped cream on top or heavy (double) cream poured over all.

CHEESE AND SAUSAGE GRITS CASSEROLE

SERVES 8

This is one *mean* casserole. You may wish to add a little salt, pepper, and paprika. I've purposely left them out because everything really depends on the spiciness of the sausage, and your own tastebuds.

1 lb (500 g) ready-made sausage meat	½ cup (4 oz, 120 g) butter
1 cup (7 oz, 200g) uncooked grits	2 large eggs, slightly beaten
4 cups (1¼ pints, 1 l) lightly salted water	½ cup (4 fl oz, 120 ml) milk
1 cup (4 oz, 120 g) grated cheddar cheese	1 small clove of garlic, minced

Form the sausage meat into patties and fry it up crisp and golden brown. Be sure you pour off all of the excess fat as you're frying. Drain your patties on paper towels, then crumble them up in a bowl. Preheat your oven to 350°F (180°C, gas 4).

While you're doing all this your grits can be cooking. You've got to boil them up in the salted water for about 5 minutes, exactly as it states on the box. When they thicken up to the consistency of porridge remove them from the heat and stir in grated cheddar. Cover and let them stand for a couple of minutes. Now stir in your butter, eggs, milk, and garlic until well blended. Stir in your sausage meat. Taste and adjust your seasonings.

Pour into a well buttered 1½ quart (1¼ UK quart, 1.5 l) baking dish and bake in your oven for 1 hour or until lightly browned and bubbling.

FRIED GRITS

Occasionally, when some grits are left over, we fry 'em up once they're cold. When there are no leftovers, cook grits according to the instructions on the box, then pour them into a cold rinsed mold or a square or rectangular loaf pan of some kind and allow them to cool down and set.

Once they're cold, just slice into ½ in (1.5 cm) strips and sauté in butter or bacon drippings until slightly crisp and golden. Serve with a slab of fried ham and red-eye gravy, hash browns, and blueberry muffins.

FINE FEATHERED FOWL

When I was a little girl visiting Granddaddy Bert's farm in Charlotte, North Carolina, Grandma Della would often ask me what I wanted for supper. Nearly always I would reply, 'Fried chicken,' and once she said, 'Well, go on out there and fetch me a chicken then.'

Now it sure wasn't from lack of trying, but, for the life of me, I couldn't even get my hands on one of those darned birds. Have you ever tried to catch a moving chicken? Believe you me, it ain't easy. After she'd finished laughing at me falling all around in the dirt, Grandma Della went straight over to the chicken coop, broom in hand, and cornered one of those little old rascals. 'Now this is the way to catch a chicken, granddaughter,' she said.

The old bird was a-flappin' and a-squawkin', but my grandmother, with one adroit flick of the wrist, snapped its neck before I even had a chance to gasp. She chopped off the head and hung the chicken out on the back porch to drain. All day long I kept watching that old bird, expecting it to come back to life and seek revenge on us all for wanting to cook it. Later, Grandma plucked the bird, threw hot water with paraffin wax all over it and, after the wax had hardened, pulled out the stubborn pin feathers. All the while, she was just a-hummin' and a-singin'. Then she singed it, cleaned it, and cut it up. She enjoyed my watching her and she sure was a sight for sore eyes. Come suppertime, we had the best fried chicken I think I have ever tasted.

If you don't keep your own chickens, it can be hard to find ones that taste so good. When buying a chicken, check the label if there is one and don't hesitate to ask how it has been raised and treated and on what it has been fed, 'cause it all comes out in the taste. Besides, what's the need for unnecessary cruelty to animals just because they are destined for the chopping block? To my mind, a free-range bird is closer to the way nature meant it to be.

Don't scorn mature birds either. They may not be so good for frying, grilling, or roasting, but if you slow cook them in plenty of liquid, they cook up really tender. Plus, the ample fat content will give your stock a rich, delectable flavor.

OPPOSITE *My Mom and Dad on 5 June 1949. My Mom always joked that she only married Dad for his culinary skills at frying chicken and fish. Although I have my doubts as to this obvious falsehood, there is always just a little twinge of underlying truth in any such jest, don'tcha think?*

*T*HE ART OF FRYING CHICKEN, OR FERGY'S FRIED CHICKEN

Make no mistake about it, my friends, frying chicken is an art. In any restaurant other than a soul food one, I never, but never, order fried chicken 'cause it never tastes like a well-fed bird should, and sometimes it even comes to the table with little bits of feathers stuck to it. Nothing like bits of feathers to kill your appetite!

Now my Dad taught me everything I know about frying chicken and I would

like to pass this family legacy on to you. We call it Fergy's Fried Chicken (no, I'm not trying to be presumptuous — it's just that my Dad and I share the nickname Fergy along with a few other people we all know). The basic principle is that if a thing's worth doing, it's worth doing well. So don't be surprised that the recipe's so long.

chicken, enough to give 2–3 pieces per person (depending on appetites)
salt and black pepper
garlic salt or powder
onion salt or powder
1 cup (4½ oz, 130 g) all-purpose flour for every 6 pieces of chicken

2 tablespoons paprika for every cup flour
about 2 cups (16 oz/fl oz, 500 ml/g) vegetable oil (or lard)
1 brown paper bag (a plastic one can be used but take care not to puncture it with a chicken bone)

Pick a young, freshly killed free-range chicken. A frozen, factory-farmed bird just won't do, even if it is a bit cheaper.

First off, clean it properly. Put some cool or cold salted water in your sink and let your chicken pieces soak for 1 hour or more. This salt helps to loosen the fat and blood and also lifts any remaining feathers so that you can see 'em.

Next, take your favorite paring knife, one that fits neatly into the palm of your hand, and begin to scrape the skin. Scrape under running water in an upward direction, raising and removing any feathers as you can see them. You're gonna be surprised at just how many tiny ones there are. If need be, you can singe off the fine ones, especially those on the wing, by holding the chicken pieces over a flame. But the scraping is still important because it removes an outer layer of scum existing on the skin. Just scrape and peel it off as you go. The chicken pieces are clean when they are featherless, smooth to the touch, and neither sticky nor grimy.

Next you wanna scrape out any filmy fat residue lurking beneath the skin. Just get as much out of there as you can, but leave the skin on. The wing is a real pistol to clean but don't be put off. It's worth every minute. Lay your finished chicken pieces on paper towels to drain and get out those glorious seasonings.

Season each piece individually with salt, pepper, garlic salt, garlic powder, and onion powder, adjusting the quantities to taste. Turn your pieces over on fresh dry paper towel and season the other side the same way.

Put the flour with the paprika in a brown paper bag and drop your chicken pieces in, two or three at a time. Shake and coat each piece evenly and thickly. Tuck and lock the little flap under the meaty side of each wing just after you flour them to form tight little triangles.

I should add here that most people I know just pour all of their seasonings into the brown paper bag along with the flour, shake each piece to coat evenly and then fry. They don't measure either, and their chicken comes out great too. And some people refrigerate their chicken after they have coated it with the flour. They say that the flavor is greatly enhanced if the seasonings are allowed to set for a spell. I can't really say, because I like to do each piece freshly and individually.

So this brings us to your skillet. Those old-fashioned, really heavy cast-iron skillets definitely fry up the best chicken. But if you're cooking with modern pans that are coated with non-stick materials, then keep a good watch over your temperature so that you don't burn the chicken skin before the inside is cooked.

You'll need about 2 in (5 cm) of fat, either vegetable oil or lard, in your skillet. Heat it, over high heat, until extremely hot but not yet smoking. For those with tidy minds, the generally accepted temperature for the deep-fat frying of chicken is 375°F (190°C). Back in the old days, down-home country folk used to throw a match into the pan of oil. When it ignited, they said it was ready for frying. I have never known of a fire resulting from this down-home technique. But, if you feel wary, just test the oil in the conventional way by tossing a drop of water into it. If it snaps, crackles, and pops, you are well on your way to some serious frying.

When the fat is ready, gently lower your pieces in, one by one, skin side up. Don't crowd the pieces, and remember that chicken pops a lot when it's frying. You may want to use a glove or mitt. I cannot work in them so I use a splatter screen, which also reduces the cleanup time afterwards.

Here you are, frying away at last! The idea is to fry the chicken so it's crisp on the outside but juicy on the inside. That means you have to fry quickly but thoroughly, turning the pieces often to keep them moving around in the pan. You poke a little and you move a little (sounds a bit like a prize fight, doesn't it?). The pieces don't have to be in constant motion, but when turning, shift their position every once in a while.

The secret is never to leave the pan unattended. No need to stand over it like an obedient dog, but stay within earshot. It's the rising and falling of the frying noise that tells you when to turn over the pieces. Don't get distracted by music or telephone calls. Never allow chicken to cook on one side longer than 5 minutes or it will begin to scorch.

Each time you turn, the fat will bubble furiously and the crackling will get slightly louder, then slowly level off. After your third or fourth turn, the pieces should be taking on a very nice shade of golden brown. At this stage, I lower the heat fractionally, cover with a lid or foil, and allow the chicken to steam for about 1 minute. This ensures there's no uncooked flesh and you don't lose any crispness.

When the crackling sound begins to intensify, you'll know it's time to remove the lid, turn the chicken again, and finish it off. Your total cooking time is around 25 to 35 minutes per panful, but you'll know when it's done by sight and sound. The crackling dies out almost completely and the chicken takes on the most beautiful golden-brown color imaginable.

Drain each piece of chicken on a paper towel. If you intend to fry more than one panful, then you should strain your oil before dropping in the next batch; otherwise the crisped-up flour particles in the bottom of your pan will burn and mess up your next batch as well as the gravy.

Believe me, after the first time, it's smooth sailing all the way and you will instinctively know exactly how to adjust the seasonings and temperature. So now you are ready to burn!

You'll have guessed by now just how fond I am of fried chicken by the pains

I've taken to explain it to you. So next time somebody mentions dipping some chicken into an artificially colored egg batter or breadcrumbs, please do me a favor and tell them that *you* know how to fry it the soul food way.

FRIED CHICKEN SMOTHERED
IN PAN GRAVY

Fergy's Fried Chicken (see above)
2 tablespoons all-purpose flour for every
   3 tablespoons fried chicken grease
about 2 cups (16 fl oz, 500 ml) water for
   every 2 tablespoons flour

salt and pepper
seasonings of your choice, such as garlic
   salt, onion powder etc.

Fry up your chicken. When it is done, crisp brown, juicy, and ready to be eaten, remove the pieces from the skillet onto a warmed serving platter and keep them warm (or better still, hide them, because inevitably some of the pieces will go missing).

Anyway, back to the gravy at hand. Pour off from your skillet all but the number of tablespoons of grease you will need, retaining all of those delicious crunchy bits of flour in the bottom of the pan (unless some are burnt, in which case you must discard them). Start by adding 2 tablespoons flour for every 3 tablespoons of grease and stir it into the crunchy residue. You can add more flour if the paste seems greasy. Stir over medium to high heat until the paste is a really dark brown. Lift your pan off the heat if it looks like it's about to smoke, but continue to stir, gathering up all the browned bits as you do.

When your paste looks right, pour in about 2 cups (16 fl oz, 500 ml) of cold water for every 2 tablespoons flour used and bring to a boil over high heat. Reduce your heat and start playing around with your seasonings. Add salt, black pepper, garlic salt or powder, seasoning salt, or whatever turns you on, and allow all this to simmer for about 5 minutes. Don't overdo it with the seasonings at this stage because as your gravy thickens up, the seasonings will become more concentrated. Do it gradually, taste, boil down, simmer, and keep tasting as you go.

Now, put your chicken pieces back into the pan. Cover and allow to simmer in the gravy for 30 minutes, stirring occasionally. Poke your chicken and make sure you spoon a little gravy over each piece so that the chicken is well smothered and the seasonings will go delightfully through and through. Near the end of this time the gravy will have thickened up and you can finally adjust your seasonings.

Just before I serve, I sometimes throw in a healthy dollop of butter and a splash of milk. I like it this way but it's not necessary. Serve directly from the skillet onto individual plates. It's a natural with long grain rice or mashed potatoes. It's even better when warmed up the next day – if there's any left.

OVEN OR GRILLED BARBECUED CHICKEN

SERVES 4

This recipe will give you a really soulful barbecued chicken all year round. But of course, there's nothing to stop you using this same sauce on the barbecue spit. It's just as good, if not better, with the added taste of smoke coming up from those coals.

$2\frac{1}{2}$ lb (1.25 kg) chicken pieces
1 cup (8 fl oz, 250 ml) tomato sauce
   (home-made, or canned sauce for
   pasta etc.)
$\frac{1}{2}$ cup (2 oz, 60 g) sliced fresh mushrooms
$\frac{1}{4}$ cup (2 fl oz, 60 ml) water
1 generous tablespoon brown sugar

1 teaspoon prepared mild mustard
$\frac{1}{8}$ teaspoon barbecue spice
1 tablespoon fresh lemon juice
$1\frac{1}{2}$ teaspoon dried onion flakes or 1
   tablespoon finely chopped onion
$\frac{1}{2}$ teaspoon Worcestershire sauce

Clean the chicken pieces (see page 64). Arrange them in a shallow 3 quart ($2\frac{1}{2}$ UK quart, 3 l) baking dish.

Combine the remaining ingredients and blend well. Pour over your chicken. Cover and refrigerate for at least 8 hours, turning occasionally.

Preheat your oven to 375°F (190°C, gas 5).

Drain your chicken pieces but reserve the marinade. Place the chicken on a rack on a shallow baking sheet or in a broiler pan, skin side up, and bake in the oven for 1 hour or until tender. Baste with your reserved marinade every 15 minutes or so, and turn occasionally. Make sure the marinade comes back to boiling point after the final basting. If any marinade is left over, throw it away and don't use it for anything else. Serve hot.

APRICOT AND HONEY ROAST DUCK

SERVES 4

This recipe is designed for a domestic duck with a milder taste and more fat under the skin than a wild one (that's in the next chapter). The stuffin' sucks up the excess fat and should be discarded after cooking. The liqueur adds a kick to the flavor.

1 duck, 3–4 lb (1.5–2 kg)
1 clove of garlic, split
1 medium onion, peeled and quartered
1 celery stalk with leaves
$\frac{1}{2}$ tart apple, cubed

$\frac{1}{2}$ cup (8 fl oz, 250 ml) honey
1 cup apricot preserves or marmalade
1 tablespoon brandy
1 tablespoon Grand Marnier or
   Cointreau

Preheat your oven to 350°F (180°C, gas 4).

Pluck, clean and singe your duck, as necessary. Rub it with your split garlic and stuff it with onion, celery, and apple. (Remember, this stuffin' is not going to be eaten.)

Lay your duck on a rack in a roasting pan and roast in the oven for 1 hour 20 minutes (or 20 minutes per lb, 40 per kg).

Combine the remaining ingredients. During the last 20 minutes of roasting, cover the duck with this sauce and baste frequently.

CORNBREAD STUFFIN'

MAKES ABOUT 8 CUPS

This delightful cornbread stuffin' is another thing entirely. I often stuff poultry with this soulful concoction. To my mind, it really adds a lot to the taste.

$\frac{1}{2}$ cup (4 oz, 120 g) butter (or half butter and half bacon grease)

$\frac{3}{4}$ cup chopped onion (1 largish onion)

1 cup (5$\frac{1}{2}$ oz, 160 g) chopped celery with leaves

4 cups (1$\frac{1}{4}$ lb, 600 g) crumbled homemade cornbread (see page 47)

4 cups (1 lb, 500 g) stale bread, cubed

1 good pinch dried ground sage

1 teaspoon dried ground thyme

2 teaspoons poultry seasoning

1 teaspoon salt

$\frac{1}{4}$ teaspoon black pepper

about 1$\frac{1}{2}$ cups (12 fl oz, 375 ml) chicken or giblet stock

Melt your butter over low heat in a large sauté pan. Add the onion and celery and sauté until soft but not brown, about 5 minutes.

Stir in your cornbread and bread cubes and continue cooking until golden brown, about another 10 minutes.

Add your seasonings and slowly stir in the stock until the stuffin' reaches your preferred consistency. I like mine on the dry side.

This is enough to stuff a 15-pound (7.5 kg) bird with you tasting along the way!

CRITTERS THAT SWIM

Growing up in Philadelphia and, at various times, in other areas along the eastern seaboard, I was fortunate enough to be exposed to many wonderful kinds of seafood. My favorite fish were porgies and spots, which I was sent down to the fish market to buy for the Friday fish fry. I learned early on from my fisherman uncle, Bill, how to stare right into those fishes' eyes to check if they were bulging and bright and how to pick up the gills to check if they were still red underneath. I'd pick out the freshest ones to take home and my Dad always said, 'Here comes Sheila with the brain food.'

Later it became one of his favorite sayings. Whenever I brought a new boyfriend home, my Dad would do his fatherly summing up. If he wasn't too fond of the guy, he'd say, 'That dude needs some brain food, honey.' But if he liked him, he'd say, 'Dahlin, you've got a good catch there, he must eat a panful of fish every morning.' Well, shur 'nuf, my husband Chris was the dude who really did not eat fish. So now it's become a family joke. My Dad says Chris proved his theory!

Sometimes these days it can be a struggle to find really fresh fish. If the kind you want are looking up from the slab at you with dull and lackluster eyes, then tell the man he's bent the truth just a little bit and choose another type with the same kind of firm, delicate, or oily flesh.

THREE WAYS FOR SOUL FRIED FISH

SERVES 4

Our family has two basic ways to fry fish soulfully; both delicious, both simple and nutritious. Aunt Peacie seasons her fish with salt and pepper, dips them in beaten egg, then in cracker meal, and fries them in a heavy skillet on medium to high heat until golden brown on both sides. Then she drains them on paper towels and serves them with French fries, stewed tomatoes, cornbread, and a salad.

My Daddy leaves out the egg. He rubs his porgies with salt and pepper, then coats them with white or yellow cornmeal, and fries them in a heavy skillet filled with oil, or fat of some kind that he's been saving up all week; then they're drained properly and served with home fries, cornbread, green salad, and large slices of tomato.

Here's my own way for fried catfish and hush puppies, one of the most cherished soul food combos. Catfish have a firm sweet flesh that Southerners dream about when they're far from home. They also have little whiskers (which are called barbels) and tough skin instead of scales. The skin is so tough that Uncle Bill, the avid fisherman, nails his to a tree and skins them with a pair of pliers.

The only time I ever caught one was when I was a kid. My Aunt Gussie told me to throw it back because catfish were becoming extinct due to so much pollution. But today they're thriving again, pond-raised, and catfish is one of the most successful ventures of all commercial fish farming. I hear tell that the farmers have improved upon the taste as well. For me, too heavy a coating spoils the texture and flavor so I keep it plain and simple.

2 lb (1 kg) thin catfish fillets, skinned
$1\frac{1}{2}$ teaspoons salt
$\frac{3}{4}$ teaspoon black pepper
1 cup ($4\frac{1}{2}$ oz, 130 g) cornmeal, yellow or white

1 cup ($4\frac{1}{2}$ oz, 130 g) all-purpose flour
about $1\frac{1}{2}$ cups (12 oz, 375 g) lard
8 lemon wedges

Rinse your fillets quickly under cold running water, then thoroughly pat them dry using paper towels.

Mix together the salt, pepper, cornmeal, and flour, then toss it with a fork. Heat up between $\frac{1}{2}$ and 1 in (1.5–2.5 cm) of lard in a heavy skillet over medium heat, and meanwhile you can be dredging the fillets in the seasoned cornmeal mixture.

When the lard is hot but not yet at the smoking stage, lay in your fillets, a couple at a time, to give those bad boys enough space to fry up crisp and brown, tender and juicy, about 3 minutes per side. Then remove them from the pan and drain on paper towels.

Serve with lemon wedges, hush puppies, cole slaw, mustard greens, and ham hocks, and fried apples or onion rings.

DAD'S SALMON CAKES
SERVES 4

My Dad did most of the cooking at our house and it's from him that I caught my passion. I could never figure out how he could come home from work and have supper ready so quickly until he started giving me some of his secrets. This is his delicious and very fast recipe for salmon cakes.

1 large can ($15\frac{1}{2}$ oz, 450 g) pink or red salmon
2 large eggs, beaten
salt and pepper to taste

1 medium onion, finely chopped
$1\frac{1}{2}$ tablespoons all-purpose flour
2 tablespoons butter

Drain your salmon of all the juices in the can, then break it apart with a fork.

Add the eggs, salt, and pepper to taste, the onion and just enough flour to tighten up the mixture or until, as Dad says, 'It's no longer juicy.'

Shape your salmon into patties and fry in the butter, turning once, until brown on both sides, about 8 minutes. Serve with mashed potatoes and stewed tomatoes, and a mixed salad to boot — I always made that for him.

Dad's sister, Aunt Ella, nicknamed 'Red Jenny' because of her sandy-colored hair, on Market Street in downtown Charlotte in 1941 when she was twenty-one years old and fresh home from qualifying as a nurse. She had a reputation for being able to really 'cut a rug', and had a pet chicken by the name of Hattie, who lived to be a ripe old broiler. Aunt Ella is one of the best soul food cooks in our family; her recipes speak for themselves.

AUNT ELLA'S FROG LEGS

Most folks think that the French have a monopoly on frogs' legs and that they carry the patent, along with some mystique on how to cook them to a T. But I'm here to tell you that the practice of frog gigging, or spearing with some kind of device, goes back a long long way.

Walter, my Dad, and Aunt Ella, his sister, were seven and nine years old when they caught their first bullfrog. They had fashioned a kind of pick by removing the two middle tines of a regular four-tined fork and securing the fork handle to a broom handle with wire.

One summer's evening, when it was completely dark, they went to the small stream close to their house in Charlotte, North Carolina. The frogs' location could always be determined by their croaking and the plopping noises they made while jumping about. They used a flashlight to pinpoint frogs on pieces of driftwood and other floating debris. Once the light was aimed at the eyes, the frog was immobile just long enough for the gig, or pick, to be stuck in its back.

They used a hunting knife to cut up and skin the frogs. They kept the legs in a cool crocus sack overnight. The next day they fried the legs just as they had seen their mother fry chicken, and Daddy made gravy from the drippings.

This first frog gigging escapade was a thrilling success, but on their next time out Daddy saw a big old snake coming at him when Aunt Ella shone that flashlight and they ran for dear life. No frogs that time.

4–5 frog legs per person, cleaned
salt and pepper
flour for dredging

butter, olive oil or fat of your choice for frying

Season your frog legs with salt and pepper and dredge with flour, just as you would when frying chicken. Heat the fat in a heavy skillet over medium heat. Add the frog legs and fry until nicely browned on all sides, about 10 minutes.

NOTE Store-bought frog legs need no preparation other than what is suggested on the package.

Some folks choose as an embellishment a lemon or garlic butter, others prefer tartare sauce and some even enjoy a little seafood cocktail sauce. If you're feeling innovative, then why not throw in some sautéed green pepper chunks or onion just for variety?

SAUTÉED SCALLOPS
SERVES 4

Quick, yes. Simple, yes. Good, absolutely. I love my scallops.

1 lb (500 g) fresh scallops (weight without shells)
$\frac{1}{4}$ cup (2 oz, 60 g) butter

1 clove of garlic, minced
salt and black pepper
1 tablespoon chopped fresh parsley

Wash your scallops and pat dry.

Melt the butter in a heavy skillet over very low heat. Stir, without letting it brown, and season it with the garlic, salt, pepper, and parsley (or any other seasoning that suits your fancy). When the butter foams, add your scallops. Sauté until just cooked, about 3 minutes. Do not overcook.

Serve hot, straight from the pan, with a lovely spinach salad, sliced beefsteak tomatoes and cracklin' bread, topped off with a glass of white Mouton Cadet. (Or in my old neighborhood, you'll have a glass of Kool-Aid and like it!)

BAKED STUFFED FLOUNDER

SERVES 4–6

Mark Twain once said that part of the secret of success in life lies in eating whatever you like and then letting the food fight it out inside. Well, here's a dish that proves him right. I like to fix this when real fish lovers come to dinner because it's splendid in appearance, as well as good brain food.

8 flounder fillets (up to 2 lb, 1 kg in all)
¼ cup plus 3 tablespoons (3½ oz, 100 g) butter
2 tablespoons finely chopped celery
¼ cup finely chopped onion (½ medium onion)
¼ cup (1½ oz, 45 g) finely sliced fresh mushrooms
2 tablespoons chopped fresh parsley
12 oz (375 g) crab meat, well cleaned
¾ cup (3 oz, 90 g) dry bread crumbs

1 teaspoon salt
red or black pepper
2 large eggs, slightly beaten
3 tablespoons all-purpose flour
¾ cup (6 fl oz, 175 ml) fresh chicken stock
¾ cup (6 fl oz, 175 ml) milk
1½ cups (6 oz, 175 g) grated Monterey Jack or Swiss cheese
½ cup (4 fl oz, 120 ml) dry white wine
½ teaspoon paprika
8 sprigs fresh parsley, washed and dried

Rinse your fillets under cold running water and pat dry. Cover them and refrigerate until ready to stuff.

Melt ¼ cup (2 oz, 60 g) butter in a medium saucepan over medium heat and sauté your celery and onion until soft but not brown, about 5 minutes. Remove from the heat and stir in your mushrooms, parsley, crab meat, bread crumbs, ½ teaspoon salt, and pepper to taste. Also throw in your eggs now and mix well.

Spread this stuffing mixture in equal amounts over your fillets, then roll each fillet from the smaller end to the larger and place them seam side down in a well greased baking dish. Make sure you pack each one solidly so that they won't fall apart while cooking.

Preheat your oven to 350°F (180°C, gas 4).

Melt the remaining butter in a medium saucepan over low heat. Blend in the flour and remaining salt. Whisk in the chicken stock and milk and cook, stirring constantly, until thick, about 5 minutes. Stir in the cheese, wine, and a dash of pepper and continue cooking, stirring constantly, for 5 minutes or until the sauce begins to bubble lightly. Pour your sauce over the fillets and sprinkle with paprika. Bake in the oven for 25 to 35 minutes or until the fillets are fork tender. When done, carefully lift out each fillet, using a spatula for ease of hauling. Transfer to individual serving plates and spoon the sauce over the top. Lay a sprig of fresh parsley on top. Add some cornbread and collard greens, and pass the Tabasco.

NOTE   This recipe is also excellent with Dover sole, halibut, or perch.

OYSTER CASSEROLE

SERVES 6

1 cup (4 oz, 120 g) coarsely crumbled
   saltine cracker (water biscuit) crumbs
1 quart (1¾ UK pints, 1 l) shucked fresh
   oysters (30–40, depending on size)
¼ cup (1½ oz, 45 g) chopped scallions
   (spring onions)
¼ cup (1½ oz, 45 g) chopped fresh parsley
1 tablespoon fresh lemon juice

salt to taste
½ teaspoon black pepper
1 teaspoon Worcestershire sauce
about ½ cup (4 oz, 120 g) butter
1 cup (8 fl oz, 250 ml) light (single) cream
½ cup (4 fl oz, 120 ml) milk
dash of Tabasco (optional)
paprika for dusting

Preheat your oven to 400°F (200°C, gas 6). Drain your oysters well.

Generously grease a shallow 1½ quart (1¼ UK quart, 1.5 l) casserole. Sprinkle half of the cracker crumbs over the bottom. Lay half of the oysters on top of the crumbs, then sprinkle with half of the onions, parsley, lemon juice, salt, pepper, and Worcestershire sauce. Dot generously with butter and pour on half of the cream and milk. Repeat these layers but save the remaining crumbs for the top. Add a dash of Tabasco if desired before covering with the crumbs. Dust the top with paprika, using enough to make it really red.

Bake for 30 minutes. Serve hot.

CRAWDAD PIE

SERVES 6

Crawdads are crawfish, crayfish to the English; small fresh- or salt-water crustaceans that closely resemble little lobsters, but taste more like shrimp. As kids we thought of them as something which got in our way when we were making mud pies, so we called them mud bugs.

This is a dish that we've been eating in our family for at least several generations. Let them call it Cajun if they like, we'll just keep on eating it and enjoying it.

1 recipe Aunt Peacie's Double Pie Crust
   (see page 158)
1 cup (8 oz, 250 g) butter
½ cup (2 oz, 60 g) all-purpose flour
1 large onion, chopped
2 large cloves of garlic, minced
1 medium green bell pepper, seeded and
   chopped
½ cup (2 oz, 60 g) chopped fresh parsley
1 cup (6 oz, 175 g) chopped celery

1 cup (6 oz, 175 g) scallions (spring
   onions), tops and bottoms separated
   and chopped
3 tablespoons tomato purée
salt and black pepper
cayenne pepper
3 cups (1¼ pints, 750 ml) fish stock
1 teaspoon fresh lemon juice
3 lb (1.5 kg) peeled and deveined crawfish
   (or peeled and deveined shrimp)

Start by making up the pie crust. Divide the pastry in half, wrap each half in clear plastic wrap, and refrigerate until ready for use.

Then melt your butter in a large heavy skillet over medium heat. When it starts to sizzle, stir in the flour. Cook, stirring constantly, for about 10 minutes or until it becomes a rich dark brown color. Now it's time to stir in your onion, garlic, green pepper, parsley, celery, scallion bottoms, and tomato purée. Continue cooking and stirring until your vegetables are tender and limp, about 5 minutes. Season with a little salt, pepper, and cayenne.

Raise the heat and pour in the fish stock and lemon juice. Bring to a rapid boil, then reduce the heat, cover, and simmer for 1 hour, stirring often. All this time is needed to blend the flavors of the herbs and spices together. You may need to add additional fish stock (or water) during this time. Take the pastry out of the refrigerator in time for it to get back to room temperature before rolling.

When the sauce is rich and creamy, throw in the crawfish. Stir and cook until tender, about 10 minutes. If the sauce starts to get too thin, thicken it up a mite with a paste of 1 to 2 tablespoons cornstarch (cornflour) and a little water. When your crawdads are tender, stir in the scallion tops. Taste and adjust seasonings. Set this filling aside to cool while you roll out your crust, and preheat your oven to 350°F (180°C, gas 4).

Line a 9 in (23 cm) pie pan with half the pastry, then pour in the lukewarm filling. Lay the top crust over the filling, remembering not to pull or stretch. Seal the top over the bottom, flute the edges, and make a few small slits to let out steam.

Bake at 350°F (180°C, gas 4) for 15 minutes. Turn the oven down to 300°F (150°C, gas 2). Cook for an additional 15 minutes or until the crust is golden brown. Serve immediately.

COOTER

Cooter is the colloquial name for a snapping turtle. The origin of the name is not really known, although it certainly comes from West Africa like so many other American expressions still in use today – for instance goober (peanut), gumbo (okra), ninny (breast), tote (carry), and of course yam (for the American sweet potato). Folklore has it that many different kinds of meat are contained within the turtle, such as chicken, fish, pork, and beef. Perhaps its taste is influenced by where and what the turtle eats.

Turtles are usually caught in the summer months, as any reader of *Tom Sawyer* or *Huckleberry Finn* can attest to, but turtle farms are now productive enterprises in the United States. When you think about it, what has lobster got on turtle anyway – one has a red shell and one a green!

Usually cooter is prepared for cooking by the person who catches it. The head is chopped off and nails cut from the toes, then the turtle is plunged into very hot water and scrubbed until the underbelly is almost white and the shell is slick and smooth. A very sharp knife is then used to remove certain venous sections from the middle, and the entire contents of the shell is removed. This portion is then cooked in just enough water to cover until fork tender. The time will, of course, depend on the size of the cooter or cooters.

You usually just season it with salt and black pepper and add in a teaspoon of vinegar or lemon juice, if you prefer, to dilute the very distinct flavor. But once this basic cleaning, de-shelling, and cooking is completed, several methods of preparation remain available to cooter connoisseurs.

Cooters vary in size from 1 ft (30 cm) long to one that a child can ride on. Therefore the amount of meat can't be determined with exact accuracy. You'll have to adjust all other ingredients proportionately. Anyway, these are not exactly strict recipes – they just describe what people do. If you live someplace you can't get cooter, forget them and make something else in this book.

COOTER STEW Combine your prepared cooter meat and juice with sautéed cubed carrots, chopped onion and potatoes. Add water if necessary. Add just enough cornstarch (cornflour) or flour to thicken the juices to the desired consistency, and simmer till the vegetables are done. Here folks, the amounts are truly up to you depending on the amount of stew you wish to prepare, which vegetables you prefer and the amount of cooter meat. Just throw in what you favor and you're set.

BAKED COOTER IN THE SHELL Add onion sautéed in butter to your cooter meat, then return it to its original shell and bake in preheated oven at 375°F (190°C, gas 5) for 25 to 30 minutes (for a small cooter). Use as much butter and onion as you wish. Now, if I were to take my choice, I'd add in a whole heap of crushed garlic and maybe a little heavy (double) cream. Then I'd spread a bit of grated cheese on top with some crisply fried herb-flavored croûtons. Yes, that would suit me very nicely.

COOTER PIE Line a baking dish with Aunt Peacie's Double Pie Crust (see page 158). Pour in your precooked cooter filling, thickened up with flour or cornstarch to the consistency of a stew. Cover with a top pastry, seal, flute, and cut in a few air vents. Bake in a preheated oven at 400°F (200°C, gas 6) for 35 to 45 minutes until nicely browned.

THE ALMIGHTY PIG

*E*very year, soon after the Christmas festivities were over and done with, Granddaddy Bert and Grandma Maggie would have their hog-killing time down on the farm in Charlotte, North Carolina.

Now this was a big annual event. The hogs were slaughtered by family, friends, and neighbors and then cut up to make use of every bit imaginable. At the end of the day, Grandma Maggie always gave the same signal so everyone could begin the big clean up. 'Well,' she would say, 'there seems to be nothing left but the squeal.' That just about sums it up for the almighty pig.

There was no waste. Hams were put out in the smokehouse or the pork barrel for the long curing process. There were side bacons; rib joints and shoulder roasts; cracklin's and fatback for seasoning vegetables; brains, ears, and tails to flavor stews and beans. Meat and fat were ground up, seasoned right there by the womenfolk and stuffed into casings to make sausage links. Valuable lard was extracted for all-year cooking. Chit'lin's – the intestines – were cleaned and stored; the hocks were chopped off as well as the jowls and maws; the trotters and other parts were pickled. Not even the snout was left unused: it was soused and made into head cheese.

Bacon grease and drippings, pure gold to the soul food cook, were saved to be used for seasoning greens, rubbing in cast-iron skillets before baking cornbreads, biscuits, and pones, adding to pancake and waffle batters, or frying up any meat or corn dishes that just had to have the sweet, deliciously bacony flavor.

I've adjusted my choice of recipes to today's tastes and lifestyles. Let's face it, folks, there aren't many takers for hog maws any more. People even get funny at the mention of chit'lin's – until they've tried them. And who's got a smokehouse or the time and patience to cure their own bacon and hams?

In a later chapter I also give a modern alternative to seasoning with fatback or ham hocks (see page 140). Today many American blacks are moving away from the use of too much pork seasoning. The reason is simple: high blood pressure. The American medical profession has pointed out that the particular social pressures experienced by African-Americans coupled with their high intake of salt and fat, primarily from pork, has been killing us off prematurely. But that doesn't mean that, from time to time, everyone shouldn't be able to enjoy the delicious flavor of ham or bacon grease in our greens. The key, as always, is in moderation.

During and after the Colonial and Civil War years, various preserving techniques were developed by farmers and meat packing houses to create a fine tradition of dry cured, beechwood or hickory smoked 'old hams' and bacons. For me their smoky ash flavor always brings to mind the aromatic scent of hickory chips gently smoldering in my Granddaddy's old smokehouse.

But today, country hams are big business, and that means big profits. The quicker you can make 'em, the faster you sell 'em. Cost effectiveness is casting aside old traditions and the time-consuming art of smoking and aging could soon be a thing of the past. Newer techniques are being implemented every day to speed up the slow traditional processes. Arterial brine injections are replacing dry salt curing. Climate-controlled environmental systems and liquid smoke are being used to simulate the variable temperatures of the old-fashioned country smoke houses. Pigs are being fed a scientifically balanced diet instead of the peanuts, corn, peaches, acorn, and other random scraps the animal would naturally devour were he allowed to roam freely in the fields.

Are all these things better? I can only say that personally I think country hams of superior quality are well worth the extra cost. They don't have the subtle smokiness of down-home hams, but they are still mighty fine. Smithfield, Virginia, is undeniably their home. Apparently, Queen Victoria received Smithfield hams on a regular basis and today they are still shipped all over the world. Smithfield pigs are fed on the peanuts which grow there in abundance, and this gives their famous flesh a distinctive flavor. Other counties in Virginia as well as other states (for example, Kentucky, North Carolina, and Georgia) also specialize in prize hams.

If you are lucky enough to get your hands on one of these country hams, cook it with tender loving care and the reward will be a tender, juicy, succulent ham, good sliced either hot or cold. My method is good for other types of ham, too, but always read the label carefully since many hams today are tenderized, pre-cooked, or partially cooked and will need little or no cooking.

BAKED COUNTRY HAM

ALLOW ¼ LB (250 G) PER PERSON

1 whole country ham
½ cup plus 1 tablespoon (4½ fl oz, 135 ml) cider vinegar
½ cup (3½ oz, 100 g) dark brown sugar
1 cup (8 fl oz, 250 ml) apple cider
1 cup (7 oz, 200 g) light brown sugar
1 teaspoon dry mild mustard

1 can (15¼ oz, 432 g) unsweetened pineapple rings
about 2 tablespoons dry sherry or juice from the can of pineapple rings
whole cloves to stud
maraschino cherries
1 cup (8 fl oz, 250 ml) beer (optional)

Start by soaking your ham in a large kettle with ½ cup (4 fl oz, 120 ml) vinegar and enough cold water to cover. Allow for some freedom of movement. After about 2 hours, pour off the soaking water. Refill and continue soaking for at least 6 more hours – you can soak it for a day or more, it sure can't hurt. Every time

I think about it, I pour off and change the water, in an attempt to soak out as much salt as I possibly can.

Now, after this long soaking period has finished, you drain off the water and rinse your ham thoroughly. Get out your old faithful stiff vegetable brush because, if ever there was a time when you were gonna need it, it's definitely now! Scrub that bad boy down to remove any traces of mold. Don't panic, mold is the telling sign of the genuine article, a really aged country ham, which is gonna yield you some fantastic flavor when you're done. Rinse your ham again.

Now it's time to simmer it – notice I didn't say boil, because that's not what we're gonna do. Put the ham back in the large kettle in fresh, clean water to cover. Add the dark brown sugar and apple cider. Simmer, uncovered, over low heat for 25 minutes per pound (50 per kg) for a whole ham (for smaller joints like picnic shoulders or butts [hands] it would be 30 minutes per pound [60 per kg]). As water begins to boil away, and it surely will, just add a little more boiling water, but try to keep an even water temperature, just under the boil, for the whole cooking time.

When your ham is tender, leave it in its own stock to cool down a bit, then remove it from the kettle and peel off the rind with a sharp knife, removing as much of the fat as you want. Your ham is now ready to be eaten; but if you want it glazed, read on.

Preheat your oven to 400°F (200°C, gas 6).

Make a paste from the light brown sugar, mustard, 1 tablespoon vinegar, and enough sherry or pineapple juice to moisten; not too runny, so it will adhere. Score the fat on the top side of your ham in a diagonal pattern with a sharp knife and stick a clove into each place where the lines intersect. Spread your paste all over the ham and lay on some pineapple rings with a maraschino cherry in the center of each one.

Place your ham in a shallow roasting pan, fat side up. Add just enough liquid – cooking liquor from the ham, or beer – to moisten the bottom of the pan. Bake in the oven for 30 minutes or until nicely browned and glazed, basting occasionally with pan drippings or more beer. Serve hot or cold.

*F*RIED PORK CHOPS
SERVES 8

These are my Daddy's simple but soulful pork chops. Just remember, the longer they cook, the tougher they be! So go for thinnish chops, 'cause if your chops are more than 1 in (2.5 cm) thick, you'll have to throw them against a wall. Serve these with smothered cabbage seasoned with ham and fatback and hot buttered cornbread. Since I once ate six of these bad boys – much to my Daddy's astonishment – I say eight servings very lightly indeed!

8 pork chops, $\frac{1}{4}$–$\frac{1}{2}$ in (around 1 cm) thick
salt and black pepper
1 cup ($4\frac{1}{2}$ oz, 130 ml) all-purpose flour
1 tablespoon paprika (optional)

about 1 cup (8 fl oz, 250 ml) vegetable oil
1 large brown paper bag

Rinse your chops clean and lay them out on paper towels right on your drain board (I find that this is the easiest way to clean up after). Salt and pepper both sides to taste.

Put the flour in the paper bag (plastic bags tend to burst when punctured by a bone and wop! you've got flour everywhere) and throw in the paprika if you're using it. Paprika's nice but not essential; it's much more noticeable when frying chicken.

Pour oil into a large heavy skillet to make a depth of $\frac{1}{2}$ in (1.5 cm) and set it over medium heat. When the oil is hot, throw your chops in the bag of flour, a couple at a time. Close the bag and shake to coat them. Remove the chops from the bag and shake off excess flour (reserve the flour if you intend making smothered pork chops – see below). Gently lay the chops in the pan. Fry them to a golden brown, quickly and no more than 4 to 5 minutes on each side. Poke at 'em so they don't stick. If you don't fry quickly, they will surely turn out tough.

When they become brown, crisp, and juicy, transfer to a warmed serving platter lined with paper towels and keep warm until ready to serve.

SMOTHERED PORK CHOPS

If you've got a hankering to smother your pork chops in some good old soulful gravy, this is what you do. Follow the previous recipe for Fried Pork Chops. After frying them up crisp and tender, drain off all but 2 tablespoons fat – but please don't lose any of those good pan bits. Stir 3 tablespoons reserved seasoned flour into the skillet and cook over medium to high heat, scraping and gathering up all the bits of browned flour and pork scraps from the bottom and sides of your pan, for about 3 minutes.

When flour turns chocolate brown, as dark as you can possibly go without burning, pour in 2 cups (16 fl oz, 500 ml) of cold water (but stand back as you do or the burst of steam will surely getcha). Bring the liquid to a rapid boil, stirring until well blended, then reduce the heat and cook it down until it thickens up, about 5 minutes. Season your gravy with salt, pepper, seasoning salt, onion powder, or whatever you feel like at the time.

You can either add the chops during the cooking-down process and braise them in the gravy, or you can cook down the gravy and pour it over the chops when you serve them. This basic pan gravy is also a shur-'nuf natural over rice or mashed potatoes.

BARBECUED SPARE RIBS

SERVES 6

Now what could be more mouth-watering than a big plate of juicy, fallin'-off-the-bone tender, and drippin'-with-barbecue-sauce succulent ribs? Oooo ... weeee ... makes me feel downright sanctified, just thinking about it!

First off, one warning. Nothin', but nothin', replaces the down-home flavor of an outdoor grill or pit. And this exceptional sauce stands up just fine on its own. So I don't advise that you risk spoiling it with the artificial flavor of liquid smoke or the like. It also keeps well in the fridge for about a month in an airtight container, so that gives you plenty of time to get out the barbecue.

And even when you bake these bad boys, they simply can't fail to give you some serious, and I do mean serious, eating enjoyment. So break out the beers and start licking your chops! It's time to greeze. This is the true meaning of finger-lickin' good, honey!

6 lb (3 kg) meaty pork spare ribs
salt and black pepper to rub
1 teaspoon paprika
2 tablespoons melted pork fat or bacon grease (or melted butter)
1 large onion, finely chopped
2 tablespoons cider vinegar
$\frac{1}{4}$ cup (2 oz, 60 g) light brown sugar
2 teaspoons mustard dry or prepared (not too strong though or it will take over the taste)

1 tablespoon celery salt or 1 teaspoon celery seed
$\frac{1}{4}$ teaspoon cayenne pepper
1 cup (8 fl oz, 250 ml) tomato ketchup
3 tablespoons Worcestershire sauce
4 tablespoons fresh lemon juice
1 cup (8 fl oz, 250 ml) water or meat stock
$\frac{1}{2}$ cup (4 fl oz, 120 ml) beer
$\frac{1}{2}$ cup (4 fl oz, 120 ml) dry white wine (optional)

TO BARBECUE   For a real smoky flavor, season the ribs by rubbing them lightly with salt, black pepper, and paprika, and throw them in the pit or on the grill, keeping them well away from direct heat. You want the smoke to do the cooking, not the flames. Cook 'em long and cook 'em slow, 2 hours or so, until the meat is about to fall off the bones.

In the meantime, make the sauce. Heat the bacon grease or butter in a large heavy saucepan over medium heat. Brown the onion, stirring frequently, for 5 minutes or so. Add in all the remaining ingredients. Bring them to a boil, then simmer over a low heat for 20 minutes, uncovered.

Begin basting with this sauce only during the last 15 or 20 minutes of cooking; otherwise the taste of the spices in the sauce will be altered significantly and will be bitter. Be sure to baste the ribs on both sides.

An alternate way of barbecuing is to make the sauce in advance and marinate your pork ribs in it for a couple of hours before grilling, turning them often. Putting them in a sealed plastic bag makes it easier to get your marinade all over the ribs. When the grill's ready, wipe off the excess sauce and just throw 'em on and cook 'em slow, turning frequently and basting in the last 20 minutes as above.

TO BAKE   Preheat your oven to 350°F (180°C, gas 4).

Parboil the ribs in water to cover for 15 minutes to eliminate as much of the unwanted fat as possible, then transfer them to a roasting pan, cover with foil, and bake in the oven for about 45 minutes or until nicely browned. Do not turn off the oven. Pour off all the excess fat, reserving just 2 tablespoons for your sauce. It is absolutely essential that you do this because nobody likes to eat greasy ribs. Also the fat will alter the taste of your sauce if it remains, and you certainly don't want that.

Put the reserved fat in a large heavy saucepan over medium heat and brown the onion, stirring frequently, about 5 minutes. Add in all of the remaining ingredients for the sauce and bring to a boil. Lower the heat, and simmer for 20 minutes, uncovered, stirring frequently.

Pour three-fourths of the sauce over the ribs in the roasting pan. Cover and continue to bake until the ribs are nicely glazed and fork tender, about 1 hour more. Baste them occasionally with the remainder of the sauce.

AUNT ELLA'S CHOPPED BARBECUED PORK SANDWICH

SERVES ABOUT 8

This is a specialty dish from down in Charlotte, North Carolina way, which comes out of the great tradition of the Southern barbecue. Once you've tasted Aunt Ella's version you'll see why it's so sought after by soul food connoisseurs. In the best soul food restaurants, the pork butt is barbecued on the spit, which gives it that decidedly smoky flavor. But you can do it this way and still obtain a delicious sandwich.

1 pork butt (hand), 4lb (2 kg) (or 5lb [2.5 kg] fresh pork shoulder)
1 tablespoon brown sugar
1 tablespoon all-purpose flour
1 tablespoon dry mustard
1 teaspoon salt
1 teaspoon black pepper
1 teaspoon paprika
1 teaspoon red pepper (or hot sauce of your choice)
1 teaspoon garlic powder (or 1 clove of garlic, minced)
1 teaspoon chilli powder
$\frac{1}{4}$ cup chopped onion ($\frac{1}{2}$ medium onion)
$\frac{1}{2}$ cup (4 fl oz, 120 ml) water
$\frac{1}{2}$ cup (4 fl oz, 120 ml) vinegar
$\frac{1}{2}$ cup (4 fl oz, 120 ml) broth from the cooked meat, or chicken stock
1 tablespoon fresh lemon juice

Place all your ingredients, except the meat, in a heavy saucepan over low heat. Simmer for 20 minutes, stirring frequently to avoid sticking. Do not boil! Remove it from the heat, cover, and set aside.

Preheat your oven to 300°F (150°C, gas 2).

Place the butt in a shallow roasting pan with 2 cups water. Cook in the oven for about 3 hours, or until very tender. (You may prefer to cook it in a pressure cooker.) When done, remove the meat from the bone, taking out any fat. Chop the meat very thinly by hand or in a food processor using the steel blade. The meat should appear shredded. Your usual yield will be 5 cups.

Put the shredded meat in a glass container. Reheat the sauce to warm and pour it over the meat. Mix well, cover, and let it marinate in the refrigerator, for 12 to 24 hours. Then remove any fat from the surface, stir well, and shape into hamburger-sized patties. There should be between 20 and 24 patties depending on their thickness.

Serve the patties hot on buns with coleslaw. You can heat the meat separately or with the buns in a 250°F (120°C, gas ½) oven.

NOTE Patties may be quick frozen without wrapping by placing them on a cookie sheet, then into individual and separate sandwich bags or foil for use at a later date. Additional hot sauce may be added to taste.

Great-Uncle Ed Lynch (Grandma Maggie Ferguson's brother), nicknamed 'The Fox,' was born around the turn of the century in Charlotte. He had no formal education but sure knew how to gamble and turn a buck. Everything he touched, including a general store, restaurant, pool hall, barber shop, and beer garden, turned to gold. His restaurant specialized in all kinds of soul food dishes, in particular chopped barbecued pork sandwiches, one of his all-time favorites.

NORTH CAROLINA FRIED HAM WITH RED-EYE GRAVY

SERVES 4

I first tasted fried country ham with red-eye gravy while recording in Mussle Shoals, Alabama. I got to sopping away with my biscuits and before I knew it I'd eaten six biscuits.

4 large slices country ham, ¼ in (6 mm) thick

1 tablespoon all-purpose flour

1 cup (8 fl oz, 250 ml) cold water

1 tablespoon strong black coffee (optional)

If your ham is particularly salty, you can, before frying, gently simmer it in just enough water to cover for about 10 to 15 minutes, turning often.

Put your ham slices in a heavy skillet over medium heat. Fry, turning frequently, for 10 minutes or until nice and brown. Any fat should be really crisp. Remove them from the pan and keep them warm.

Pour off most of the fat, leaving no more than 1 tablespoon. (You will see that the ham residue has left a slightly reddish hue in your pan, which is how this old Southern recipe got its name.) Throw in the flour, raise the heat, and stir until it browns. Pour in the cold water and coffee. Bring to a boil, stirring constantly, and scraping up the bits in the bottom of the pan with a fork. Lower the heat and simmer for 5 minutes. You can also throw your ham back in the red-eye to simmer for a spell. Then start sopping!

CHIT'LIN'S

SERVES 6

Chit'lin's, as they are commonly known, or chitterlings if you wanna be formal, are the intestines of the pig. When properly cooked and highly seasoned with vinegar, salt and Tabasco they are some kinda good. I like mine to be so hot that my head threatens to pop off. However, I shall start by giving you a basic recipe. Then you're on your own with the hot pepper sauce.

10 lb (5 kg) chit'lin's

1 large onion, quartered

1 clove of garlic, peeled

1 bay leaf

1 tablespoon salt

2 teaspoons black pepper

¼ cup (2 fl oz, 60 ml) vinegar (to start)

1 tablespoon Tabasco sauce (or other hot pepper sauce) to start

Chit'lin's have to be washed and washed and washed again. Put them in your sink in warm water and scrub them like you would a pair of socks. No, I'm not joking. You mustn't be afraid of them, because you've got to get rid of all the excess fat, grease, and grime. Change the water often, at least 5 or 6 times, until it rinses clear.

Place your nice clean chit'lin's in a large pot together with the onion, garlic, bay leaf, salt, pepper, vinegar, and Tabasco. Do not add water as the chit'lin's will produce their own liquid throughout the cooking process. The onion is in there not only for flavoring but to reduce the considerable smell. Am I frightening you? Come on now. Be brave.

Bring them slowly to a boil over medium heat, then quickly reduce the heat and allow to simmer slowly for about 2 hours, during which time you must remove excess water as it builds up – use an ordinary cup. The chit'lin's will remain watery, but you don't want them to be saturated. Stir every 25 minutes or so to prevent sticking.

When your 2 hours are up, cut the chit'lin's into 2 to 3 in (5–8 cm) long pieces, using a sharp knife and a fork.

Continue simmering them, and removing the excess liquid, for another $1\frac{1}{2}$ to 2 hours or until they become fork tender. When they are done, season them to taste with salt, additional pepper, vinegar, and Tabasco or other hot sauce. Serve with greens and potato salad.

Pigs' Feet

SERVES 10–12

Pigs' feet are commonly referred to as trotters. I had always presumed that trotters were characteristically from the deep South, but, having eaten my way through Germany and Austria, I now suspect that the art of cooking them was brought to America via the German immigrants back in the 1800s. I have noticed a distinct difference in the way they are seasoned though. American trotters are decidedly hotter and more highly seasoned. Either way, I love 'em.

12 pigs' feet, split in half lengthwise
4 bay leaves
2 teaspoons crushed red pepper flakes
4 large onions, thickly sliced
6 stalks celery with leaves, cut into
    chunks

10–12 whole black peppercorns
4 cups ($1\frac{3}{4}$ pints, 1 l) cider vinegar
2 cloves of garlic, split
3 tablespoons salt
1 tablespoon Tabasco sauce (or your
    preferred hot sauce)

Your butcher will split the trotters for you. Then you scrub each one until it is super-clean. Singe off any excess hairs, paying particular attention to the area between the toes. (Some folks now wrap each trotter in cheesecloth to help it retain its shape, but I don't find this to be necessary since you want the meat to be tender enough to fall off the bone anyway.)

Put the pigs' feet and all of your other ingredients in a large pot and cover with cold water. Cover tightly and bring to the boil over high heat. Now immediately reduce your heat and simmer slowly for 3 or 4 hours or until fork tender.

Now please yourself. Put some on a plate, douse them with as much vinegar and hot sauce as you care for, and dine!

IF YOU SEE IT, SHOOT IT

Granddaddy Bert was a great believer in living off the fat of the land and in making use of all the things that the good Lord made it possible for us to enjoy. Hunting was a way of life for him.

Many a time he'd get down that old hunting rifle and go out into the backwoods. When he returned he would always have a full crocus sack and a bounty of wonderment for our eyes: wild turkeys and geese, squabs and rabbits, guinea hens and quail, grouse, and occasionally a Canadian wild duck that had made its way down to Charlotte. He always had too much for just us, so after he put away the stores for our family, he would share his fare with neighbors and friends, a tradition which they say dates back to African tribal customs.

Today we eat few animals from the wild because we are acutely aware of endangered species and don't take so easily to tougher, strongly flavored meats. But it is important to remember that to some people eating wild animals was, and in some parts of the world still is, a means of survival and part of their culture. Squirrel, raccoon, even grizzly bear, but especially 'possum were all appreciated by slaves who otherwise often had only fatty cuts of pork.

Granddaddy Bert knew just how to determine the age of a squirrel. If it was young he would fry it up like a batch of chicken, but if it was too tough for that, he would tenderize it with salt and bake it up to serve with a creamy gravy.

Recently there has been something of a return to wild game birds. Some people prefer them to beef, lamb, pork, or fowl because the conditions under which they live and die are far healthier than those on factory farms. Equally, they are free of the hormones injected into farm animals, leaner, and with far less saturated fat. The point is, surely, that we are lucky to have a choice to exercise according to our own tastes and beliefs.

ROASTED WILD DUCK
SERVES 6

If a woodsman or a hunter ever makes you a gift of wild duck, thank him profusely and take it quickly before he changes his mind. For wild duck is a true delicacy, leaner and tastier than its domestic cousin. It should always be hung, undrawn, for a couple of days to a week to develop its full, rich flavor.

You've no doubt heard the expression 'a tough old bird.' Well, there's a lot of

Granddaddy Bert Ferguson (on the right) was born in 1892. He had nine brothers and sisters and lived his entire life in Charlotte, North Carolina. Up until the day he died he could swing one of his legs up to touch the top of any doorway. A boilermaker by trade, he was also an avid hunter and fisherman who loved his family, his farm, and his old Buick. He would preside over the evening meal by swiftly saying, 'Bless the cook and bless the meat, good God, let's eat!'

truth to that old cliché when it comes to wild birds who get a chance to use their muscles. So never try using a recipe for farmyard duck. Since wild birds don't store an awful lot of fat under their skin, always lard them by placing strips of bacon or salt pork over the breast, and baste often to ensure that the more tender meat stays moist, while the tougher legs and wings cook through.

This is Granddaddy Bert's recipe. Like most good hunters, he understood exactly how to cook a bird simply and well. Often he'd cook one out in the open when he chose to stay out overnight. Salt, pepper, lemon slices, and 30 minutes to the pound for well done was what he told anybody who asked. (That would be 1 hour to the kilogram.) It was always delicious but, being a keen believer in garlic and the best aromatic herbs and spices, I've taken his recipe one step further.

3 large or 6 small wild ducks
salt and black pepper
$\frac{1}{3}$ cup ($1\frac{1}{2}$ oz, 45 g) all-purpose flour
    seasoned with $\frac{1}{4}$ teaspoon salt and $\frac{1}{8}$
    teaspoon black pepper
3 cups chopped onion (6 medium onions)

3 cups green bell peppers, seeded and
    chopped (3 large peppers)
1 large apple, peeled, cored, and cubed
1 tablespoon fresh lemon juice
1 teaspoon grated fresh lemon rind
2 tablespoons olive oil

$\frac{1}{3}$ cup ($2\frac{1}{2}$ oz, 75 g) butter

$\frac{1}{3}$ cup ($2\frac{1}{2}$ fl oz, 75 ml) vegetable oil

2 cloves of garlic, minced

2 cups (16 fl oz, 500 ml) fresh chicken stock (or water)

1 cup ($5\frac{1}{2}$ oz, 160 g) coarsely chopped celery with leaves

1 bay leaf

1 teaspoon dried thyme

6 strips bacon

2 oranges, peeled and sliced

parsley for garnish

Wash and clean your ducks thoroughly and pat dry. Season by rubbing salt and pepper inside and out. Put the seasoned flour in a bowl and, using your hands, lightly dust each duck with the flour.

In a bowl, combine one-third each of the chopped onions and peppers, and all the cubed apple, lemon juice, and lemon rind. Add the olive oil and mix well. Stuff each duck cavity with this mixture and truss the legs.

Preheat your oven to 350°F (180°C, gas 4).

Heat up your butter and oil in a heavy 10 quart (8 UK quart, 10 l) iron roaster with a lid, or a very large open roasting pan. Quickly brown your ducks on all sides. Remove the ducks and pour off nearly all the fat. Stir in the remaining onions and the garlic, and sauté for 3 minutes. Return the ducks to the roaster and add the chicken stock, celery, remaining green peppers, bay leaf, and thyme. Lay one strip of bacon across each duck breast. Cover (if you don't have a lid, lay foil loosely over the pan), and cook in the oven for about 2 hours, basting often. Add more stock if necessary. Whatever you do, don't let the ducks dry out.

The ducks are done when the meat begins to separate at the breastbone and the drumsticks move about loosely at the joint. Transfer the ducks onto a warm serving platter and garnish with orange slices and parsley sprigs. Keep warm.

Place the roaster on top of the stove over medium heat. Skim off any excess fat and cook the juices down to a wonderful glazed consistency, which takes about 5 minutes. Serve this gravy on the side.

NOTE The gravy is excellent over white or brown rice. Green beans, gently boiled or sautéed in a little butter or garlic butter and covered with slivered almonds, are another good accompaniment. And, of course, a little Spider Cornbread (see page 47) wouldn't hurt!

BRUNSWICK STEW

SERVES 6

There has been considerable controversy surrounding the origin of this famous Southern stew. In *Fading Feast*, a collection of essays on disappearing American regional foods, Raymond Sokolov, food critic for the *New York Times*, passes on the story that a black cook named Jimmy Matthews concocted a squirrel stew for his master Creed Haskins in Brunswick County, Virginia, in 1828, and that Brunswick Stew evolved from this. But in Brunswick County, North Carolina, and in the city of Brunswick on the coast of Georgia, there are other stories. As

My maternal great-uncle Dr Reverend Frank Leon Bullock, who often came up North as a guest preacher at many of our local Baptist churches, including that of my uncle Reverend Theodore Bullock, in North Philadelphia. His recipe for Brunswick stew remains as cherished as his inspirational sermons.

John Egerton comments in *Southern Food*, 'In cookery, proof of origin is always a difficult task at best. It seems safe to say that Indians were making stews with wild game long before any Europeans arrived, and in that sense there was Brunswick stew before there was a Brunswick.'

In my own family, we use the recipe of my late great-uncle Frank Bullock, who was a Baptist minister to a large congregation down in Enfield, North Carolina. As a child, I used to love to hear Uncle Frank preach. He was a stout rotund man who commanded a lot of space when he entered a room. When he got going with that bellowing, deep, and resonant voice of his, the whole church got to hootin' and hollerin', hoppin' round and standin' on its feet 'cause when the spirit hit you then you just had to move something.

One lady used to get excited and she would start to speak what they called the unknown tongue. Then she would commence to falling all out and the sisters of the church, clad in white from head to toe, would have to come over and revive her and carry her out. Gerald, my cousin, and I always got there early enough to be able to sit close by her pew, so we could get a good look at her when she started her thing. But even a non-religious person *had* to be moved by the charged and caring delivery of Great-Uncle Frank's sermons. If he couldn't give you the spirit, then nobody could.

His wife, Aunt Bertha, used to make this stew according to his precise instructions, in the original way using fresh squirrel meat. It's almost as flavorful without the squirrel and just as belly-warming. And if this dish doesn't give *you* the spirit, then nothing will.

1 stewing chicken, 4 lb (2 kg), cut into service pieces (or a mixture of chicken and squirrel)
6 oz (175 g) sliced bacon
butter to make $\frac{1}{4}$ cup (2 fl oz, 60 ml) when melted with the bacon grease, plus another 1 tablespoon
2 medium onions, chopped
2 cups (16 oz, 500 g) seeded and chopped tomatoes
2 cups (12 oz, 375 g) baby lima beans

3 cups ($1\frac{1}{4}$ pints, 750 ml) water
1 tablespoon salt
$\frac{1}{2}$ teaspoon cayenne pepper
2 teaspoons Worcestershire sauce
splash of Tabasco sauce
2 cups whole kernel corn, freshly cut off the cob (from 4 cobs)
sprinkling of white sugar (no more than 1 teaspoon)
1 tablespoon all-purpose flour

Wash your chicken, pat dry, and set aside. Traditionally the pieces are not skinned.

Fry your bacon until crisp. Drain on paper towels, crumble it and set aside.

Now, add enough butter to the skillet to make $\frac{1}{4}$ cup (2 fl oz, 60 ml) fat. Gently sauté your chicken, turning frequently, until light brown on all sides, about 10 minutes. Add the chopped onions and sauté for 5 minutes or until nice and soft.

Pour your chicken and onions into a flameproof casserole. Throw in the chopped tomatoes, lima beans, water, salt, cayenne, Worcestershire sauce, and Tabasco. Stir well and bring to a boil. Now reduce the heat, cover tightly, and simmer until your chicken is just about done, perhaps about 40 minutes. Stir in the bacon, corn, and a sprinkling of sugar. Continue to cook for 30 minutes or until the vegetables are tender. About 15 minutes before serving, thicken your stew with a paste of 1 tablespoon melted butter beaten into 1 tablespoon flour (or more if necessary). Adjust the seasonings and serve hot.

RABBIT FRICASSEE
SERVES 4

Rabbit is very good fricasseed like chicken. Granddaddy Bert used to skin and roast his over a spit out of doors, while my Dad fried rabbit just the way he fried chicken.

2 fresh rabbits, cut into serving pieces (or 2 lb, 1 kg frozen boned rabbit)
$\frac{3}{4}$ cup ($3\frac{1}{2}$ oz, 100 g) all-purpose flour seasoned with 2 teaspoons salt and 1 teaspoon black pepper
$\frac{1}{4}$ cup (2 oz, 60 g) butter
$\frac{1}{4}$ cup (2 oz, 60 g) bacon grease

1 cup (8 fl oz, 250 ml) stock
2 bay leaves
1 onion, sliced
1 cup (4 oz, 120 g) sliced mushrooms with stems
1 cup (8 fl oz, 250 ml) light (single) cream

If you're using fresh rabbits then you've got your work cut out for you in skinning, cleaning, and cutting into individual servings. But then, most people love a challenge! If you're using frozen rabbit, then just thaw and rinse. Pat the pieces dry.

After this is done, you dredge your rabbit pieces in the seasoned flour. Melt your butter and bacon grease in a heavy skillet which has a lid, over medium heat. Add the rabbit pieces and cook, turning frequently, until brown and crisp, about 15 minutes. When this has been accomplished, pour off all but 3 tablespoons of the grease. Add your stock, bay leaves, and onion. Cover, lower the heat and gently simmer until your rabbit is nice and tender, 1 hour or so.

Ten minutes before serving, throw in your mushrooms and cream, but don't allow it to boil again – just heat it through. Adjust your seasonings before serving.

NOTE You may need to thicken the sauce by using 1 tablespoon flour mixed into 2 tablespoons milk. If so, do it before you add the cream, because the flour must be cooked and you can't boil the sauce after the cream goes in.

Roast Pheasant with Wild Rice Stuffin'

SERVES 4

There are interesting variations to the basic wild rice stuffin' which I'm giving you. For example, you can hold back the cooked gizzards, chop them, and throw into the roasting pan at the end, while you're making the gravy. Or you can add 1 cup (4 oz, 120 g) mushrooms sautéed in a little butter along with $\frac{1}{2}$ cup (2 oz, 60 g) chopped water chestnuts or pecans. The possibilities are endless. Remember though, if you choose to use these you'll be increasing the volume.

1 pheasant, 3 lb (1.5 kg)	2 slices fatty bacon
salt and black pepper	$\frac{1}{4}$ cup (2 oz, 60 g) melted butter
1 clove of garlic, split	1 tablespoon all-purpose flour
Wild Rice Stuffin' (see below)	1 cup (8 fl oz, 250 ml) fresh chicken stock

Pluck, clean, and singe your pheasant. Preheat your oven to 350°F (180°C, gas 4).

Rub the pheasant cavity with salt, pepper, and garlic. Stuff with Wild Rice Stuffin', tie the legs together, and tuck the wings under.

Place your pheasant, breast side up, on a rack in a roasting pan and lay the strips of bacon across the breast. Roast in the oven for about 30 minutes per pound (60 per kg), basting frequently with melted butter. The blend of butter and bacon will finish off your bird delectably.

When done, transfer onto a warm serving platter and keep it warm while you thicken up the pan juices. Pour off the excess fat, leaving no more than 1 tablespoon. Stir in the flour and cook, until brown, stirring and scraping up all of the delicious brown bits in the pan. Pour in the chicken stock and let it cook down until it thickens up to the creamy consistency you desire, about 3 minutes. Adjust the seasonings and serve alongside your pheasant.

*W*ILD RICE STUFFIN'

1 cup (8 oz, 250 g) giblets (from game bird with additions as needed)
4 cups (1¾ pints, 1 l) salted water
1 cup (6½ oz, 185 g) wild rice
¼ cup (2 oz, 60 g) butter
2 tablespoons grated onion

¼ cup (1½ oz, 45 g) chopped celery with leaves
1 tablespoon chopped fresh parsley
1 teaspoon salt
½ teaspoon black pepper
1 teaspoon poultry seasoning

Start by cleaning and chopping up your giblets. Bring them to the boil in the salted water. Simmer until tender, but note that gizzards and hearts take up to 5 times longer to cook than livers, maybe over 1 hour. If time is a problem, use chicken livers instead. Remove each item with a slotted spoon when done. Leave them to cool, chop finely and set aside.

Bring your giblet stock to a rapid boil, then pour in the wild rice. Reduce the heat and simmer the rice till almost tender, at least 30 minutes.

During this time you can melt your butter in a skillet over low heat and sauté your onion, celery, and parsley for 3 or 4 minutes.

Now drain the rice and fluff it, either by shaking the pan over a very low heat for about 10 minutes or with a few seconds in a microwave (not in the metal pan!). Throw your rice, giblets, cooked vegetables, and seasonings into a bowl and blend well. Taste and adjust the seasonings, then stuff the bird.

NOTE This recipe is sufficient for a 3 to 4 lb (1.5–2 kg) game bird – that is, if you can resist eating half the stuffing before it goes into the bird.

*Q*UAILS WITH PORT
SERVES 6–8

Usually you serve one quail to a customer, but I've known guests who wanted more. When quail or partridge or bobwhite have been out of season, I've given Cornish hen (guinea fowl) this treatment and it's come out nearly as good.

8 quails, cleaned
1 cup (4½ oz, 130 g) all-purpose flour seasoned with 2 teaspoons salt, ⅛ teaspoon black pepper, and a pinch of thyme
¼ cup (2 oz, 60 g) unsalted butter
¼ cup (2 oz, 60 g) bacon grease
4 bay leaves
4 teaspoons salted butter

2 cups (½ lb, 250 g) sliced mushrooms
2 cloves of garlic, minced
1 large onion, chopped
2 cups (16 fl oz, 500 ml) hot fresh chicken stock
1½ cups (12 fl oz, 375 ml) port
2 cups (13 oz, 400 g) uncooked rice
salt and black pepper

Wash your quails under cold running water then pat dry. Lightly dust each quail in seasoned flour, shaking off any excess flour.

In a large skillet, over medium heat, melt the butter and bacon grease. Brown the quails on all sides. The best way to turn the birds is to grasp their legs. If space is a problem, brown them in several batches.

When they're nicely browned, remove them from the skillet and place in a roasting pan. Place half a bay leaf and $\frac{1}{2}$ teaspoon salted butter into the cavity of each bird. Set aside.

Preheat your oven to 350°F (180°C, gas 4).

Now, in that same skillet, sauté your mushrooms over medium heat for about 5 minutes, then stir in the garlic and onion. Continue cooking until the onion is nicely browned, about another 5 minutes. Pour in the hot chicken stock and simmer for 2 or 3 minutes. Remove from the heat. Stir in the port and rice and pour over the quails.

Cover the pan (if it has no lid, drape foil over it) and cook in the oven for 45 minutes to 1 hour, basting every so often. When the birds are tender and the rice is cooked, taste and adjust your seasonings. Transfer to a large chafing dish and serve one quail to a person, splayed over a delicious bed of rice. I usually serve string beans with ham hocks with this dish.

COUNTRY FRIED VENISON STEAKS IN CREAMY PAN GRAVY

SERVES 6

Here is an old family recipe, traditionally eaten for breakfast with fried eggs, grits, and hot buttered biscuits. This one'll keep you going for a long time, so if you're having it for dinner, make dessert something very light.

2 lb (1 kg) young venison steak
2 cloves of garlic, split
$\frac{1}{2}$ cup ($2\frac{1}{2}$ oz, 75 g) all-purpose flour
    seasoned with 1 teaspoon salt,
    $\frac{1}{4}$ teaspoon pepper and $\frac{1}{8}$ teaspoon
    paprika, plus another 3 tablespoons
    unseasoned

$\frac{1}{2}$ cup (4 fl oz/oz, 120 ml/g) vegetable oil
    or bacon grease
$2\frac{1}{2}$ cups ($1\frac{1}{4}$ pints, 750 ml) milk
salt and black pepper

Pound your venison steaks to about $\frac{1}{2}$ in (1.5 cm) thick. Cut them into individual serving pieces, trimming off excess fat. Rub each with garlic then dredge in seasoned flour. Shake off any excess flour.

Heat your oil or bacon grease in a heavy skillet over medium heat. When hot, sauté your steaks for 10 to 12 minutes or so, turning frequently. Don't overcook them or they'll be tough. (I always cook them to well done because that is my own preference.) Transfer them to a warmed platter and keep the steaks warm while you attend to making the gravy.

Pour off all but 3 tablespoons of fat from the skillet. Please don't lose any of the residue in the bottom of the pan, but do get rid of most of the fat — you see, venison fat is really strong if left in a gravy. Stir in your flour and blend well. Pour in the milk, stirring constantly, and cook your pan gravy until it thickens up, 3 minutes or so. Season it to your liking. To my taste 1 teaspoon salt and about $\frac{1}{2}$ teaspoon of black pepper is just about right. I just keep on adding and tasting until I get that special chill down my spine.

Spoon a little gravy over the steak and pass the rest around in a gravy boat. If you have this for dinner, serve it with mashed potatoes and perhaps throw a few sliced or button mushrooms into the gravy.

ROAST 'POSSUM WITH APPLES AND YAMS

SERVES 6

People immediately think of Jed Clampet, Granny and the Beverly Hillbillies whenever they hear of 'possum. But it's a real enough critter. You'll know the expression 'playing possum.' That derives from some species of 'possum which when caught or frightened pretend to be dead. Outside the States the only people I've ever met, aside from my own soul food lovin' family, who are familiar with the taste of 'possum are New Zealanders who love the meat cooked in an outdoor pit like a suckling pig. 'Possum tastes like a cross between rabbit and wild fowl. If you can't find one, make this recipe with a couple of wild rabbits.

1 large or 2 small 'possums	6 yams (sweet potatoes), peeled and
$\frac{1}{4}$ cup (2 fl oz, 60 ml) fresh lemon juice	halved lengthwise
3 tablespoons all-purpose flour	4 apples, peeled, cored and quartered
salt and pepper	1 cup (7 oz, 200 g) light brown sugar
1 teaspoon dried ground thyme	1 teaspoon ground cinnamon
2 cups (16 fl oz, 500 ml) water	$\frac{1}{2}$ teaspoon ground nutmeg
2 tablespoons butter	

Skin and clean your 'possum, removing as much of the unwanted fat as you can find. Get rid of all the innards, and be certain to remove the small reddish musk glands from the small of its back and from under each foreleg between the shoulder and the rib. (Granddaddy Bert, like most hunters, used to soak his 'possums overnight in salted water, then rinse really well before roasting the next day.) Douse the 'possum with lemon juice and rub it in as best you can.

Preheat your oven to 350°F (180°C, gas 4). Mix together your flour, salt, pepper, and thyme. Rub the 'possum, both inside and out, with the flour mixture. Now lay it on a rack in a roasting pan and pour the water in.

Cover with a tightly fitting lid or foil, and roast in the oven for 45 minutes, or 1 hour for a big 'possum.

Drain off all but about 1 cup (8 fl oz, 250 ml) of the juice from the pan and throw in your yams. Dot each half yam with a generous dollop of butter. Cover again and continue to roast for an additional 45 minutes or until almost tender.

Now throw in the apple quarters. Mix the brown sugar, cinnamon, and nutmeg, and sprinkle it over the yams and apples. Uncover and roast for 20 minutes or until nicely browned and tender. Serve immediately.

BRAISED SQUIRREL

SERVES 4

Squirrel meat is one of the ingredients of two famous Southern stews: Brunswick Stew (see page 92); and Burgoo, the traditional dish of the state of Kentucky, which is still served to thousands of anxious people each year at the famous Kentucky Derby horse race.

Squirrel is usually braised or cooked in stews because the meat from an older animal can be very tough. Since it's virtually impossible for anyone other than an experienced hunter to determine the age of a squirrel, it's safer to cook it those ways. Slow cooking brings out the best in squirrel meat, but here again, some people like my Granddad and Dad would just as soon fry up squirrel as chicken.

The native American species is the gray squirrel, which is now rampant in much of Europe. However the red squirrel is a small and endangered species and should never be abused. More realistically, you can also use this recipe for any small game animal that might be tough.

2 squirrels
salt and pepper
$\frac{1}{4}$ cup (2 oz, 60 g) butter, plus
   1 teaspoon
$\frac{1}{4}$ cup (2 oz, 60 g) bacon grease
2–3 tablespoons all-purpose flour
2 cups (16 fl oz, 500 ml) chicken stock or
   water

salt and pepper
onion powder
seasoning salt
$\frac{1}{4}$ cup chopped onion ($\frac{1}{2}$ medium onion)
$\frac{1}{2}$ cup (4 fl oz, 120 ml) heavy (double)
   cream

Skin, clean and quarter your squirrels, then rub each piece with salt and pepper. Wrap in foil or clear plastic wrap and refrigerate for at least 2 hours or overnight (you don't have to take this step, but the salt serves to tenderize the squirrels).

Melt your butter and bacon grease in a large skillet and sauté the pieces until golden brown all over, about 10 minutes. Transfer to a roasting pan. Preheat your oven to 350°F (180°C, gas 4).

Pour off all but about 3 tablespoons of fat, but make sure you don't lose any of the delicious residue in the bottom of the pan. Stir in 3 tablespoons flour and brown it, stirring constantly, for 3 minutes or so, then pour in the chicken stock or water. Raise the heat and bring to a rapid boil, then reduce the heat and allow to simmer until it thickens up, about 10 minutes. Season as you would any pan gravy. I use a little salt, pepper, onion powder, seasoning salt, whatever I feel like at the moment. Then add in your chopped onion.

Pour this gravy over your squirrel pieces. Cover with a tight-fitting lid or foil, and cook in the oven for about 1 hour. Baste and move the pieces around from time to time, paying attention to the liquid level. Add more stock or water if you see fit.

When the flesh is fork tender and falling off the bone, stir in the cream and just 1 teaspoon of butter. Adjust the seasonings and allow the cream to heat through. Serve over white, brown, or wild rice, or with home fried potatoes and Spider Cornbread (see page 47).

BEANS 'N' RICE

*I*n soul food cooking, beans and rice always go together. They say there's a nutritional reason for this, but I reckon on another one. Simmered slow and easy the soul food way (with a ham hock, bone, or stock, and some celery, onion, and hot or sweet peppers), your beans come out with a sumptuously thick and soulful gravy that can make a big man weep. And what better to pick up the flavor and make sure it reaches all of your tastebuds than a generous bed of rice?

Now of all the different beans we cook – pinto, kidney, and so forth – the black-eyed pea, also known as the cowpea, has to be the most soulful. It was brought to America by the slaves and, according to expert John Thorne, often planted by them on the borders of the cornfields, from which comes its other names, like the field pea or the cornfield pea. I sure could've burnt up some serious pages with the black-eyed pea. George Washington Carver, the great black statesman, once wrote, 'As a food for man, the cowpea should be to the South what the White, Soup, Navy, or Boston bean is to the North, East, and West; and it may be prepared in a sufficient number of ways to suit the most fastidious palate.'

For a long time tradition had it that rice, too, came to the New World from Africa, arriving via Charleston, South Carolina, in the latter half of the seventeenth century as a gift of thanks to the townsfolk from a distressed ship from Madagascar which they had helped. But in fact the first rice was grown by the British in Virginia and its cultivation seems to have spread southward, with new varieties arriving from various places.

None the less, rice had been known in Africa for thousands of years and, in particular, cultivated in the delta and coastal regions of West Africa for several centuries by the time the slave trade started. Historians believe that the slaves' knowledge of lowland cultivation techniques contributed a great deal to the success of rice as a commercial crop in South Carolina.

Today that area remains a world leader in the trade, and we consider Carolina extra-long grain rice to be the very best for smothering with soul food gravies and sauces, mixing into gumbos or jambalayas and – I confess – eating with sugar and a dash of cream. With game we prefer wild rice, the seeds of a native swamp grass. But now, of course, it's an expensive delicacy.

These dishes adapt beautifully to vegetarian eating, seasoned simply with herbs and spices and perhaps flavored with additional vegetables like green pepper and celery. And if you're one of those people who get paranoid when they learn a vegetarian is coming to dinner, remember they'll probably be more thankful for something substantial like this than for a rabbit-food salad.

SOAKING BEANS

I'm indebted for my bean knowledge to an absorbing book called *Beans & Rice* by John Thorne, who has researched the subject through many centuries and cultures. He also gives the most accurate and practical advice I have ever read, so I would like to quote him here:

> Soak them in good spring water and let them plump out to their own rhythm: don't hustle things along by boiling them and then letting them soak — which is just pre-cooking them and tends to turn them into mush. Eight hours is the length of soaking time to shoot for ... start them the night before for day cooking or first thing in the morning for cooking in the evening. Beans tend to absorb (after soaking) three to four times their weight while cooking: there is no set rule and every chart is different!

He also explains that the only consideration to prevent you from using the soaking water as part or all of the cooking water is that it encourages flatulence, the bane of a dedicated bean-eater's life. This is caused by oligosaccharides, complex sugars that are removed from the bean by soaking. The problem varies with the bean and with the eater. To avoid it, change the water several times during the soaking. Some nutrients are lost, but the problem is greatly lessened.

To me, this encompasses all that needs to be said about soaking beans. Thank you, John!

HOPPIN' JOHN

SERVES 12

Hoppin' John is about the most famous black-eyed pea dish to come out of the American South. It is traditionally eaten on New Year's Day to ensure good luck and prosperity for the coming year. Some folks even say that if you add cabbage to the menu, money will come flooding in as well. John Thorne explains why this dish is considered to be good luck by citing the saying, 'Eat poor on New Year's and eat fat the rest of the year.'

There are various theories about how this dish came by its name. One tells of a certain John who came a-hoppin' when his wife took the dish out of the stove, another of children hopping once around the table before the dish was served. Yet another says that it was named after a lively waiter. John Thorne also writes that etymologists believe the name is a corruption of *pois à pigeon*, French for pigeon pea, another bean brought from Africa to the Americas and which flourishes throughout the Caribbean. There beans and rice are always cooked together. In fact Helen Mendes, author of *The African Heritage Cookbook*, has suggested that since this is the only American dish in which beans and rice are

cooked together, it may have been brought over from the West Indies by slaves. With its name anglicized and the origin forgotten, folk legends naturally evolved to explain it. Choose your own theory, but first try the recipe so you'll know what all the fuss is about.

$2\frac{1}{2}$ cups (1 lb, 500 g) black-eyed peas
2 ham hocks
2 bay leaves
1 large or 2 medium Bermuda (mild Spanish) onion, coarsely chopped
1 cup (5 oz, 150 g) diced celery, leaves included

$\frac{1}{2}$ teaspoon crushed red pepper flakes
salt and black (or cayenne) pepper
2 tablespoons finely diced green bell pepper (optional)
2 cups (13 oz, 400 g, but see below) long grain rice

Wash and sort out your peas the night before, taking care to sort out any damaged or discolored peas as well as any that float. Soak as directed on page 101.

Now, if you've never cooked ham hocks before, then you need to know that they have to be scrubbed with a vegetable brush until they are clean and free of any unsightly hairs. Then throw your hocks into a large saucepan, cover with water, bring it to a boil, and simmer for about 30 minutes.

Then put in your peas, bay leaves, onion, celery, pepper flakes, green pepper, and any other seasonings you wish to add, along with enough water to just cover the peas. You must be careful with green pepper as it tends to take over the taste of any dish unless used in strict moderation. Allow all this to simmer for about 2 hours. Stir every now and then, but take care not to pulverize your peas. If they begin breaking up before they are tender, you are cooking them too fast.

About 30 minutes before you estimate the peas to be done, boil your rice. Use your favorite method or this one. Measure out the rice with a cup into a pan, then use the same cup to measure an equal amount of water. Bring the water to a fast boil, stir the rice once, turn the heat right down, cover the pan, and *don't lift that lid* for 20 minutes. Then you can either turn the heat off and let the rice rest for 10 minutes, still covered, or fluff it by putting it in a colander over a pot with a little boiling water. Add salt only after cooking.

When your peas are nice and tender but not broken up, your dish is done. Your mixture should be of a creamy texture. Adjust your seasonings to taste and blend well. In my family the rice and peas are never combined until they hit our plates, because we like the juiciness that gives, but a lot of folks will fluff the rice right into the pot of peas and ham hocks.

There you have it — Hoppin' John. Serve at once with cornbread and collards or, if you really wanna be lucky, with cabbage.

OPPOSITE *My great-great-grandfather Peter Johnson (Grandma Maggie Ferguson's grandfather), who was a slave in South Carolina, almost certainly on a rice plantation. That is sadly the sum total of everything we know about him.*

UNITED STATES SENATORIAL BEAN SOUP

SERVES 8

This famous soup is alleged to have been created in Washington, DC, for President Abraham Lincoln by his black cook at the White House. Several versions are in existence today, but the original recipe, and the one I like, calls for the use of marrow beans and sorrel. This soup is still on the menus of many Washington restaurants frequented by Congressmen and government officials.

(In case you don't know, marrow beans are ordinary white haricot beans. If you prefer, you can use any kind of kidney beans, or navy or lima beans – large dried lima beans are known as butter beans.)

1 cup (6½ oz, 190 g) dried marrow beans
1 ham bone with some meat still on it
4 oz (120 g) ham or salt pork, in a piece
1 bay leaf
4 whole cloves
½ teaspoon salt
5 whole peppercorns
4 quarts (3½ UK quarts, 4 l) water
2 cups (10 oz, 300 g) chopped celery, including leaves

½ cup (3 oz, 90 g) peeled, trimmed, and sliced carrots
¼ teaspoon saffron
2 garlic cloves, crushed
1 medium onion, chopped
1 cup (8 oz, 250 g) freshly cooked mashed potatoes
1 cup (4 oz, 120 g) chopped sorrel
fried croûtons (optional)

Wash and sort your beans, and soak them according to the instructions on page 101.

Put the beans, ham bone, ham or salt pork, bay leaf, cloves, salt, and peppercorns with the water in a large saucepan. Bring to a boil, then simmer for about 3 hours or until the beans are cooked.

About 30 minutes before you estimate that your beans will be done, throw in your celery, carrots, saffron, garlic, onion, mashed potatoes, and sorrel.

When all your vegetables are ready, remove your chunk of ham or salt pork and dice it up. Scrape all of the meat from the ham bone. Purée the soup with a blender or a fine sieve. Now add your meat to the soup. If you need to thin it out any, use warm milk or cream. Season to taste and serve. This soup is delicious topped with fried croûtons.

RED KIDNEY BEANS WITH RICE AND SAUSAGES

SERVES 6

Down Louisiana way, around New Orleans, Creole and Cajun lore explains that red beans and rice was a favorite Monday evening meal. Monday was washday, so Sunday's left-over ham bone was thrown in a big old pot with a heap of red beans and left to simmer on all day long, affording the lady of the house the time she needed to devote to her washing and scrubbing. A more modern point of interest is that this dish freezes extremely well and seems to taste even better each time it's reheated.

$2\frac{1}{2}$ cups (1 lb, 500 g) dried red kidney
    beans
$\frac{1}{3}$ cup bacon grease
1 large onion, diced
1 stalk celery with leaves, sliced
2 cloves of garlic, minced
large ham bone with some meat on it (or
    $1\frac{1}{2}$ lb [750 g] ham hock)
4 quarts ($3\frac{1}{2}$ UK quarts, 4 l) water
1 teaspoon Tabasco sauce
$\frac{1}{4}$ teaspoon salt
$\frac{1}{4}$ teaspoon black pepper
1 bay leaf
$1\frac{1}{2}$ teaspoons sugar
1 teaspoon dried thyme

1 teaspoon dried marjoram
$\frac{1}{3}$ cup coconut cream (optional)
1 peeled, trimmed, and sliced carrot
    (optional)
$\frac{3}{4}$ cup (6 fl oz, 175 ml) beer (optional)
$\frac{1}{2}$ cup chopped green bell pepper (1
    smallish pepper; optional)
cayenne pepper (optional)
3 tablespoons vegetable oil
12 hot sausages (or frankfurters)
3 cups ($1\frac{1}{4}$ lb, 600 g) long grain rice

Garnish (optional):
$\frac{1}{2}$ cup ($2\frac{1}{2}$ oz, 75 g) sliced scallions
$\frac{1}{4}$ cup (1 oz, 30 g) chopped fresh parsley

Rinse your beans, discarding any bruised or discolored ones. Soak as directed on page 101. (There is a short cut, although soul food cooks scoff at it. If you must, you can bring the beans to a rapid boil, then boil gently for about 3 minutes. Remove the pot from the heat and let it stand for about 1 hour, then continue as usual.)

Drain your beans and rinse again.

In a large pot, melt your bacon grease over medium heat, then gently sauté your onion, celery, and garlic until the onion is soft and transparent but not yet browned. Throw in the kidney beans, ham bone (or ham hock), 4 quarts ($3\frac{1}{2}$ UK quarts, 4 l) water, Tabasco sauce, salt, pepper, bay leaf, sugar, and herbs (and any other flavorings you choose). Stir well and bring the mixture to a boil.

Reduce your heat, cover, and allow to simmer until beans are tender and juice is nicely thickened, about 1 to $1\frac{1}{2}$ hours. Stir your beans frequently to prevent sticking. Adjust the seasoning after the beans have cooked down and thickened up, for only then can you judge the true taste. Creole people believe that whoever finds the bay leaf on their plate will be awarded good luck, so, if you're superstitious, don't discard that old bay leaf.

When your beans are almost done, cook the rice by your preferred method (or see page 103). Heat your oil in a large heavy skillet and sauté your sausages until they are well cooked and nicely browned on all sides, about 10 minutes.

To serve, spoon a portion of rice onto each plate, cover with a generous helping of beans and gravy and sling a couple of sausages (or frankfurters) on the side. If you like, garnish with a sprinkling of sliced scallions and parsley.

NOTE That is your basic way of eating basic red beans, rice and sausages. But, of course, there are plenty of twists to the recipe. Soul food cooks usually prefer slicing up the sausages or frankfurters into quarters and adding them right into the pot during the last 30 minutes of cooking to combine the flavors. Some throw in a little ham hock meat and skin, rice, and some Tabasco, and serve a large wedge of Spider Cornbread (see page 47) on the side. Coconut cream and carrot add a Caribbean twist. Beer, along with green pepper and cayenne pepper, will lend a distinct Cajun taste.

DIRTY RICE

SERVES 6

Yet another delicacy from the deep, deep South. It is delicious just on its dirty own, or as an accompaniment to quail, pheasant, turkey, roast beef, or a Cajun barbecue.

2 cups (13 oz, 400 g) long grain rice
2 cups (16 fl oz, 500 ml) beef stock
$\frac{1}{4}$ cup (2 oz/fl oz, 60 g/ml) bacon grease
  (or vegetable oil or butter)
$\frac{1}{4}$ cup (1 oz, 30 g) all-purpose flour
8 oz (250 g) chicken gizzards, cleaned
  and minced
4 oz chicken livers, minced
1 large onion, chopped

$\frac{1}{2}$ medium green bell pepper, chopped
1 stalk celery, finely chopped
2 cloves of garlic, minced
$\frac{1}{2}$ cup (2 oz, 60 g) chopped mushrooms
1 cup (8 fl oz, 250 ml) water
$\frac{1}{2}$ cup (2 oz, 60 g) sliced scallion (spring
  onion) tops (green part only)
3 sprigs of parsley, chopped
salt, pepper and Tabasco to taste

Start by washing your rice, then cook it in the beef stock by the method given on page 103. Meanwhile prepare all of your vegetables and mince the gizzards and livers. Heat the bacon grease (or oil or butter) in a heavy skillet over high heat. When hot, add in your flour and cook, stirring constantly, until brown, about 5 minutes.

Now throw in your gizzards and livers and sauté until they're no longer pink, about 4 minutes. Add the onion, pepper, celery, garlic, mushrooms, and water, then lower the heat and simmer until nicely thick, 45 minutes to 1 hour. Stir often, remembering to scrape any residue from the bottom of the skillet. Just before you are ready to serve, throw in your cooked rice, scallion tops, and parsley and season to taste with salt, pepper and Tabasco.

SAFFRON RICE

SERVES 8

Saffron rice is a contribution from the early Spanish immigrants and is found across the whole of the Southern delta region. It is one of my favorite side dishes with subtly flavored fish, chicken, or meat.

2 cups (13 oz, 400 g) white long grain
  rice
5 cups (2$\frac{1}{4}$ pints, 1.3 l) cold water
2$\frac{1}{2}$ teaspoons salt

$\frac{1}{2}$ teaspoon crushed saffron
2 tablespoons boiling water
4 teaspoons melted butter
salt and pepper

Add the salt to the water, bring to a fast boil, throw in your rice and cook, uncovered, for 18 minutes. Drain it and rinse well in a colander. Place this over a pan of boiling water and let the rice steam through until nice and fluffy, about 10 minutes.

Drop your crushed saffron in a cup and add the two spoons of boiling water. Mash and stir it thoroughly. Stir in the melted butter.

Turn your rice into a serving bowl. Add the saffron butter and salt and pepper to taste, and blend well. Serve piping hot.

DADDY'S PINTO BEANS WITH RICE
SERVES 8

2 cups (13 oz, 400 g) dried pinto beans
4 cups (16 fl oz, 500 ml) water
1 small onion, coarsely chopped

8 oz (250 g) salt pork, diced (or Virginia [mild cured] ham)
salt and pepper

Wash your beans, discarding any rotten or discolored ones. Soak them as directed on page 101.

After soaking, drain the beans and put them in a large pot with the water (you can use the soaking water if you like), onion, and salt pork. Bring this to a boil, lower the heat, and simmer, uncovered, until tender, $1\frac{1}{2}$ to 2 hours. Do not let the pot boil again. Season to taste.

Serve just as they are over hot steamed rice with C. J.'s Pickled Peaches (see page 197) on the side. A big wedge of cornbread could take an active part too.

LIMA BEAN POT
SERVES 6

In the dead of winter, nothing warms you better than a big pot of lima beans. This dish keeps well in the fridge and tastes better warmed up days later. It also freezes extremely well.

2 cups (13 oz, 400 g) dried lima (butter) beans
$\frac{1}{2}$ teaspoon salt
pepper

$1\frac{1}{2}$ tablespoons brown sugar
1 medium onion, chopped
4 oz (120 g) salt pork, sliced (or ham with 2 tablespoons bacon fat added)

Wash and sort your lima beans, discarding any rotten or discolored ones, and soak them as directed on page 101 for at least 12 hours. I always soak mine overnight.

Cook them in the soaking water, if you dare, or in fresh water, adding your salt, pepper, brown sugar, onion, and salt pork (or ham with bacon fat). Bring to a boil, reduce the heat, and simmer until the beans are tender, stirring gently so as not to mash them. The longer they cook the thicker the juice will naturally become. Add water if necessary, but you want to keep a rich gravy-like consistency. Taste and adjust your seasonings as you go. Total cooking time should be 2 or 3 hours. Then sit back and enjoy.

LIMA BEAN CAKES
SERVES 6

Just a soulful little old cake, similar to a potato pancake but made out of lima beans instead. A nice change, and it's oh so easy to make.

$1\frac{1}{2}$ cups (12 oz, 375 g) cooked, mashed lima (butter) beans

1 cup (4 oz, 120 g) soft breadcrumbs

$\frac{1}{2}$ cup finely chopped onion (1 medium onion)

2 tablespoons chopped fresh parsley

1 teaspoon salt, or to taste

$\frac{1}{4}$ teaspoon pepper (white, black, or cayenne)

$\frac{1}{2}$ teaspoon dried ground sage

$\frac{1}{4}$ cup (2 oz, 60 g) butter (or bacon grease or other fat)

1 recipe Creole Sauce (see page 115)

Combine your mashed lima beans, breadcrumbs, onion, parsley, salt, pepper, and sage. Using your hands, shape your mixture into flat little cakes about the size of a small hamburger. Refrigerate the cakes for 1 hour or so, during which time you can be preparing the sauce.

Sauté your cakes in a skillet, very gently, in butter or other fat, for about 3 minutes a side. When they're nicely brown on both sides, they're ready to serve. Just pour on your Creole Sauce.

BAKED LIMA BEAN AND PORK CASSEROLE
SERVES 6

One day I was making this and I didn't have any cooked pork, and I didn't want to go out until I'd put the casserole in the oven. So I used what I had, some frankfurters, and it turned out to be quite delicious.

$1\frac{1}{2}$ cups ($1\frac{1}{4}$ lb, 600 g) dried large lima (butter) beans

8 oz (250 g) slab of salt pork, sliced almost to the rind

1 lb (500 g) lean cooked pork (or 1 lb [500 g] frankfurters)

5 cups (2 pints, 1.2 l) water

2 tablespoons peanut oil

1 medium onion, chopped

1 clove of garlic, minced

$\frac{1}{3}$ cup ($2\frac{1}{2}$ oz, 75 g) dark brown sugar

1–2 teaspoons sorghum molasses (or ordinary dark molasses)

1 teaspoon salt

1 teaspoon dry mustard

2 tablespoons cider vinegar

4 tablespoons tomato ketchup

1 tablespoon Worcestershire sauce

1 tablespoon chilli powder

1 teaspoon curry powder (optional)

about $\frac{1}{4}$ cup (2 fl oz, 60 ml) beer (optional)

Wash and sort your beans in a colander, under running water, discarding any discolored or rotten ones. Soak as directed on page 101.

Put the beans in a large saucepan with the salt pork and water (you can use the soaking water) and bring to a boil. Lower the heat and simmer until tender, about $1\frac{1}{2}$ hours.

Now drain your beans but reserve the liquid and salt pork. Put the beans in a greased casserole and set aside.

Preheat your oven to 350°F (180°C, gas 4).

Heat the oil in a saucepan over medium heat. Add the onion and sauté for about 3 minutes. Then add the garlic and sauté for an additional 3 minutes.

Meanwhile combine your brown sugar, molasses, salt, mustard, vinegar, ketchup, Worcestershire sauce, and chilli powder (and curry powder if you want) in a large measuring cup. Mix well. Pour enough reserved bean liquid into the measuring cup to bring the level up to $1\frac{1}{2}$ cups (12 fl oz, 375 ml). If using beer, use part beer and part bean liquid to make up the volume. Set aside.

Pour this mixture into the saucepan with the onion and garlic and bring to a boil. Reduce the heat and allow it to simmer for 5 minutes. Cut your other piece of pork or frankfurters into bite-size pieces and throw them into your saucepan. Just let them heat through, then pour the whole thing into your casserole with the beans. Stir gently, just enough to mix everything. Decorate the top by splaying the salt pork slab in the center.

Bake, covered, in the oven for about 40 minutes. If your beans begin to look dry, add a little more of the reserved bean liquid. Remove the lid at the end of the 40 minutes and continue baking for an additional 30 minutes or so.

KISSIN' COUSINS

A kissin' cousin is someone with whom you share such a closeness that you could be related, even though there's no direct blood tie. Take my Uncle Mutt. He was raised by Granddaddy Bert and when my Dad moved to Philly he came too. When my Dad got married, Mutt became part of the household. He was just always there. He was a true kissin' cousin. I know some of you cynics out there are thinking he sounds like a parasite. Well, it's not the same thing at all. The closeness between kissin' cousins is a blend of respect and pride in mutual background.

From that comes the use of the expression for any two things which relate to one another in a special and intimate fashion. Now soul food has lots of kissin' cousins, because white and black have been stirrin' pots and sharin' dreams for hundreds of years in the South.

The closest one is the wonderful Gullah cuisine. The Gullahs, who live along the coasts of South Carolina, Florida, and Georgia and on offshore islands, are folks who have stuck with their own complex language of old plantation English mixed into African tribal tongues. We don't know for sure, but their name may come from Angolan ancestors. They have always been a poor people and their food is simple: rice from the plantations, crabs, oysters, and fish from the shallows and inlets, and all kinds of greens. They season all these up with onions, garlic, green peppers, and small amounts of bacon or game, and come out with meals that are some kinda good.

Then come Creole and Cajun. These days everyone knows about them, but a lot of people still aren't clear about the distinctions. First let's take Creole. It's considered to be a cosmopolitan city style, the product of the rich cultural blend in New Orleans. The Creole people are descended from African, Caribbean, French, and Spanish roots — a spicy combo if ever I heard one — and this heritage is strongly reflected in their cooking. Many of the Creole sauces have a tomato base and use Spanish or French seasonings.

We shouldn't forget that there's also a lot of soul blended in there, as Paul Prudhomme explains in his book *Louisiana Cooking*:

> The position of cook was highly esteemed and the best paid position in the household. Those cooks, most of whom were black ... learned how to cook for a variety of nationalities, and they incorporated their own spicy, home-style way of cooking into the different cuisines of their employers. This is the way Creole food was created.

Well, to my humble tastebuds, Creole food is more satisfying than even the most exquisite pure *haute cuisine*, maybe because it is blessed with such a wide range of flavors, or maybe because it has that smack-dab essence of soul that I love.

Cajun, on the other hand, is pure country. The Cajuns were originally Acadians – French settlers in the southeastern Canadian province of Acadia – who relocated to the swampy marshes, or bayou country, in and around Louisiana. They adapted their native dishes to local ingredients and spices that grew wild in the area: bay leaves, filé powder from sassafras, and an abundance of different peppers, learning many of their uses from the native Indians. Like the Gullahs (or the hillbillies of Kentucky or the Amish of Pennsylvania) they've remained outside mainstream American culture and, by doing so, have kept alive their own language and cooking.

Now Cajun food is some kinda hot and don't let anybody tell you any different! The soul food heat of hot peppers tempered with onion and vinegar has nothin' on this. Oh, no. Cajun heat wallops your taste buds with a KO punch of lots of garlic and cayenne pepper topped off with Tabasco, then ricochets around your salivary glands like an out-of-control brushfire. When it's tested, tasted, tried, and true, it can be exquisite.

I've also included here a few mainstream classics, the kinds of dishes that everybody ate in the neighborhoods where I grew up, regardless of their ethnic or social background. I'd call them Northern city soul, because you will notice that somewhere along the way they have acquired a soulful twist – maybe a few more peppers or a fried-up crispness.

VERTAMAE'S FRIED CRAB 'N' GRITS

SERVES 4

Here are my adaptations of two Gullah recipes from Vertamae Smart Grosvenor, author of the soul food classic, *Vibration Cooking, or The Travel Notes of a Geechee Girl*. Coincidentally, she also grew up in Philadelphia, after moving up North.

Her wonderful book tells you exactly what Gullah cooking is all about. Vertamae writes, 'I never weigh or measure anything. I cook by vibration. Just turn on the imagination, be willing to change your style and let a little soul in.' These are special versions of her recipes, with quantities and cooking times, taken from the *Orlando Sentinel*.

1 cup (7 oz, 200 g) uncooked grits
2 tablespoons butter or margarine
1 lb (500 g) crab meat
¼ cup (2 fl oz, 60 g) vegetable oil
1 medium onion, chopped
¼ teaspoon sugar
2 cloves of garlic, minced

1 green bell pepper, seeded and chopped
¼ cup (1 oz, 30 g) all-purpose flour
¾ teaspoon salt
½ teaspoon black pepper
1 cup (8 fl oz, 250 ml) water or milk
Tabasco sauce (optional)

Boil the grits according to the instructions on the box. When cooked, slap your butter or margarine on top, cover, and keep 'em warm.

Now clean and pick over the crab meat and remove any bits of shell or cartilage. Careful, because there's always one lurking in the shadows.

Heat up your oil in a heavy skillet, over medium heat, and sauté the onion until soft and transparent, about 5 minutes. Add your sugar, garlic, and green pepper and stir for 3 minutes. Stir in your crab meat and just heat it through – don't kill it. Now stir in the flour, salt, and pepper, making sure the crab meat and vegetables are well coated. Cook for about 2 minutes or until the flour begins to stick to the bottom and the sides of the skillet. Add in the water or milk and cook, stirring continuously, until the sauce boils up and thickens sufficiently, about 3 minutes.

Serve over your hot buttered grits and season with Tabasco sauce if you like. Vertamae says that with this dish she serves cold beer, lemonade, or a crisp Sauvignon Blanc. Sounds delightful.

NOTE   Also may I point out that this dish can be even fancier if you make up a batch of cheese grits and add a topping of grated cheese. But of course the dish can stand on its own merit, it's simply out of this soul world.

*V*ERTAMAE'S GEECHEE OYSTERS 'N' RICE

SERVES 4

Whenever I asked for a second portion of rice as a child, I can vividly remember my dad calling me a geechee – the nickname for a Gullah. All the grown-ups at the table would laugh. I grew up assuming that a geechee was anyone who ate lots of rice. This skillet dinner with a lotta rice and just a few oysters is, to me, true Gullah style eating.

1 pint (sparing UK pint, 500 ml) shucked fresh oysters (15–20, depending on size)	1 cup (6$\frac{1}{2}$ oz, 190 g) uncooked long grain rice
2 slices thick-cut bacon	1 teaspoon salt, or to taste
1 medium onion	$\frac{1}{2}$ teaspoon black pepper
2 cloves of garlic	cayenne pepper (optional)
1 medium green bell pepper	1$\frac{1}{2}$ cups (12 fl oz, 375 ml) water

First you drain your oysters, but reserve the liquor. Chop the oysters into thumbnail-sized chunks and set aside.

Choose a heavy skillet which has a lid. Dice up your bacon and fry it over medium heat until crisp, about 5 minutes. While it's cooking, dice your onion and green pepper, and mince the garlic. I dice my green pepper up very finely to help disguise it from my family. They like the taste it gives to foods, but they don't like to crunch down on any the way I do.

When the bacon is nicely browned, add in your onion and cook for 3 minutes or until soft and translucent, but not browned. Add the garlic and green pepper and cook for another 2 minutes or so. Now stir in the rice, salt, pepper, and cayenne if desired. Make sure your rice is well and truly coated with the mixture. Pour in the reserved oyster liquor along with the water. Cover, simmer for about

10 minutes, then add your oyster bits, stirring well. Lower the heat and cook for another 10 minutes or longer, until the rice is tender. Serve immediately with Tabasco sauce on the side for those who want it. Vertamae says that her dish goes really well with a tall glass of ice-cold lemonade or sweetened iced tea.

NOTE If you insist on a meatier dish, then stir in some shrimp, fish fillets or ham; if you like a spicier outcome, then add in $\frac{1}{2}$ teaspoon cayenne pepper along with the rice.

OKRA GUMBO

SERVES 4

Centuries ago in Africa, young okra pods, called *ngombo*, were made into a soup to which the same name was given. The pods were also dried and ground to a fine powder to be used as a seasoning for other native foods. And when the Africans were sold into slavery in America, the vegetable, its name, and the soup came with them.

In America there are basically two kinds of gumbos: those using okra as their base; and those, like Uncle Boykin's, which contain no okra but use gumbo filé powder – from the sassafras tree – instead. So here is your basic African-American stew – a delicious okra gumbo.

2 tablespoons butter	2 large tomatoes, peeled and chopped
$\frac{1}{2}$ medium onion, finely chopped	$\frac{1}{2}$ lb (250 g) fresh okra, sliced
$\frac{1}{2}$ green bell pepper, seeded and chopped	2 cloves of garlic, minced
2 celery stalks, chopped	salt and pepper
1 level tablespoon all-purpose flour	pinch of cayenne pepper
2 cups (16 fl oz, 500 ml) hot fresh chicken stock	

Melt the butter in a large pot over medium heat. When it begins to sizzle, throw in your onion, green pepper, celery, and flour. Cook, stirring constantly, until your vegetables are soft but not brown, about 3 minutes, then add your chicken stock, okra, tomatoes, and garlic. Lower the heat and cook, with lid just askew, for about 1 hour.

Season your gumbo with salt, pepper, and cayenne just before serving.

UNCLE BOYKIN'S GUMBO

SERVES 6

When I lived with Uncle Boykin and Aunt Gussie in Jamaica, Long Island, New York, Uncle Boykin used to tell me stories about his childhood. He grew up in the state of Louisiana, an area inhabited by the Choctaw Indians until they were resettled around the Oklahoma territory in 1803. When I was eight years old, he told me that his grandmother had been a Choctaw. This fascinated me and I wanted to know what teepee life was all about.

Oftentimes, though, it was hard to get Uncle Boykin to talk. His grandfather had been a slave and many of his own experiences with racial bigotry were obviously very painful to discuss. When I pressed him about teepees or his own childhood, he would change the subject or fall into a deep, wan silence. But after a considerable amount of Rock and Rye (rye whiskey, rock candy and some slices of orange, lemon or other fruits) he would either start crying or would recount tangled tales of his childhood.

The clearest legacy he passed down is this recipe for gumbo. The Choctaws were the first Indian tribe known to use gumbo filé, which both flavors and thickens gumbos.

2 tablespoons bacon grease

1 large green bell pepper or 2 smaller red peppers, seeded and finely diced

1 cup chopped onion (1 large onion)

2 cloves of garlic, minced

$\frac{1}{4}$ cup (1 oz, 30 g) diced scallion (spring onion) tops (green part only)

$\frac{1}{2}$ cup (2 oz, 60 g) chopped fresh parsley

1 cup (8 oz, 250 g) cubed cooked ham

1 cup (8 oz, 250 g) cubed cooked chicken

1 cup (8 oz, 250 g) cubed cooked chicken giblets

1 lb (500 g) fresh shrimp, peeled and deveined

2 cups (1 lb, 500 g) peeled, seeded, and chopped tomatoes

5 cups (1 quart, 1.2 l) boiling water

$\frac{1}{4}$ teaspoon black pepper

$\frac{1}{4}$ teaspoon paprika

1 tablespoon Worcestershire sauce

2 cups (1 lb, 500 g) fresh crab meat, cartilage removed

$\frac{1}{2}$ teaspoon salt

1 tablespoon gumbo filé

After all your ingredients are prepared, you can begin to make a gumbo. Heat your bacon grease in a large heavy skillet over medium heat and sauté your pepper, onion, garlic, scallions, and half of the parsley until the onion starts to turn soft but has not browned, about 10 minutes. Turn all these vegetables out into a large pot with a lid.

In the same skillet, sauté your ham, chicken, and giblets for about 2 minutes over medium heat. Now throw in the shrimp, raise the heat and toss them around for about another 3 minutes. Remember you should never overcook shrimp. Pour this mixture into a bowl and set it aside for the moment.

Go back to the large pot and pour in your tomatoes and the boiling water. Add in the pepper, paprika, and Worcestershire sauce, stir, and allow to simmer over low heat, uncovered, for 1 hour. Toss in the shrimp mixture and crab meat. Gently stir and let it warm through, about 10 minutes.

Remove your gumbo from the heat and add the salt and gumbo filé. Stir and adjust the seasonings to fit your own individual taste. Take care when adding the gumbo filé because it will thicken up on you if you don't watch out, so do it in stages, bit by bit. Serve hot, sprinkled with the remaining parsley.

Eat it as a soup or as a stew. You may want to serve it over white rice. But any way you eat it, it's mighty good eating. If you like you can serve it on a large platter surrounded by freshly cooked crab or lobster claws. Lay a bit of parsley on top and by gum, they'll be singing your praises.

Remember that gumbos are extremely flexible. If there is something in this recipe that you don't particularly like, you can easily make substitutions. Keep the vegetables in equal proportion with the meats or fish. You can make an all-seafood gumbo, or all-chicken or beef, or whatever. If you use your imagination you'll never have to worry about what to do with leftover meats again. Just make a gumbo!

CREOLE SAUCE
MAKES APPROXIMATELY 2 CUPS

This is an amazing sauce over boiled white rice, with seafood or on top of an omelette. It is also my choice as an accompaniment to my Lima Bean Cakes (see page 108).

2 tablespoons butter (or other fat)
$\frac{1}{2}$ cup finely chopped onion (1 medium onion)
1 clove of garlic, minced
$\frac{1}{4}$ cup seeded and chopped green bell pepper ($\frac{1}{2}$ medium pepper)
$1\frac{1}{2}$ cups (12 oz, 375 g) canned plum tomatoes
$\frac{1}{2}$ cup (4 fl oz, 120 ml) water
1 teaspoon vinegar (cider or malt)
1 teaspoon sugar

$\frac{1}{2}$ teaspoon salt
$\frac{1}{2}$ teaspoon cayenne pepper
1 teaspoon chopped fresh parsley
pinch of ground thyme
dash of Tabasco sauce
$\frac{1}{4}$ cup (2 oz, 60 g) ham, cut into tiny cubes (optional)
$\frac{1}{4}$ cup (2 fl oz, 60 ml) hot chilli sauce (for the daring)
$\frac{1}{2}$ cup (2 oz, 60 g) sliced mushrooms (optional)

Melt the butter in a skillet over medium heat and sauté your onion, garlic, and green pepper for 2 or 3 minutes. Now pour in your tomatoes, water, vinegar, sugar, salt, cayenne pepper, parsley, thyme, and Tabasco sauce and any or all of the optional ingredients, and mix well. Lower the heat and simmer, uncovered, for about 1 hour or until your sauce thickens up sufficiently.

Adjust the seasonings and serve hot.

AFRO-CAROLINA PILAU
SERVES 8

Most folks who know a bit about American cooking are aware that pilau – or pilaf or purlo or purloo and so on – is a delicious rice dish that you find throughout the Southern states. But not many of them realize that it is a hot soul food specialty. Many cookbooks will tell you that pilau is primarily a French or Spanish dish. (But British readers who have encountered *pulao* in Indian restaurants will realize that this ain't the whole story.)

Now it is true that pilaus are especially linked with South Carolina and Louisiana, that they began appearing there about the same time as rice did, along with the Spanish and French influx, and that today they are still alive and kicking, particularly in the French quarter in New Orleans. But what most writers skip over is that pilau dates back centuries to the Middle East and was introduced into Africa by the Persians, and that's the Persian name for the dish. All this was before black people were extradited into slavery in the Americas and a long time before Charleston became the rice capital of the world, and if I'm lying I'm flying and pigs ain't pork. So now you understand why I call my recipe, which combines rice with okra, chicken and shrimp, Afro-Carolina Pilau. Can I get an Amen?

1 stewing chicken, 3–4 lb (1.5–2 kg), cut into pieces

2 tablespoons butter or bacon grease

1 large onion, finely chopped

1 clove of garlic, minced

1 cup (5½ oz, 160 g) diced celery

⅓ cup seeded and finely chopped green bell pepper (1 small pepper)

1¼ cups (12 oz, 375 g) canned plum tomatoes with juice

1 cup (5 oz, 150 g) trimmed, sliced fresh okra

½ teaspoon dried thyme

1 cup (6½ oz, 190 g) uncooked Carolina long grain rice

1 teaspoon salt

black pepper

Wash your chicken and pat dry. Put it in a deep kettle with just enough water to cover and bring to a boil, then lower the heat and simmer until very tender, 2 hours or so depending on the age of the chicken. The meat should be falling off the bone. When it's done, reserve the stock. Chop all of the meat from the bone and cut it into mouth-sized morsels. You can leave the skin on or remove it as you prefer.

Towards the end of the cooking time of the chicken, heat up your butter or bacon grease in a large pot and gently sauté your onion, garlic, celery, and green pepper until tender but not yet brown, about 3 minutes. Pour in your tomatoes, juice and all, and the sliced okra and thyme. Mix well and bring to a rapid boil, lower the heat and allow to simmer for about 30 minutes.

While that's going on, pour 2½ cups (1 generous UK quart, 1.25 l) of your reserved chicken stock into a saucepan (if there's any left, I always freeze it for later use). Add the rice and salt, bring to a boil, and cook uncovered for 18 minutes or until the rice is tender and all of the liquid has been absorbed. If you've timed it right, the vegetables and the rice should be coming to a head at about the same time. When the vegetables have boiled down and blended nicely, throw in the cubed chicken and fluff in the rice. Adjust your seasonings to fit your taste, allow the chicken and rice to heat through, and serve immediately.

PHILADELPHIA PEPPERPOT SOUP

SERVES 4

If you enjoy the taste of tripe, and perhaps even if you think you don't but are open-minded, then you must surely try Philadelphia Pepperpot Soup. It was first issued to General Washington's troops when they were on the brink of starvation and freezing to death during the great winter battle at Valley Forge, Pennsylvania, during the War of Independence. This is how the story goes. One day, after making an inspection of his troops, Washington furiously demanded to see the cook and ordered him to feed the men. The cook replied that all he had was some tripe and some peppercorns. So out of necessity came this original creation. To my mind this makes the cook a real war hero, since without his ingenuity Washington's men wouldn't have been able to outlast the British, win a decisive victory, and go on to win the war.

Everyone I know in Philadelphia makes Pepperpot Soup differently. Some use up to a dozen large potatoes while others add up to 4 lb (2 kg) of tripe. My Aunt Ella says that the soul way to cook tripe is to boil it till it's nice and tender, then roll it in seasoned flour and fry it.

But I'd like to give you the recipe that I created to pass a cooking exam back in school. The main change I made was to add a variety of peppers. This enhances the flavor of the soup and also seems to alter the texture. The recipe also contains more herbs and spices than General Washington's cook was probably able to obtain. But then, we're no longer at war with the British either. Now to the soup!

4 slices of fatty bacon
1 large green bell pepper, finely chopped
$\frac{1}{2}$ cup onion, finely chopped (1 medium onion)
$\frac{1}{2}$ cup ($2\frac{1}{2}$ oz, 75 g) celery, finely chopped
1 teaspoon paprika
$\frac{1}{2}$ teaspoon thyme
2 tablespoons parsley, finely chopped
$\frac{1}{2}$ teaspoon marjoram
1 lb (500 g) honeycomb tripe, cooked and finely shredded
8 cups ($3\frac{1}{2}$ pints, 2 l) beef bouillon or chicken stock

1 bay leaf
$\frac{1}{2}$ teaspoon black peppercorns, finely pounded (this time!)
$\frac{1}{2}$ teaspoon red pepper flakes, crushed
2 teaspoons salt
1 cup raw white potatoes, peeled and cubed
2 tablespoons butter or margarine
2 tablespoons all-purpose flour
$\frac{1}{2}$ cup (4 fl oz, 120 ml) heavy (double) cream

Cut up your bacon into tiny bits and sauté them in a skillet until they are transparent but not totally crisp. Throw in your green peppers, onion, and celery, and continue to sauté for another 5 minutes or so, until all your vegetables are tender. Now stir in your paprika, thyme, parsley, and marjoram; then set your frying pan aside for the time being.

Place your shredded cooked tripe in a large pot along with the bouillon or stock, bay leaf, black and red pepper, and salt. Bring the mixture to a boil, then put in your cubed potatoes. When it boils again reduce the heat and gently simmer, uncovered, until your potatoes are nice and tender, about 15 minutes.

Melt your butter or margarine in a small pan over low heat and stir in the butter to make a roux. Tip it into the pot of tripe. Bring this back to the boil, pour in your bacon and vegetable mixture, reduce the heat again, and mix well. Adjust your seasoning at this point.

Just before you are ready to serve, warm the cream. Take the pot of soup off the heat and stir in the cream. Don't allow the soup to boil again.

VARIATION This soup is truly a main course and really needs no accompaniments. But Grandma Battle used to add these dumplings to hers, and they do make a delicious addition. Simply sift 1 cup ($4\frac{1}{2}$ oz, 130 g) all-purpose flour with

$\frac{1}{2}$ teaspoon salt and $\frac{1}{2}$ teaspoon baking powder. Cut in 2 tablespoons butter, margarine, or bacon grease, and add enough water to make a soft dough. Shape into small balls no more than 1 in (2.5 cm) across and add to the pot 15 minutes before you add the cream. Raise the heat for a few seconds to return the soup to a simmer, then lower it again.

TERRY THOMPSON'S CAJUN POPCORN

SERVES 12

I'm giving you two splendid recipes for Cajun popcorn. This one comes from Cajun-Creole cooking expert Terry Thompson. The second version comes from renowned chef Paul Prudhomme. In these two recipes the basic methods of dredging and frying are the same, and the difference comes in their choice of seasonings and herbs. If one were to try to make a clear distinction between Cajun and Creole cooking, these two recipes would do just that. One seems to me pure country Cajun, and the other is clearly city Creole.

Serve either of these hot as an appetizer or at a party.

Terry Thompson uses yellow cornmeal as a base for her batter, which is familiar to me since we use it in soul food cooking for frying fish. But let me warn you, her recipe is hot.

about 4 cups (1$\frac{3}{4}$ pints, 1 l) vegetable oil
4 large eggs beaten into 3 cups (1$\frac{1}{4}$ pints, 750 ml) milk
4 cups (14 oz, 430 g) all-purpose flour
2 cups (7 oz, 210 g) yellow cornmeal
2 cups (7 oz, 210 g) cornstarch (cornflour) (or very finely ground cornmeal)

2 tablespoons red cayenne pepper
1 tablespoon salt
1 tablespoon finely ground black pepper
3 lb (1.5 kg) peeled and cleaned crawfish tails

For this you'll need a large deep pan, such as a deep-fat fryer, with a basket. Pour in vegetable oil to a depth of 3 in (8 cm).

Now you'll also need to have three bowls: one for your beaten egg and milk mixture; one for your all-purpose flour; and the third for your cornmeal, cornstarch, and all of the seasonings, which you toss till well blended.

Start heating the oil, until just under the smoking stage – 365°F (185°C) on a cooking thermometer.

Dredge your crawfish tails in all-purpose flour and shake off any excess. Next plunge them into the egg and milk mixture and coat well. Then dredge them in the seasoned cornmeal, and shake off any excess of that.

Drop a few at a time into your fry basket and cook until brown and crisp – each batch will take 3 to 5 minutes. The thing to remember is that for the tails to be crisp they must not be touching when they fry. If they're clumped togther they'll come out soggy, so don't crowd them, give 'em plenty of room. As each batch is ready, drain on paper towels.

I think you'll find, as I have, that no sooner do you cook 'em, someone will eat 'em, which is the way it should be.

PAUL PRUDHOMME'S CAJUN POPCORN
WITH SHERRY WINE SAUCE

SERVES 12

This is a much more complex recipe as far as seasonings are concerned. The fancy sauce takes the whole thing upmarket, though I have to admit that my kids like it with ketchup too. Don't worry, the sauce is a piece of cake to make. I find it goes well with other dishes like fried chicken wings or any deep-fat fried hors d'oeuvre. It is delicate and just a touch spicy. Creole mustard is a brown mustard with some whole mustard seeds in it, full-bodied and mellow but slightly tart. Since I can't find it where I live, I use a brown French mustard in its place. Judging from my own experience, you'd better make twice as much of this recipe as you think you'll need, unless your family are pretty unenthusiastic eaters.

2 large eggs, well beaten
1¼ cups (10 fl oz, 300 ml) milk
½ cup (2½ oz, 75 g) cornstarch (cornflour)
½ cup (2½ oz, 75 g) all-purpose flour
1 teaspoon sugar
1 teaspoon salt
½ teaspoon onion powder
½ teaspoon garlic powder

½ teaspoon white pepper
⅛ teaspoon black pepper
½ teaspoon cayenne pepper
¼ teaspoon dried thyme
⅛ teaspoon dried sweet basil
2 lb (1 kg) peeled and cleaned crawfish tails, small shrimp, or crab meat
about 1½ cups (12 fl oz, 375 ml) vegetable oil

For the sauce:
1 egg yolk
¼ cup (2 fl oz, 60 ml) tomato ketchup
3 tablespoons finely chopped scallions (spring onions)
2 tablespoons dry sherry

1 teaspoon Creole (or brown) mustard
¼ teaspoon Tabasco sauce
¼ teaspoon white pepper
¼ teaspoon salt
½ cup (4 fl oz, 120 ml) vegetable oil

Whisk your eggs and milk together until well blended and frothy. Toss together your flours, sugar, salt, and all other seasonings until well distributed. Now pour half of your egg and milk mixture into the seasoned flour and whisk until well blended. Pour in the other half of your egg and milk mixture and blend it in thoroughly. Mr Prudhomme lets this mixture stand at room temperature for 1 hour to allow the flour to expand in the batter.

While this is going on, cut your fish into bite-size pieces if necessary, and make the sauce. Now this is really difficult, folks. Throw all the sauce ingredients except the oil into a blender or food processor and blend for about 30 seconds. Now, with the blender still running, pour in your oil in a slow thin stream, and when it's all in let the blender run for about another 50 seconds. If the mixture begins to rise up the side of the blender, push it back down so it all blends evenly. Boy, that was really hard, huh?

When your batter is ready, heat up 1 in (2.5 cm) of oil in a deep-fat fryer to 370°F (188°C) on a cooking thermometer; or you can use a large heavy skillet. Coat your fish well with the batter, letting any excess drop off, and fry in small batches until crisp and brown, 3 to 4 minutes. Don't crowd the pan, and do try to keep the oil at a steady temperature. Mr Prudhomme points out that you should cook the fish quickly so that it is crisp but not overdone, and that won't happen if the temperature falls below 350°F (177°C). However, since I prefer to fry it in my skillet, I just use my ears and eyes, and when I think it's done I whisk it out of the pan.

As each batch is done, drain it on paper towels and keep warm (and hidden, or it'll disappear). Serve piping hot with the sauce on the side.

JAMBALAYA

SERVES 4

This is a traditional Southern Louisiana Creole dish made up of ham, rice, and any leftover meats that may be hanging around. It's a great way to revamp leftover chicken or turkey. 'The word jambalaya,' says Chachie Dupuy, in *New Orleans Home Cooking*, 'comes from the French word *jambon* meaning ham and the African word *ya* which means rice. The *à la* means with.' When you put it all together, folks, you've got one helluva smoking dish.

2 tablespoons vegetable oil
1½ cups (12 oz, 375 g) diced cooked ham
1 cup chopped onion (1 large onion)
¾ cup (4 oz, 120 g) finely diced celery
1 green bell pepper, seeded and julienned
1 clove of garlic, minced
¾ cup (5 oz, 150 g) uncooked rice
2 cups (16 fl oz, 500 ml) tomato sauce, home-made or canned (such as sauce for pasta)

1 cup (8 oz, 250 g) chopped cooked chicken
1½ cups (12 fl oz, 375 ml) fresh chicken stock
1 bay leaf
2 tablespoons minced fresh parsley
¼ teaspoon dried thyme
¼ teaspoon Worcestershire sauce
⅛ teaspoon cayenne pepper

Heat your oil in a large skillet over medium heat and cook your ham, onion, celery, green pepper, and garlic until the onion is soft but not brown, 5 minutes or so. Stir in the remaining ingredients and bring to a boil. Lower the heat, cover, and simmer for about 30 minutes, stirring once or twice. Be sure your rice is well cooked before serving.

AUNT PEACIE'S BRAISED SHORT RIBS OF BEEF DINNER

SERVES 4

Succulent and mouth-wateringly delicious – that's about the best way to describe short ribs. They're cut from the lower end of the ribs between the rib roast and the plate (brisket), they are usually about 2 to 4 in (5–10 cm) thick and 4 in (10 cm) long with a blade-like flat piece of rib attached. You can make this dish with any good cut of braising steak, but it's much better if you have a piece with a bone. Allow at least 8 oz (250 g) of meat, weight without bone, for each person, and cut it into pieces about the same size as the real short ribs.

8 short ribs of beef
salt and pepper
$\frac{1}{2}$ teaspoon garlic powder, or to taste
about 1 cup ($4\frac{1}{2}$ oz, 130 g) all-purpose flour
$\frac{1}{4}$ cup (2 fl oz, 60 ml) vegetable oil (or other fat)

6 medium potatoes, quartered
6 medium carrots, sliced
1 medium onion, diced
1 medium green bell pepper, seeded and cubed
$\frac{1}{4}$ cup (2 fl oz, 60 ml) water

Season your short ribs with salt, pepper, and garlic powder to taste. Dredge them in flour until they are well coated. Preheat your oven to 350°F (180°C, gas 4).

Heat your oil in a skillet and when it's hot, just under smoking, brown the ribs on both sides. Place them in a casserole or pot large enough to take them in one layer with room to spare. Put your potatoes, carrots, onion, and green pepper around the meat, then sprinkle it with a little salt and pepper. Pour in the water, cover, and cook in the oven for 1 hour and 20 minutes or until your ribs are tender and falling off the bone.

Serve immediately to a family who by now are simply ravenous from having this delicious smell wafting through the house for so long.

POT ROAST DINNER
SERVES 8

American pot roast recipes are all much the same, though some people prefer cooking in the oven and others the top of the stove. In America this is seen as quite an ordinary meal. Now that I live in England, where beef is more expensive, I think of it as more of a delicacy, and I pick a good cut for it.

Remember that the secret of a juicy, melt-in-your-mouth pot roast is slow, slow, slow cooking. We're talking 3 to 4 hours cooking time to tenderize the meat and give a really good stock for your gravy. So no short cuts, please!

$\frac{1}{3}$ cup ($2\frac{1}{2}$ fl oz/oz, 75 ml/g) vegetable oil or fat (you can cut a chunk of fat from the meat)
5 pounds (2.5 kg) good beef (rump, round, or chuck)
1 clove of garlic, split
2 tablespoons all-purpose flour
salt and black pepper

1 large onion, sliced
1 cup (8 fl oz, 250 ml) hot water
1–4 tablespoons diced celery (optional)
10 medium carrots, washed, trimmed, and halved lengthwise
10 medium potatoes, washed and halved
14 white pearl onions

Heat the oil or fat in a large pot or Dutch oven over medium heat. Rub the meat all over with garlic. Blend the flour, salt, and pepper together and rub the mixture well into the meat.

When the oil is hot, throw in the onion and cook, stirring occasionally, until lightly browned, about 5 minutes. This gives the fat a nice oniony flavor. Add the meat and brown it evenly on all sides, keeping the onion to the sides of the pot so it doesn't burn. Use two forks to turn the meat.

Remove the browned roast and place a trivet in the bottom of the Dutch oven so that the meat is not sitting directly on the heat. (If you don't have a trivet, you'll need to turn the meat a few times so that it cooks evenly.) Return the meat to the pot and pour in the hot water (and celery if you like). Cover with a tight-fitting lid and cook, over very low heat, until tender. *Never* allow the liquid to boil. You may need to add a little more water after a while. I cook pot roast for 45 minutes to 1 hour to the pound, which makes a cooking time of 3 to 4 hours.

One hour before EDT – estimated dining time – lay in your carrots, potatoes, and pearl onions, and leave them to cook gently.

When your pot roast is done, transfer the meat to a large hot serving platter and carefully arrange the vegetables around it. Keep it warm while you make a rich, delectable gravy.

Skim any excess fat or scum from the top of the pan juices. For each cup of pan juice measure out 1 level tablespoon flour and 3 tablespoons cold water. Put that flour and water combo in a small lidded jar or receptacle of some kind and shake until all of the lumps are gone and the flour and water are well blended.

With the pan juices simmering, slowly add the flour and water mixture, stirring constantly, until the gravy is thick, rich, and delightfully smooth, about 3 minutes. Allow the gravy to bubble just under the boil for 1 or 2 minutes while you adjust your seasoning to suit your taste. (This is my favorite part of gravy making – the tasting and adding of the seasoning.) Pour the gravy into a gravy boat and serve with the pot roast and vegetables. Get ready to enjoy a truly great meal.

NOTE My Aunt Peacie does her pot roasts differently. She loves green bell peppers and tomatoes, and the vegetables she uses for a roast this size are half a dozen potatoes, a couple of medium onions, a medium green pepper seeded and chopped, and a small (8 oz, 227 g) can of plum tomatoes. She sprinkles the meat with salt, pepper, and garlic powder, then rolls it in flour before browning it. And after she's browned it she cooks the roast in the oven at 300°F (150°C, gas 2) for as long as needed, which is at least 2 hours and maybe 3. Then she spoons her juices right over the meat, which gives more of an *au jus* effect.

AUNT ODESSA'S MACARONI AND TUNA BAKE CASSEROLE

SERVES 4

When I think of Aunt Odessa's cooking, the first dish that comes to mind is her macaroni and tuna casserole. Whenever Gerald and Oliver, her sons, and I would come home from school to find that tuna casserole waiting for us, we would do just about anything to get out of supper. Don't get me wrong, it was delicious,

Three generations on a horse and buggy! Grandma Battle (my maternal grandmother), her daughter Aunt Odessa, and her grandson (and Odessa's son) Oliver, on the boardwalk in Atlantic City, New Jersey. Aunt Odessa now travels around the United States representing the Governor of Pennsylvania and lecturing on the importance of unions in America.

but we had it at least once a week and it was a reminder that times were hard. I still cannot face it often, but my kids really love it.

1 cup (6 oz, 175 g) uncooked short macaroni
1 cup hot thin White Sauce (see below)
1 cup shredded sharp cheddar cheese
1 small (6½/7 oz, 185/198 g) can tuna
¼ cup chopped onion (½ medium onion)

¼ cup seeded and chopped green bell pepper (½ small pepper)
¼ teaspoon garlic powder
1 cup (8 oz, 250 g) butter
1 cup (4 oz, 120 g) fried croûtons

Boil your macaroni in plenty of salted water over high heat. It will take 10 to 15 minutes. When it's just tender but not limp, tip it into a colander and rinse under cold running water. Drain well and pour into a 2 quart (3½ pint, 2 l) casserole greased with a little of the butter.

While the macaroni is cooking, make your Thin White Sauce. Stir in your cheddar cheese, remove from the heat, and leave the cheese to melt. Preheat your oven to 375°F (190°C, gas 5). Drain your tuna and break it up into shreds with two forks, then stir in your onion and green pepper.

Put your tuna mixture into your casserole along with the cheese sauce and mix well. If it seems too dry, add a smidgen of milk or water. Bake in the oven for 30 minutes.

During this time melt the rest of the butter, blend in your garlic powder, and stir in the croûtons.

When the 30 minutes of cooking time is up, stir your casserole around, then sprinkle the buttered croûtons on top and bake uncovered for another 10 minutes.

WHITE SAUCE

One of the most basic requirements for any good cook is a white sauce. I make three kinds for various purposes, and here's how.

Thin	Medium	Thick	
1 tablespoon	2 tablespoons	3 tablespoons	butter or margarine
1 tablespoon	2 tablespoons	3 tablespoons	flour
$\frac{1}{2}$ teaspoon	$\frac{1}{2}$ teaspoon	$\frac{1}{2}$ teaspoon	salt
dash	dash	dash	white or black pepper
1 cup (8 fl oz, 250 ml)	1 cup (8 fl oz, 250 ml)	1 cup (8 fl oz, 250 ml)	milk

Melt your butter or margarine in a saucepan over low heat, then remove it from the heat. Slowly add in the flour and stir until smooth, then add the salt and pepper. Keep stirring while you slowly trickle in the milk. Return the pan to the stove, stirring constantly, turn the heat up to medium, and bring the mixture to a boil. Turn the heat down, and let it boil gently for 1 minute, still stirring.

Please do as this recipe suggests, for I have burnt white sauce, boiled it over onto my stove, and done everything imaginable to mess up this very simple recipe. *You must keep stirring!*

MONSTROUS BAKED MACARONI AND CHEESE

Aunt Peacie makes about the best macaroni and cheese that I have ever tasted. But no matter how hard I tried — and believe me, I tried — I just couldn't seem to duplicate her subtle, creamy blend of flavors and velvety-smooth texture. Mine was not bad, but not nearly good enough. I became obsessed. So on my last trip to the United States, I dropped my bags and I dropped straight in on dear Aunt Peacie. I had already decided upon my strategy.

First I told her my own recipe. She turned her spectacles up to me and kinda frowned, pinching up her nose. 'What in the world kinda stuff d'you call that?' she sniffed. So she wrote her recipe on the back of an old calendar. 'Eggs. Extra sharp cheese. Creamettes. Evaporated milk. Butter. Salt.' That was it. You see,

Aunt Peacie assumes that everyone can deal with incidentals like quantities for themselves.

Eventually I found out just how much, for how long, and so on. It was not hard to see my mistake. By trying to make my macaroni more daring, more adventurous, hotter, and spicier, I had been moving further and further away from the simplicity of soul food cooking. I never did find out how many the recipe would serve. When I asked, Aunt Peacie said, 'Just as many as it has to feed, honey.'

2 large eggs, well beaten

2 tablespoons salt

2 cups (12 oz, 375 g) uncooked elbow or short macaroni

$\frac{1}{4}$ cup (2 oz, 60 g) butter, softened

2–2$\frac{1}{3}$ cups evaporated milk (16–20 fl oz, 500–600 ml)

1$\frac{1}{2}$ lb (750 g) extra sharp cheddar cheese, grated

paprika

cayenne pepper (completely optional)

Bring plenty of water to a boil in a large saucepan over high heat while you beat the eggs. Add the salt, then add your macaroni slowly so that the water never stops boiling. Boil for 12 minutes, stirring constantly. *Do not overcook, and do not stop stirring*, as it helps to keep the water from boiling over. Meanwhile, preheat your oven to 350°F (180°C, gas 4).

After 12 minutes remove your macaroni from the heat and drain. Pour a little cold water over the drained macaroni in the pot, swish it around, and quickly pour it off. Quickly stir in the butter. Pour the beaten eggs into the evaporated milk. (I use 1 large and 1 small can [14.5 and 6 fl oz, 410 and 170 ml]. That makes it the way Aunt Peacie likes it — really moist, not gummy and dry.)

Put a layer of macaroni into a buttered 2 quart (1$\frac{3}{4}$ UK quart, 2 l) casserole, then a layer of grated cheese, a layer of macaroni, another of cheese until you use them up, ending with a layer of cheese on top. Pour the milk and egg mixture over all, forking it through evenly, and top with a healthy sprinkling of paprika. Bake, uncovered, in the oven for 45 minutes or until brown and bubbilicious.

There you have it, the most soulful macaroni and cheese that I have ever tasted. Oh go on then, if you want, add just a pinch of cayenne pepper, but you really don't need it.

SOULFUL SALADS

*B*oy, does it get hot and sticky in Philadelphia in the summer. I remember it when I was a child. It was then that the block parties would start, and the kids would cool off with the fire hydrants. That was one of our favorite summer pastimes. We would knock the rim off the hydrant and take turns running through the gushing water and wallowing around in the deep puddles until the cops came. The real fun was waiting for them to leave and then trying it again. Well don't knock it. That was the closest some of us ever came to a swimming pool!

And on those hot dog days of summer the last place anybody wants to be is in a kitchen slaving over an even hotter stove. This is the time for water ices bought from the vending cart – those wonderful paper cones filled with crushed or chipped ice flavored with a fruit syrup poured over the top. And for salads.

But, my friends, there are salads and there are salads. The first time I ordered one in England I thought the waiter could not be serious. There were a few limp leaves of lettuce, two hard-boiled eggs, and a watery hothouse tomato with a stream of yellow salad cream poured across them. I called the waiter over and explained my predicament. He said, 'You ordered egg salad, madam, you got egg salad.'

Well here I am as proud as Lucifer to present true American specialty salads. A wonderful variety of chopped meats, fish, egg, and pastas blended together with crunchy fresh vegetables like celery and onion, seasoned to a fever pitch and then bound together with a good mayonnaise or salad dressing. In the immortal words of Chico Marx, *now dat's a lotta salad*. They're all practical as well as tasty because they're good travelers, almost serve themselves, can be eaten in sandwiches, and are even better after the've been allowed to chill for a while – which means you can easily make up one of them the night before, thus giving you the time you need to devote to other things.

To my American tastebuds, mayonnaise is a bit too bland for some of these salads, maybe because I grew up with the spicy taste of Miracle Whip, a Stateside product which for me strikes just the perfect balance. I realize this is a controversial view, but each to his or her own taste, go. So I like to make my own mayonnaise, spicing it up with extra vinegar or lemon juice, seasonings, and maybe a little garlic; or, if I'm feeling laid back, mix good bought mayonnaise with salad cream, usually in half-half quantities, and that gets me pretty darn close to the real deal.

COLESLAW

SERVES 8

Making good coleslaw is not an exact science, so if you can bear with me, I'd like to explain how to make it the soul food way, by sight and sound and taste.

Let's start with your dressing. This is enough for half a large white cabbage. Plop 4 tablespoons of mayonnaise into a glass or china bowl. I mean really heaping. Grate an onion over it or maybe $\frac{1}{2}$ teaspoon onion juice. I don't like to crunch down on whole onion chunks in my coleslaw, that's why I prefer to use the juice, but take care because onion juice is stronger than you think and the flavor develops with time. Then add in $\frac{1}{2}$ teaspoon or so of dry mild mustard and up to three heaping tablespoons of sugar. I like a sweet salad but you might want to add the sugar a bit at a time. Next, a splash or two of vinegar. Mix your dressing well, stirring until all the sugar has dissolved, then taste. It should be more sweet than vinegary, with only the slightest hint of onion. Cover and refrigerate for at least 1 hour. Taste and adjust, as the onion will have come out powerfully. You may want to add in a touch more sugar, vinegar, mayonnaise, lemon, mustard, onion juice, or whatever to suit your own taste. But do it in small stages because every little change is a major event in this dressing. Cover and refrigerate until ready to use.

Take half of a nice firm, large head of white cabbage and, after removing the outer leaves and cleaning, cut it through from top to bottom. Remove the main stem from each piece. You can use this if you like, but it has to be cut up separately. (Personally, I eat 'em myself – cook's prerogative.) Place each quarter cut side down on a cutting board and with a long sharp knife cut each quarter into very fine shreds. The finer the better, but it will depend on just how patient you are. If you are including the stem, slice this finely first lengthwise, then across into shreds.

Next, take 1 or 2 carrots, depending on their size of course, and grate them into your cabbage. I usually judge it by color. If you like the taste of green bell pepper, as I do, dice no more than one half of a small pepper very finely and add to the slaw. Then, if you want, add 1 or more stalks of very finely diced celery. When you toss the slaw, it should be colorful with finely cut ingredients. When you are satisfied that it's right, you can pour on your dressing.

Mix well by folding in the dressing little by little. The slaw should look glossy, not too white. Cover with clear plastic wrap and refrigerate for at least 2 hours. Overnight is OK too, if you like the cabbage to marinate and soften a little. Afterwards you can add more dressing if you like. Don't judge the dressing until your coleslaw has been refrigerated or you might make it too soupy. Just before serving I usually garnish with the other half of that green pepper cut into rings, or with slices of beefsteak tomato each topped with a stuffed olive.

Coleslaw is a classic side dish with fried chicken, cornbread, and collard greens, but I like to keep a supply in the fridge because it goes well with so many things – the likes of soul fried fish, barbecued spare ribs, braised short ribs of beef, corn on the cob. Use it any time you want to picnic or just eat a big bowl of it on its own.

Chicken Salad

SERVES 6–8

2 cups (1 lb, 500 g) diced cooked chicken
2 cups (10 oz, 300 g) finely diced celery
2 tablespoons sweet (cucumber) relish
2 coarsely chopped hard-boiled eggs
   (optional)

1 teaspoon finely diced onion (optional)
2 tablespoons mayonnaise
2 tablespoons salad cream (or use all
   mayonnaise)
lettuce, to serve

Mix together the chicken, celery, relish, and chopped egg and onion if you choose. Lightly stir in the mayonnaise, and salad cream if used. Add more of these if you want, but only enough to make a smooth salad.

To serve, spoon onto a bed of lettuce or eat between two slices of toast.

VARIATIONS Here are some delicious ideas.

Walnut and Apple Add $\frac{1}{4}$ cup (1 oz, 30 g) chopped walnuts and $\frac{1}{2}$ cup peeled, cored, and cubed apple ($\frac{1}{2}$ medium apple).

Almond Sprinkle $\frac{1}{2}$ cup (2 oz, 60 g) chopped toasted almonds over the top.

Cucumber and Raisin Substitute 2 tablespoons of finely chopped cucumber for the celery and add 2 tablespoons seedless raisins.

Lemon Flavor the mayonnaise with 1 teaspoon fresh lemon juice, or to taste.

Curry Add $\frac{1}{2}$ teaspoon curry powder, or more if you like, to the mayonnaise.

Hot Seafood Salad

SERVES 6–8

Kids love the addition of potato chips (crisps) to this dish, and that alone seems to make it worth eating as far as they're concerned. If you're dubious about using them, substitute breadcrumbs – but even the gourmets I know don't think they're half as good.

1 cup (7 oz, 200 g) flaked crab meat
1 cup (7 oz, 200 g) peeled, cleaned, and
   deveined shrimp
1 cup (8 fl oz, 250 ml) store-bought
   mayonnaise
$\frac{1}{4}$ cup (2 fl oz, 60 ml) light (single) cream
$\frac{1}{3}$ cup (2 oz, 60 g) finely minced green
   bell pepper

3 tablespoons finely minced onion
1 cup (5 oz, 150 g) finely chopped celery
1 tablespoon finely chopped fresh parsley
$\frac{1}{2}$ teaspoon salt, or to taste
$\frac{1}{8}$ teaspoon black pepper
dash of cayenne pepper or Tabasco sauce
$\frac{1}{2}$ teaspoon Worcestershire sauce
$\frac{3}{4}$ cup (5 oz, 150 g) potato chips (crisps)

Preheat your oven to 350°F (180°C, gas 4).

Combine all the ingredients except the potato chips. Taste and adjust your seasonings. Fill 8 well buttered ramekins or scallop shells, or a $1\frac{1}{2}$ quart ($1\frac{1}{4}$ UK quart, 1.25 l) casserole with the seafood mixture. Sprinkle crushed potato chips on top and bake in the oven until lightly browned and bubbling, 15 to 20 minutes for ramekins or 25 to 30 minutes for a casserole. Serve at once.

BLACK OLIVE AND MUSHROOM SALAD

SERVES 8

1 firm head of lettuce (preferably iceberg)
2 large cucumbers
2 large beefsteak tomatoes
8 oz (250 g) fresh mushrooms, sliced

1 lb (500 g) black olives
salad dressing of your choice
chopped fresh oregano (optional)

Wash and dry your lettuce, and break it into bite-size pieces. Throw them into a salad bowl. Peel and slice the cucumbers. Cut the tomatoes into wedges. Add the cucumbers, tomatoes, mushrooms, and olives to the lettuce. Pour on your favorite dressing and toss to mix. Serve at once. If you like, sprinkle on a little fresh oregano just before serving.

TUNA FISH SALAD

SERVES 4–6

1 small ($6\frac{1}{2}$/7 oz, 185/198 g) can tuna
$\frac{1}{2}$ cup ($2\frac{1}{2}$ oz, 75 g) finely chopped celery
$\frac{1}{3}$ cup chopped onion (1 smallish onion)
$\frac{1}{3}$ cup ($2\frac{1}{2}$ oz, 75 g) sweet (cucumber) relish
4 tablespoons mayonnaise
1 tablespoon salad cream (or use all mayonnaise)

1 coarsely chopped hard-boiled egg (optional)
salt and pepper
dash of celery salt or celery seed (optional)
dash of fresh lemon juice (optional)
lettuce, etc., to serve (see below)

Drain your tuna well. Put it in a small bowl and break it apart with a fork. Blend in the celery, onion, and relish. Spoon in the mayonnaise and salad cream, and mix again. The consistency should now be about right, not liquid and not too stiff. Add in your chopped egg at this point if you choose to use it. (I have one twin who refuses to eat eggs, so I like to slide them by her in disguises like this. Most times she doesn't notice.) Season with salt, pepper, and perhaps a little celery salt or celery seed or both, it's up to you! You can add a splash of lemon juice if you're of a mind to do so. Refrigerate, covered, until ready to serve.

Tuna fish salad tastes great served on a bed of crisp lettuce, on crackers, or in a sandwich with lettuce and sliced tomatoes. My grandmother, Martha Battle, sometimes used a cubed tart apple instead of the sweet relish. She was also known to throw in a few raisins, and so do I. My kids love it that way too.

MACARONI SALAD
SERVES 6

This amazing salad is usually found in most soul food restaurants to accompany barbecued ribs or chicken. The best one I have ever experienced was at a place called Piggy's in North Philadelphia, and this is the closest you could get to it. The only thing you *must* do is to refrigerate overnight; otherwise the flavor of the salad doesn't have time to develop and it won't taste right.

4 cups (1 lb, 500 g) cooked macaroni
1 cup (5 oz, 150 g) finely chopped celery
½ cup finely minced onion (1 medium onion)
¼ cup (1 oz, 30 g) finely chopped fresh parsley
¼ cup seeded and coarsely chopped green bell pepper (½ small pepper)

¼ cup canned pimiento or finely chopped sweet red pepper (½ small pepper)
1 teaspoon salt, or to taste
½ teaspoon celery salt, or to taste
½ teaspoon ground black pepper
1 cup (8 fl oz, 250 ml) mayonnaise
¼ cup (2 fl oz, 60 ml) vinegar

Make sure your macaroni is well drained and place it in a bowl along with the celery, onion, parsley, green and red pepper, salts, and black pepper. Mix the mayonnaise and vinegar and blend until smooth. Pour on your dressing and mix well. Cover and refrigerate overnight. The longer this salad chills the more the flavor develops.

Then, and not before, taste it and adjust your seasonings.

POTATO SALAD
SERVES 6

To me, potato salad is the backbone of any picnic or barbecue. You just do not barbecue without having some potato salad on the scene. It takes to fried chicken, spare ribs, corn on the cob, devilled eggs and collard greens like a fish to water. I have made enough potato salad at one time to feed about fifty people and that's the kind of big bowlful I like to see. But don't panic, I've scaled my recipe down to feed about six.

2 lb (500 g) firm potatoes
½ cup (2¼ oz, 75 g) chopped celery
¼ cup finely chopped onion (½ medium onion)
2 tablespoons seeded and finely diced green bell pepper
1 teaspoon salt
⅛ teaspoon black or white pepper
½ teaspoon dry mustard
1 teaspoon celery salt
1 tablespoon sugar
1 tablespoon vinegar

1 hard-boiled egg
½ cup (4 fl oz, 120 g) mayonnaise
⅓ cup (2½ fl oz, 75 ml) salad cream (or use all mayonnaise with extra vinegar and seasonings)
2 tablespoons celery seed
7–8 small sweet pickles (pickled gherkins), or 4 heaping tablespoons sweet (cucumber) relish (see below)
paprika
garnishes (optional, see below)

The author, all dressed up as a drum majorette, sitting on the top of Dad's new green Chevrolet, looking forward to later on that day when the decorations, card tables, and food would come out and the block party would get rolling.

I usually boil my potatoes the night before. Wash them and put into a pot of boiling salted water to cover. Cover tightly and cook for about 20 minutes or until tender. Test them with a fork or knife. They should be soft enough to cube easily but not mushy and falling apart. Drain in a colander and refrigerate until they are cold enough to work with.

Peel the potatoes and cut into coarse chunks or cubes. Throw in your celery, onion, and green pepper, but do not stir yet. Add salt, pepper, dry mustard, celery salt, sugar, and vinegar, still not stirring.

Now take the yolk from the hard boiled egg and mash it up with a fork. Add a bit of mayonnaise to it to make a lumpy paste. Mix this with the rest of your mayonnaise and salad cream, then pour it on the potatoes. Sprinkle 1 tablespoon of the celery seed on top of this mountain. Using a wooden spoon, toss until well blended. Taste and adjust your seasonings.

Coarsely chop the sweet pickles. (These must be sweet. I use Heinz, and find others too bitter. If you can't find suitable ones, use relish.) Coarsely chop the egg white, and add both of these and the rest of the celery seed to the salad. Again taste and adjust – you may need a touch more salad cream, seasonings or whatever. When blending, try not to pulverize the potatoes, or the salad will be mushy.

Now turn your potato salad into a serving bowl. Liberally sprinkle paprika over the top until it's quite red. Cover with clear plastic wrap and refrigerate for at least 2 hours or until ready to serve.

Just before serving, if you like you can garnish the salad with green or red pepper rings, slices of tomato with a stuffed olive in the center, or sliced hard-boiled eggs with a dab of caviar on each.

The best part about making potato salad is the tasting. Sometimes I taste so much that by the time I'm finished I'm no longer hungry. And don't worry if it turns out too mushy. I've discovered that as long as it tastes great no one will even notice.

*H*OT POTATO SALAD WITH
BACON DRESSING

SERVES 8

3 lb (1.5 kg) firm potatoes
6 slices fatty bacon
$\frac{1}{4}$ cup finely chopped onion ($\frac{1}{2}$ medium onion)
2 tablespoons all-purpose flour
6 tablespoons cider vinegar
$1\frac{1}{2}$ cups (12 fl oz, 375 g) hot water

2 teaspoons salt
$\frac{1}{2}$ teaspoon dry mustard
3 tablespoons sugar
1 teaspoon celery seed
$\frac{1}{2}$ teaspoon freshly ground black pepper
about 1 teaspoon paprika
$\frac{1}{4}$ cup (1 oz, 30 g) chopped fresh parsley

Peel and cube your potatoes. Boil 1 inch (2.5 cm) depth of salted water in a saucepan over high heat. Add the cubed potatoes, cover tightly, and cook until just tender, which may take from 15 minutes to over 30 for hard new potatoes. Don't let them overcook.

Meanwhile fry your bacon over medium heat until nice and crisp, about 10 minutes, then drain on paper towels and set aside. Throw the onion into the bacon fat and cook for 5 minutes or until soft. Now stir in the flour and blend well. Remove the skillet from heat and stir in your vinegar and hot water. Then put the pan back on the heat and bring to a boil, stirring constantly. Lower the heat and allow to simmer until it thickens up, about 3 minutes. Stir in the salt, dry mustard, sugar, celery seed, and black pepper, and continue cooking for another 4 or 5 minutes while all of the seasonings become settled.

When your potatoes are ready drain them, return them to the pot, and crumble the bacon slices into them. Carefully toss the potatoes and bacon in the hot dressing. The salad should be quite warm; if not, return to the stove to heat through. Pour it onto a large serving platter and garnish with paprika and chopped parsley.

DEVILLED EGGS

SERVES 6

The secret to these eggs is in the seasoning of the yolks. Make sure you choose a sweet relish without too harsh a flavor or it will ruin your eggs. Once you get the balance right you've got it made. This is one of my British friends' favorite dishes, so I usually find myself making up a batch of double or triple quantities.

6 hard-boiled eggs
2 teaspoons finely minced onion
2 teaspoons finely chopped celery
$\frac{1}{4}$ teaspoon dry mustard
2 teaspoons sweet (cucumber) relish or finely chopped sweet pickles (pickled cucumbers)

$\frac{1}{4}$ teaspoon salt
2 or more tablespoons mayonnaise
paprika
2 tablespoons sliced olives, or chopped sweet pickles, or sweet red bell pepper (optional)

Cut your hard-boiled eggs in half lengthwise while they're still hot. Put the yolks in a small bowl and quickly mash with a fork. Add your onion, celery, dry mustard, relish, salt, and enough mayonnaise to make a soft paste (don't make it too watery). Now taste and adjust your seasonings.

Rinse your egg whites if necessary, then refill each one with egg yolk mixture. Arrange on a serving plate and sprinkle lavishly with paprika. Cover with clear plastic wrap and refrigerate for at least 1 hour. This will set your egg mixture. Before serving, you may garnish with slivers of olives, pickle, or sweet red pepper.

GINGER ALE SALAD

SERVES 8

This is such an unusual salad that I thought you might like to try it on for size. It comes from a delightful cookbook entitled *Spoonbread and Strawberry Wine*, written by Norma Jean and Carole Darden, two sisters who sure know how to burn a mean pot and turn a neat phrase. In reading their book, I felt as though I could reach out and touch their family and friends. This recipe is the invention of their mother, Mamie Jean Darden Sampson, and to my mind typifies the imaginative ingenuity of the black soul food cook.

Feel free to alter the combination of fruits, but be sure that they go well together in color, shape, texture, and ripeness. Both overripe and underripe fruits make dreadful molds. Coordinate them properly and you've got a colorful, tasty, and truly spectacular salad that can be prepared in advance.

Don't use fresh pineapple, papaya, or figs: they all contain enzymes which prevent gelatin from setting. Canned fruit, and fruit which has been heated briefly to boiling point, don't have this effect.

There are also a few practicalities to consider about turning out the salad. Ever had a mold slide out so fast that it falls on the floor? Or had one break and collapse on the plate? No? Well, you haven't lived yet. To avoid a struggle I lightly coat the inside of the mold with oil, or dip it into cold water before filling. Before turning out, check that the salad is properly set and holds together well.

⅓ cup (2 oz, 60 g) peeled and sliced fresh peach

⅓ cup (2 oz, 60 g) pitted fresh cherries

⅓ cup (2 oz, 60 g) peeled and sliced fresh pear

½ cup (3 oz, 90 g) drained, crushed *canned* unsweetened pineapple (reserve the juice)

½ cup (3 oz, 90 g) seedless grapes

2 tablespoons seedless raisins

2 tablespoons unflavored gelatin

2 tablespoons fresh lemon juice

2 cups (16 fl oz, 500 ml) dry ginger ale

¼ teaspoon powdered ginger

½ cup (4 fl oz, 120 ml) mayonnaise

⅛ teaspoon (large pinch) salt

sprinkling of paprika

2 tablespoons slivered almonds

lettuce, watercress or parsley, and a small bunch of grapes, to serve

Prepare and slice your fresh fruits over a strainer placed across a mixing bowl to catch the delicious juices needed for the salad. Put the prepared fruits into a bowl and add the pineapple, grapes, and raisins.

Add some juice from the canned pineapple to the fresh fruit juice to make ¾ cup (6 fl oz, 175 ml) liquid. Pour this into a small saucepan and stir in the gelatin. Let it stand for a couple of minutes, then set it over a low heat and simmer, stirring slowly, until the gelatin has completely dissolved. Remove from the heat and blend in the lemon juice, ginger ale, ginger, mayonnaise, salt, and paprika. Refrigerate until the gelatin thickens to the consistency of a lightly beaten egg white, 30 minutes or longer.

When the gelatin has thickened, remove it from the refrigerator and fold in your fruits and nuts. Pour your salad into a decorative ring mold, or several smaller ones. Chill until firmly set, which may take 4 hours.

Unmold and serve on a bed of lettuce garnished with grapes and watercress or parsley.

GOD'S GREEN ACRES

When the African slaves first came to America, they carried with them seeds of many plants which had been abundant in their homelands. One of them, the collard green, a kind of kale with greyish leaves, flourished throughout the South. This staple of soul food is cooked in the same way as spinach, or ordinary kale or cabbage; and the nutritious juice that results, called pot likka, is eaten as well as the leaves.

Greens were vital to the health of the slaves and were adopted throughout the South by the poor whites when they realized their nutritional value. Today the collard green is undoubtedly the most favored soul food vegetable.

Slaves also introduced okra, black-eyed peas, sesame, and yams – that is, yams from Africa, not the native sweet potato – to American tables. John Taylor, the foremost expert on Low Country cooking, has pointed out that recipes for eggplant (aubergine), under the name Guinea squash, appeared in old Charleston recipe books long before this Asian vegetable was supposed to have arrived with the Spanish. All of these plants took readily to the climate and soil of the Southern states and became soul food favorites.

The slaves learned to cook the whites' own vegetables which had been brought over from the Old World, including turnip greens and mustard greens. They also took to native vegetables favored by the Amerian Indians: creasy greens and the young shoots of poke sallet (which starred in the old folk song 'Poke Sallet Annie') are among soul food favorites. All of these greens are cooked in the same way as collards. The secret is timing. When you cook mixed greens, cook each separately before combining them.

It had also been the American Indians who had taught the first settlers to plant and harvest corn (maize), how to roast it, and how to grind it into meal. This became a year-round staple of most black kitchens, and so did many dishes borrowed from the Indians, such as pones and succotash.

When purchasing greens of any kind be sure you buy only fresh, unblemished, brightly colored ones: 1 lb (500 g) will serve two people generously. Start preparing them by looking them over and discarding any bruised or discolored leaves. The stems cook up tough, so get rid of those really heavy ones. Wash your greens in a sink, in several waters. The first two rinses should be slightly warm to remove the sand and grit effectively. The last waters should be cold. Always lift the greens *from* the water, never just let the water drain off. This way the sand and grit will settle to the bottom of the sink and will drain away rather than remaining on the leaves.

SEASONING VEGETABLES

Traditionally the soul food cook seasons most vegetables, especially our wonderful leafy varieties, with bacon grease or pork fat drippings, which adds an unmistakable smokey flavor. Today, this is often the only pork that soul folks will allow themselves since everyone is concerned, and quite rightly so, with their salt and fat intake.

The problem for us comes in the fact that we absolutely refuse to sacrifice or compromise our flavorings and the taste of our foods. But luckily there's a new

My sister Peaches, Cousin Gerald and I in front of Aunt Gussie's vegetable garden in Jamaica, Long Island, New York. Aunt Gussie brought her collard green seeds up from the South with her and we used them well, yes suh! She taught me to tell when a collard green was ready to be pulled up from the garden before the frost set in and it became too bitter.

idea and it's some kinda good, and healthy as well. Traditional cooks are now seasoning vegetables with smoked turkey butts instead of pork fat. These are less fattening and lower in cholesterol, and give as good a taste as you're likely to find. (In case you're not familiar with the term, a turkey butt is just what you'd expect, it's the bird's butt – or more commonly the parson's nose. Smoked turkey is now quite easy to find at delicatessens, especially Jewish ones, and if you can't find butts just get a small piece of any kind.)

This is how Aunt Peacie uses them. You will need 1 butt (or another piece weighing about 3 oz [90 g]) for every $1\frac{1}{2}$ lb (750 g) of vegetables. Let them simmer slowly in a large pot with a lid, in water to cover, for 4 or 5 hours or until they start to fall apart and the water has cooked down to a nice juice. The turkey butts will break up when you add the vegetables, so you can take them out or leave them in – it's totally up to you. Then put in your vegetables and cook them over a very low heat till tender, about 1 hour.

You can save time by cooking your turkey butts in advance and freezing them with the juice till needed.

Other seasonings include ham hocks and cubed ham (to which you can add a tablespoon of bacon grease). Recipes later in this chapter show you how these are used.

COLLARD GREENS

SERVES 8

Collard greens are my absolute favorite and accompany any soul food meal beautifully. I find spring greens a bit timid in flavor by comparison. I cook all greens in the same way as I do collards, adjusting the cooking time as necessary. I season them and douse them with vinegar and they are all nearly as delicious and delectable.

1 ham hock
$\frac{1}{2}$ teaspoon crushed red pepper flakes
4 lb (2 kg) collard greens
$\frac{1}{4}$ cup (2 fl oz, 60 ml) cider vinegar

1 tablespoon chopped onion
about 1 teaspoon sugar
salt and black or cayenne pepper

Scrub and clean your ham hock with a vegetable brush under cold running water. Place it in a pot with cold water to cover. Add the red pepper flakes, put on the lid, bring to a boil, reduce the heat, and simmer until tender, 45 minutes to 1 hour. Add more water if necessary.

During this time you can be washing your greens as instructed on page 140. Collards have such large leaves that they need to be prepared in one of several ways. One is to fold a bunch in half, then fold again and cut; then again, until you have pieces of a palatable size. Another way is to slide a knife down the main stem to remove the leaves and then tear them up Or cook them whole and chop them up in the pot when they're done.

When the hock is done, add the greens and remaining ingredients to the pot. Lower the heat and simmer until tender, which usually takes 45 minutes to 1 hour. Stir occasionally during this time.

Season to taste and serve with extra vinegar and hot sauce on the side, and a little chopped raw onion if you like.

POT LIKKA That's how you pronounce pot liquor in proper Southern style. It's the liquid that remains after you've cooked up a mess of collards, mustard greens, turnip greens, or whatever greens. It's packed full of the vitamins and minerals that have cooked out of the greens. It's not just nutritious but decidedly delicious, so whatever you do, don't waste it. We just dunk our cornbread right into it or break up bits of cornbread into a bowl and sop up all of that rich goodness by swirling the cornbread around the plate. It can also be used as a vegetable stock for soups.

*W*ILD GREENS

Wild greens are a true delicacy to greens lovers, who gather them from the wild or sometimes grow them specially.

POKE SALLET This plant, otherwise known as pokeweed, grows in open fields, along fences, and especially in areas where food scraps may have been deposited. The plant can get to a height of several feet and has a distinct odor which makes it easy to find. The thin tender leaves are picked during the spring before the plant matures. A mature plant has red berries and will cause illness if eaten. Poke sallet tastes best when mixed with other types of greens, says my Aunt Ella, and believe you me, she should know, 'cause Aunt Ella loves her greens.

Leaves should be checked for insects, then put in a container or sink of warm water to which salt has been added (about 1 teaspoon to each gallon [5 l] of water used). This will cause any foreign matter to float to the surface. Wash carefully, then rinse until the water is clear. Cook the leaves in boiling water until tender, 10 to 15 minutes. Drain, then season with salt, pepper, and hot bacon grease.

CREASY GREENS This plant, sometimes called wild watercress, grows in clumps along creek beds with sandy shoulders (and is now being grown commercially in the United States). Creasy greens, like poke sallet and other wild varieties, may be eaten on their own but are at their best in combination with other greens (such as mustard, kale, or turnip greens). To gather, cut from the base of the growth, keeping the long thin stems intact. To clean, gently separate clumps of the stems, cut through the base root leaving the leaves attached, and wash in as many changes of tepid water as needed, until no sand or grit can be seen or felt in the bottom of the bowl or sink. Break, rather than cut, individual stems from their base, and discard the root piece.

Cook the stems gently in a small amount of water with the seasoning of your choice: fatback, ham drippings, smoky bacon fat, or hocks. They will take 10 to 15 minutes. Add salt and pepper to taste, and greeze.

SAUTÉED OKRA

SERVES 4

Okra, nicknamed lady's fingers because of its delicate shape, has been a Southern favorite since the first black slaves brought it from Africa. It has a gluey (some people even say slimy) sap when cut which is a natural thickener for any stew, soup, or gumbo. But don't feel that you have to use it in special recipes. It is also good boiled and smothered with butter, sautéed, creamed, or steamed. When selecting okra, choose small, green, tender, and slightly flexible pods between 2 and 4 in (5–10 cm) in length.

1 lb (500 g) fresh okra	1 clove garlic, minced (optional)
6 tablespoons butter	salt and black pepper

Wash your okra thoroughly, then cut off the stems. Now blanch the pods by submerging them in a pot of rapidly boiling water for 1 or 2 minutes, or until light green but still crisp. Drain them and pat dry. Slice your okra crosswise into 1 in (2.5 cm) pieces.

Heat the butter, and garlic if used, in a large skillet over medium heat, and sauté the okra, stirring frequently, for 5 minutes or until they are nice and brown and tender. Season with salt and pepper to taste and serve.

NOTE Some people prefer okra sautéed in breadcrumbs. Wash and blanch as above. Drain and pat dry. Brown $\frac{1}{2}$ cup (2 oz, 60 g) freshly made breadcrumbs in the butter. Add garlic if you like, and 2 tablespoons milk. Sauté as above, adding a little more butter if it starts to look dry.

SMOTHERED OKRA AND TOMATOES

SERVES 6

4 tablespoons bacon grease or butter	1 tablespoon Worcestershire sauce
2 lb (1 kg) fresh okra, washed and sliced	1 tablespoon sugar
into $\frac{1}{2}$ in (1.5 cm) pieces	1 teaspoon salt
2 cups (16 oz, 500 g) peeled, chopped	pinch of dried oregano
tomatoes (or a 14 oz [397 g] can)	pinch of dried basil
1 large onion, chopped	$\frac{1}{2}$ teaspoon black pepper or cayenne
1 tablespoon fresh lemon juice	

Heat up your bacon grease or butter in a large heavy skillet over medium heat, throw in the sliced okra, lower the heat and gently sauté until the seeds take on a pinkish tint, about 3 minutes. Use a spatula to keep the okra moving as the juice will cause it to stick. Throw in your tomatoes, onion, lemon juice, Worcestershire sauce, sugar, salt, oregano, basil, black pepper, or cayenne if you prefer, tossing all these together until there is virtually no liquid left in the pan.

VARIATION To make *Creole Okra*, increase the amount of bacon grease to 6 tablespoons. Add $\frac{3}{4}$ cup seeded and chopped green pepper (1 smallish pepper) and 2 minced cloves of garlic, and sauté along with the onion until this is soft but not browned, about 3 minutes. Now add your sliced okra and continue cooking until its seeds take on a pinkish tint. Throw in your tomatoes, the above seasonings, and $\frac{1}{2}$ teaspoon cayenne pepper. Allow to simmer for 20 minutes, stirring every so often, then pour in $1\frac{1}{2}$ cups (12 fl oz, 375 ml) chicken broth. Simmer, covered, for another few minutes, until the okra is nice and tender. Sprinkle it with 1 tablespoon chopped parsley before serving.

SMOTHERED FRIED CABBAGE
WITH HAM

SERVES 6

Boiled cabbage does nothing for me. But fried with ham or bacon, smothered and steamed until slightly tender but still with a crunch, well then, it becomes something altogether different.

1 large green cabbage, about 3 lb
    (1.5 kg)
4 slices of fatback, scored almost to the
    rind
2 tablespoons butter (if necessary)
salt
$\frac{1}{2}$ teaspoon black pepper, or to taste

1 medium onion, chopped (optional)
dash of cayenne pepper or crushed red
    pepper flakes (optional)
1 lb (500 g) smoked ham, cubed (omit
    from the recipe if serving with ham or
    pork)

Discard the outer leaves of your cabbage. Tear it apart and wash the leaves. Cut them up coarsely and let them drain in a colander.

Fry your fatback in a heavy skillet over medium heat for 10 minutes or until crisp and brown. Remove the fatback. (Discard it, or dice it and add to the cabbage later, or just eat half of it as I always do.) There should be enough fat in your skillet to fry the cabbage; if not, add butter.

Turn the heat right up. Plunge your·shredded cabbage into the skillet and quickly toss, coating it all over. Cover with a lid, forcing the cabbage down into the pan. Lower the heat and steam for about 5 minutes. Remove the lid and season with salt, pepper, and any of the optional ingredients including the ham. Now remember, you don't want your cabbage to be cooked to death by any means. So replace the lid and continue cooking for no more than 10 minutes, so that the cabbage still has a slight crunch and is highly seasoned with the taste of salt pork.

NOTE Try serving cabbage with fried pork chops; sweet potatoes quartered, boiled in sugar water, and seasoned with cloves or nutmeg and cinnamon; and cornbread or. Apple Brown Muffins (see page 58). Keep it simple. This is truly soulful eating.

Bacon fries up some mean cabbage too, and then you can crumble up the crispy bits right into it. Don't forget, though, it must be fatty enough to give you some real down-home flavor for frying.

Aunt Gussie, really a cousin but always referred to as an aunt as a sign of all the respect we felt due her. A fearless poker player, she grew all kinds of vegetables in her garden in Jamaica, New York — collard greens, big juicy tomatoes, turnips, cabbages, and all kinds of squashes. She was a wonderful woman whose culinary skills extended to every aspect of soul food cooking.

STRING BEANS WITH HAM HOCKS

SERVES 6–8

Green beans go well with virtually any dinner. I do mine with ham hocks because that is the flavor that I prefer — but you can also use cooked ham chunks, ham bones, bacon bits, or smoked turkey butts. Snapping beans was one of the first things I learned to do in the kitchen, or out on the back porch, when I was knee-high to a grasshopper. Now I've taught my kids. It's quick and easy and — unlike many kitchen tasks — carries no risk of them cutting or burning themselves.

2 lb (1 kg) string beans   1 small onion, quartered (optional)
1 ham hock   salt and pepper

Scrub and clean your ham hock with a vegetable brush under cold running water. Simmer it in a deep pot with a lid, in water to cover, until fork tender but not falling apart, for 45 minutes or 1 hour depending on size. Add more water if necessary. Try not to cook your hock too fast, or you'll leave the seasoning residue on the side of the pot instead of in the liquid.

During this time you can be sorting, snapping, and stringing your beans. (In fact most modern varieties don't require stringing, so you may only have to break off the stem end and snap them.) I prefer mine snapped to a length of just under 2 in (5 cm), the right size for a fork. Rinse the beans in a colander under cold running water.

When your hock is done throw in the beans, and the onion if you want it. Add just enough water to cover, then turn up the heat and bring to a quick boil. Lower the heat, season with salt and pepper, and simmer very slowly, partially covered, until the beans are tender and liquid has boiled down a bit. Adjust your seasonings and keep warm until ready to serve.

NOTE   That's the way I like mine, but my Dad likes to throw potatoes (4 peeled and quartered medium ones) right in that ol' pot and forget about them. Dad says it saves pots, but really, he prefers the flavor of the potatoes when they've been cooked in the ham hock and string bean juice. If you want to try Dad's method, adjust the water level to cover the potatoes and then leave 'em alone until you're ready to serve.

BROCCOLI AND RICE CASSEROLE

SERVES 6–8

Broccoli is such a robust vegetable that it can accompany any meal. This is great with steak.

2 cups (13 oz, 400 g) long grain rice
5 cups (2 pints, 1.2 l) cold water
1–2 cups (8–16 fl oz, 250–500 ml) chicken stock
3 cups (1 lb, 500 g) tightly packed broccoli florets (may be frozen)
1 cup (8 oz, 250 g) unsalted butter or margarine
1 cup (4 oz, 120 g) finely chopped fresh mushrooms
1 cup finely chopped onion (1 large onion)

1 cup (4½ oz, 130 g) all-purpose flour
3 cups (1¼ pints, 750 ml) cream, equal parts heavy and light (double and single, or use all whipping cream)
2½ teaspoons salt, or to taste
pepper
dash of cayenne pepper (optional)
2 cloves of garlic, minced
1 crumbled bay leaf
2 cups (8 oz, 250 g) fresh breadcrumbs

Boil the rice in salted water for about 18 minutes. Drain it in a colander over a large pot, reserving the cooking water. Add just enough chicken stock to the reserved cooking water to give it a taste of chicken. Make sure you have enough liquid to cover the broccoli. Bring it to a boil over high heat, add the broccoli, reduce the heat, and simmer for 4 minutes or until almost tender. Preheat your oven to 350°F (180°C, gas 4).

In a medium-sized saucepan, over medium heat, melt ¼ cup butter (or margarine). Add the mushrooms and onions and sauté until soft, about 5 minutes. Moisten them with just enough chicken stock to give a chicken flavor. Blend in the flour, then whisk in the cream. Stir well, adding salt, pepper, and a pinch of cayenne pepper if you choose to give it an added kick. Pour this sauce into a bowl and set aside.

Melt the remaining butter in the same saucepan and gently sauté your garlic and bay leaf for about 4 minutes. Throw in the breadcrumbs and toss well.

Lightly butter a 3 quart ($2\frac{1}{2}$ UK quart, 3 l) casserole and spread your rice over the bottom. Arrange the broccoli on the rice. Pour your mushroom sauce over it, then top with the seasoned breadcrumbs. Bake in the oven for 20–30 minutes or until lightly browned and bubbling.

SLICING CORN

Dot, my stepmother, is definitely the queen of corn in my family. She just seems to step all in it, and she makes it taste better than the rest of us ever can. She reckons the difference is her Southern way of shucking and slicing the corn off the cob to draw out all the milk.

This is Dot's method. Shuck the corn (that is, pull off the leaves), then wash it thoroughly, removing all of the silk. Holding each ear vertically, score down through each row of kernels with a sharp knife, cutting them in half. Then, holding the cob down against the work surface, cut horizontally away from you to slice a very thin layer of the kernels off the cob. Turning the ear as you go, keep slicing thin layers until all of the corn has been cut off. Scrape off and catch all of the milk you can, and add it into your cut kernels.

At this stage your corn mixture should look like a thickish curdled cream. Since corn varies so, according to the season, you may have to thicken it up a wee bit with a tablespoon or so of flour, or you may have to thin it out a bit with a little more cream or milk. You must use your own discretion and remember to keep tasting as you go.

CREAMY SOUTHERN FRIED CORN

SERVES 4

I like my corn boiled and eaten right off the cob, but with Dot around you've gotta be quick because she'll turn it into this delicious fried corn no sooner than you can say skillet. It makes a nice vegetable accompaniment to almost any soul food meal.

6 ears fresh white or yellow corn
$\frac{1}{4}$ cup (2 oz, 50 g) bacon grease
2 tablespoons all-purpose flour
2 tablespoons sugar

$\frac{1}{2}$ cup (4 fl oz, 120 ml) milk
$\frac{1}{2}$ cup (4 fl oz, 120 ml) water
salt and pepper

Prepare your corn as instructed above.

Heat up your bacon grease in a frying pan over medium heat. When it's hot but not yet smoking, add in your corn. Lower the heat and stir in the flour, sugar, milk, and water. Mix well and cook gently until nice and tender, about 15 minutes.

Raise the heat to high. Slightly brown your corn mixture on the bottom only – don't burn it. Blend the browned crusty bottom into the rest of the corn, season with salt and pepper and, if need be, add just a touch more cream or milk if the corn seems to be dry. It should be slightly moist, never soupy or crusty.

*S*UCCOTASH

SERVES 4

Succotash is a Narragansett Indian word. Literally translated it means something that is broken into bits, but Americans today associate it only with this vegetable dish. When it was first introduced to the white settlers by the Algonkian, Powhatan, and other tribes, the bits were sweet corn kernels and lima beans.

It has survived these past five centuries along with many of the other Indians' contributions, and today it's made and eaten everywhere.

Elbert Solomon Ferguson, my father's great-grandfather, and his wife Sally, an Indian, who were married as slaves and worked on Lady Knox's farm down in Westminster, South Carolina. Elbert was the chief horse trainer and it was his job to hide away the horses and to stop the Yankees from taking them during the Civil War. At the end of the war they were given their freedom and became sharecroppers.

1 cup (6 oz, 175 g) cooked whole kernel
  corn
1 cup (6 oz, 175 g) cooked shelled green
  lima beans

$\frac{1}{2}$ cup (4 fl oz, 120 ml) light (single) cream
2 tablespoons butter or bacon grease
$\frac{1}{2}$ teaspoon salt, or to taste
black pepper

Simmer your corn and lima beans in a saucepan over low heat with the cream and butter or bacon grease for 15 minutes or until very tender. Add salt and pepper to taste. Serve immediately. What could be simpler?

NOTE You can also make this with canned or frozen corn and lima beans if need be. Simply put in $\frac{1}{2}$ cup (4 fl oz, 120 ml) water and simmer the vegetables until they are nice and tender. Drain, add your cream, butter, salt, and pepper just before serving and heat through. My dear Aunt Cleo gives this a soulful touch by adding in some okra. Top and tail whole fresh okra and simmer for 20 minutes, or until tender, in a little salted water. Drain, then add to the above recipe. If using canned or frozen okra, add it directly to the cooked corn and beans and heat through.

SOUTHERN CORN PIE

SERVES 6–8

You've just gotta taste this to believe it. Be sure to use Dot's way of cutting the kernels off the cob because you don't want to lose any of that sweet corn milk.

4 cups corn, freshly cut off the cob
  (8 cobs)
3 large eggs
1$\frac{1}{2}$ cups (12 fl oz, 375 ml) milk
1–2 tablespoons sugar, or to taste
salt and white pepper to taste

$\frac{1}{8}$ teaspoon onion powder
$\frac{1}{2}$ cup (4 fl oz, 120 ml) heavy (double)
  cream
3 tablespoons melted butter
paprika

Preheat your oven to 325°F (160°C, gas 3).

Slice your corn (see page 147) right into a well buttered 3 quart (2$\frac{1}{2}$ UK quart, 3 l) casserole.

Beat the eggs until light and foamy. Pour in the milk, sugar, salt, pepper, and onion powder, beating until well blended. Stir this into your corn. Now pour the cream on top and top with melted butter and a sprinkling of paprika.

Bake, uncovered, in the oven for 35 to 40 minutes or until your pie sets firmly.

AUNT ELLA'S EGGPLANT
AND TOMATO BAKE

SERVES 4–6

Eggplant has never been one of my favorite vegetables, but when Aunt Ella mixes it up with some of her luscious home-grown tomatoes, that changes things and eggplant becomes something very special indeed.

1 lb (500 g) fresh eggplant (aubergine)

about 1½ cups (12 fl oz, 375 ml) vegetable
  oil

about 1 cup (4½ oz, 130 g) all-purpose
  flour

4 medium partially ripened tomatoes (or
  2 red and 2 green)

2 tablespoons butter or margarine

2 tablespoons seeded and chopped green
  bell pepper

2 tablespoons chopped onion

2 tablespoons chopped celery

1 teaspoon salt

1 teaspoon black pepper

2 tablespoons brown sugar (light or dark,
  your choice)

8 fl oz (250 ml) tomato sauce (home-
  made or canned, as for pasta)

Wash and peel your eggplant, removing any soft spots, then cut crosswise into ¼ in (6 mm) thick slices. Heat ¼ in (6 mm) depth of oil in a frying pan over medium heat. Dredge the eggplant slices in flour and brown in the hot fat, being careful to avoid burning. As the eggplant is browned, remove each slice to a flat dry surface.

Now cut the tomatoes across into ¼ inch (6 mm) slices. Dredge these in flour and fry as above, adding more oil if necessary. When done, remove to a flat surface as well. Clean out the skillet.

Melt the butter or margarine in the skillet over medium heat. Sauté your green pepper, onion, and celery until just soft and limp but not brown, about 5 minutes. Mix together the salt, pepper, and sugar.

In a well greased 1 quart (1¾ UK pint, 1l) baking dish, layer eggplant slices alternating with tomato slices, green pepper, onion, celery, sugar, salt, and pepper, ending with tomatoes. Pour tomato sauce over all and let it set for 15 minutes while you preheat your oven to 375°F (190°C, gas 5).

Place in the oven and bake for 35 to 45 minutes or until bubbling.

NOTE Sometimes Aunt Ella puts on a topping made up of grated cheddar cheese or breadcrumbs.

*A*UNT ELLA'S SQUASH BAKE WITH CHEESE

SERVES 6–8

Aunt Ella is one of the finest soul food cooks in our family and she makes squash taste like something out of this world. If you can't find the right kind of squash, this is almost as good made with courgettes.

5 cups (1¾ lb, 850 g) sliced thin-skinned
  yellow squash

3 tablespoons butter or margarine

¼ cup chopped green pepper (½ small
  pepper)

¼ cup chopped onion (½ medium onion)

¼ cup (1½ oz, 45 g) chopped celery

1 can (10½ fl oz, 300 ml) condensed cream
  of mushroom soup

1 egg, slightly beaten

1 teaspoon salt

1 teaspoon black pepper

½ cup (2 oz, 60 g) grated cheddar cheese

¼ cup (1 oz, 30 g) fresh breadcrumbs

paprika (optional)

Cook the squash in $\frac{1}{4}$ to $\frac{1}{2}$ cup (2–4 fl oz, 60–120 ml) water for 10 to 15 minutes or until fork tender. Drain well and purée it. Melt 2 tablespoons butter or margarine in a skillet over medium heat and sauté your onion, celery, and green pepper until soft, about 5 minutes. Add the can of mushroom soup, undiluted, and cook, stirring constantly, until the soup is smooth and well blended with the vegetables.

Preheat your oven to 375°F (190°C, gas 5).

In a medium-sized bowl, mix but do not beat your squash purée, mushroom soup, and vegetable mixture, with the egg, salt, pepper, and half of the cheese. Pour into a well-greased $1\frac{1}{2}$ quart ($1\frac{1}{4}$ UK quart, 1.5 l) baking dish. Mix the remaining butter with the breadcrumbs and the rest of the cheese, and spread this over the top of the squash. Sprinkle with paprika if desired. Bake in the oven for 35 to 45 minutes or until your squash bake is brown and bubbly.

THE GLORIOUS SWEET
POTATO

Ah, welcome! You have just entered into the realm of the sublime. This thick, sweet, tuberous root may not look like anything special, but its glorious flavor and flesh lies behind some of the most exquisite soul food dishes. I used to take it somewhat for granted. Yet now I know that family get-togethers just wouldn't have been the same without a sweet potato pudding or a flamed sweet potato and apple casserole.

I was shocked when I discovered that Europe has been missing out on them for four hundred years! It all comes down to climate. Sweet potatoes (or sweets as we call them) arrived there from the Caribbean during the sixteenth century and before common white potatoes came from South America — in fact the word potato comes from *batata*, the Haitian name for a sweet potato. They caused a brief sensation when they arrived, and are even mentioned in Shakespeare: in *The Merry Wives of Windsor* Falstaff says, 'Let the sky rain potatoes.' But they just got pushed to one side because they could only grow in warm regions and were quite perishable. On the other hand they flourished in the Southern states of America. Who knows, maybe we wouldn't have had all our sweet potato specialties if George Washington Carver, the great black statesman, hadn't come along and taught the American South to appreciate just how versatile the root could be. He is revered for many things, and that comes close to the top of the list in my book.

It is very characteristic in soul food cooking to combine sweet things with savory ones, resulting in a blending of flavors that burst in your mouth. The sweet breads or biscuits that we eat for breakfast can just as easily be eaten for dinner; the sweet potatoes left over from last night's dinner can be fried up for breakfast the following morning.

All you need to know if you're a beginner is that there are two types of sweets. There are those which have yellowish flesh, and the larger orangey-red-skinned ones (which we call yams in the States). They are totally interchangeable in any of the recipes to come. Once you begin to try these your imagination will take over because the flavor of sweets is so open to experiment. Try vanilla, lemon, orange, brandy or other liquor, brown or white sugar, cream, or butter as flavorings. Or add in nuts, raisins, crushed pineapple, and so on. Just go with the flow.

As if the recipes in this chapter weren't sensational enough, there's one more at the beginning of the next chapter (page 159): the glorious Sweet Potato Pie.

BAKED, ROAST, AND BOILED SWEET POTATOES

To BAKE You bake sweet potatoes just as you would white potatoes. If they are a bit larger, then obviously they will take a while longer. After washing them, rub the skins with butter or oil. Bake in a preheated 450°F (230°C, gas 8) oven for 45 minutes to 1 hour. Prick with a fork about halfway through the baking process to allow the steam to escape. Cut one in half, lengthwise, on your plate; then simply slap a dollop of butter on each half and mash it in just as you would for a baked white potato.

To ROAST Just throw small sweet potatoes into your roasting pan alongside a plump pheasant, quail, or mallard to add a soulful zest to a gourmet meal.

To BOIL This is quick soulful top-of-the-stove stuff. Boil your sweets, still in their jackets, until almost tender, about 20 minutes. Meanwhile, in a saucepan, make up a sugar syrup using $\frac{1}{4}$ cup (2 oz, 60 g) light or dark brown sugar and 1 cup (8 fl oz, 250 ml) water. Simmer this over low heat for 15 minutes or until thick. Drain the cooked sweets. When cool enough to handle, peel and either slice them thickly or quarter them. Add them to the syrup and season with ground cinnamon, nutmeg or cloves, a dash of salt, a piece of fatback, and a splash of fresh lemon juice or orange juice. Simmer over low heat for 10 minutes or until your sweets are nice and tender.

SWEET POTATO FRENCH FRIES

Wash and scrub your sweet potatoes, then parboil them in salted water for about 10 minutes and drain. Now, as soon as you can handle them, peel them and cut into thin strips the same size as for ordinary French fried potatoes (chips). Heat 3 cups (or more) vegetable oil over high heat to 395°F (202°C) on a cooking thermometer. Fry them for 3 minutes or until golden brown. Drain on paper towels or, as I prefer, on newspaper – it seems to leave them crisper. Serve hot, sprinkled with salt, or you can use a little brown sugar and ground nutmeg as well as the salt.

SWEET POTATO AND APPLE CASSEROLE

SERVES 6

This concoction is possibly the most favored of all the sweet potato casseroles to be found on American tables at Thanksgiving or Christmas.

The most important thing to remember when making any sweet potato casserole is that the potatoes must hold together when you cut them or they'll be falling apart by the time you spoon them onto the plates. You don't want to go into overdrive with the boiling. Here, for instance, you want to be able to distinguish the apple texture from that of the sweets.

3–4 medium sweet potatoes (total about 1¼ lb, 600 g)

2 medium tart apples

2 teaspoons fresh lemon juice

⅓ cup (2½ oz, 75 g) dark brown sugar

½ teaspoon salt, or to taste

½ teaspoon ground cinnamon

3 tablespoons butter

Wash your sweet potatoes, then boil them in their skins, covered, until they are nearly tender but a bit on the firm side, about 10 minutes. Drain. When they are cool enough to handle, peel and slice them ½ in (1.5 cm) thick.

While they are cooking, wash, core, and slice your apples. Preheat your oven to 350°F (180°C, gas 4).

Place half of the sliced sweet potatoes in a buttered 3 quart (2½ UK quart, 3 l) baking dish, and cover with half of apples. Splash on 1 teaspoon lemon juice. Sprinkle with half the sugar, salt and cinnamon. Dot with half of the butter. Repeat the process with the other half of the ingredients. Bake in the oven for 45 minutes or until the top is brown and potatoes and apples are tender. Serve hot.

NOTE   Treat yourself by topping your casserole off with colorful marshmallows a couple of minutes before serving, so that they melt down and lightly brown. You can also add 2 tablespoons of brandy to the potatoes for an added kick.

BAKED STUFFED SWEET POTATOES WITH MARSHMALLOW TOPPING

SERVES 6

6 large sweet potatoes (total about 3 lb, 1.5 kg)

1 tablespoon butter, softened, or vegetable oil, plus at least 3 tablespoons butter

¼ teaspoon cinnamon

¼ teaspoon nutmeg

2–4 tablespoons brown sugar

¼ cup (2 fl oz, 60 ml) heavy (double) cream

2 tablespoons bourbon whiskey (optional)

½ cup (2 oz, 60 g) chopped black (or English) walnuts

about 8 oz (250 g) marshmallows

Preheat your oven to 450°F (230°C, gas 8).

Scrub your sweet potatoes, then rub the skins with butter or oil. Bake in the oven until tender, 45 minutes or 1 hour. Prick each one halfway through the baking to allow steam to escape. Don't turn off the oven.

When the sweet potatoes are done, cut them in half lengthwise and scoop out the insides with a teaspoon, taking care not to break the skins. Now use a fork to mash your butter, cinnamon, nutmeg, and brown sugar into the pulp, then stir in the cream and bourbon (if used). Beat until nice and fluffy, then add the nuts and stir well. Heap the mixture into the skins. Place them on a baking sheet and bake for 15 minutes or until light brown.

Remove the potatoes from the oven and top each one with marshmallows — kinda push them into your mixture as much as you can. I prefer to use miniature colored marshmallows, but the larger ones taste just as good. Bake an additional 5 minutes or so until the marshmallows are melted and lightly browned.

ORANGE-GLAZED SWEET POTATOES
SERVES 6

6 medium sweet potatoes (total about 2 lb, 1 kg)
1 cup (8 fl oz, 250 ml) fresh orange juice
$\frac{3}{4}$ cup (6 oz, 175 g) white sugar

1 tablespoon cornstarch (cornflour)
$\frac{1}{2}$ teaspoon salt
$\frac{1}{2}$ teaspoon grated lemon peel
3 tablespoons butter

Preheat your oven to 350°F (180°C, gas 4).

Scrub your sweet potatoes. Parboil them, still in their skins, in boiling salted water for 10 minutes. Drain. As soon as they can be handled somewhat, peel them and slice in half lengthwise. Place them in a buttered 2 quart ($1\frac{3}{4}$ UK quart, 2 l) casserole.

While the sweets are parboiling and cooling, you can be making up your orange glaze syrup. Slowly simmer your orange juice, sugar, cornstarch, salt, lemon peel, and butter until it thickens up into a nice syrup, about 5 minutes. Pour this syrup over your sweet potatoes and bake, covered, in the oven for 1 hour or until lightly browned. Baste occasionally.

NOTE You can top this with marshmallows about 5 minutes before the end of baking, if you choose to — *I always do.*

SWEET POTATO MOUNDS
SERVES 4

3 medium sweet potatoes (total about 1 lb, 500 g), boiled and still hot
2 tablespoons butter
2 tablespoons light brown sugar, or to taste
1 large egg yolk
pinch of salt

$\frac{1}{8}$ teaspoon ground nutmeg
1 teaspoon rum (or pure vanilla extract)
$\frac{1}{4}$ cup (2 fl oz, 60 ml) heavy (double) cream
1 large egg white, stiffly beaten
1 cup (4 oz, 120 g) crushed walnuts (or pecans)

Preheat your oven to 450°F (230°C, gas 8). Peel and mash your sweet potatoes, and beat in the butter, brown sugar, egg yolk, salt, nutmeg, rum, and cream. Fold in your stiffly beaten egg white.

Divide the mixture into 8 individual lumps and pat them until firm. Spread the nuts out on a plate and roll the lumps in the nuts to coat them. Form them into mounds on a well greased baking sheet and bake in the oven for 12 to 15 minutes or until light brown. Keep them warm until ready to serve. They are simply scrumptious as a side dish with meat.

CANDIED YAMS

SERVES 4

This is a soul food classic. If possible make it with the orangey-red sweet potatoes that we call yams (but not with real yams, of course). However, it's just as delicious made with the yellow kind.

4 medium-sized sweet potatoes (total about 1½ lb, 750 g)
½ cup (4 oz, 120 g) butter

1 tablespoon fresh lemon juice
½ cup (3½ oz, 100 g) brown sugar
½ cup (4 fl oz, 120 ml) water

Wash your sweet potatoes. Boil them in their skins, covered, for 10 minutes or until nearly tender (or bake them if this is more convenient). Meanwhile, make up a syrup with the remaining ingredients, and cook it in a small saucepan over high heat until the syrup coats a spoon, about 3 minutes. Also preheat your oven to 375°F (190°C, gas 5).

When the sweets are cool enough to handle, peel them and cut lengthwise about ½ in (1.5 cm) thick. Lay them in a buttered shallow 2 quart (1¾ UK quart, 2 l) baking dish. Pour your hot syrup over the sweet potatoes and bake, uncovered, for 30 to 40 minutes or until light brown. Baste a couple of times during baking. Serve with anything you like, but this goes especially well with roast ham or pork chops.

NOTE   Add in some nuts or brandy or top with marshmallows, if you like. Just let your feelings go and taste, taste, taste. Soon you'll know the exact taste you want.

SWEET POTATO PUDDING

SERVES 4

4 medium sweet potatoes (total about 1½ lb, 750 g)
½ cup (4 oz, 120 g) butter
2 large eggs
½ cup (3½ oz, 100 g) brown sugar
1 teaspoon pure vanilla extract
½ cup (4 fl oz, 120 ml) warmed heavy (double) cream

¼ cup (1 oz, 30 g) chopped pecans (optional)
½ cup (1½ oz, 45 g) miniature marshmallows (optional)
about 5 pineapple rings (may be canned)
about 5 maraschino cherries

Wash your sweet potatoes and boil in their skins, covered, until fork tender, about 20 minutes. Meanwhile, preheat your oven to 375°F (190°C, gas 5).

You've got to work quickly when your sweets are ready. Peel them while they're still hot, mash them up with a fork and beat in your butter until it melts. Next beat in the eggs, one at a time, until well blended. Then throw in your brown sugar, vanilla, and cream and blend well. At this stage you may add your nuts and marshmallows should you choose to use them – which you should.

Turn your mixture out into a well buttered 2 quart ($1\frac{3}{4}$ UK quart, 2 l) casserole. Decorate with pineapple rings and maraschino cherries and bake in the oven for about 20 to 25 minutes or until light brown.

NOTE   You can also put this pudding into some halved orange cups as described below.

SWEET POTATOES IN ORANGE CUPS

SERVES 6

This is an old family favorite.

3 large sweet potatoes (total about $1\frac{1}{2}$ lb, 750 g), boiled and still hot
salt
$\frac{1}{4}$ cup (2 oz, 60 g) butter, softened

3 tablespoons fresh orange juice, or to taste
$\frac{1}{4}$ cup (2 oz, 60 g) light brown sugar
6 cleaned orange half shells

Peel and mash the boiled sweet potatoes. Working quickly, beat in the salt, butter, orange juice, and sugar. Pile the mixture into your orange shells. Serve warm.

I like to decorate each with a maraschino cherry and a mere drop of cherry juice, as seen on pages 138–9.

SWEET THANGS

Y ou may be wondering why there are so many recipes in this chapter. Well, the answer is quite simple. I have a sweet tooth. Blueberry cobblers, cherry fritters, and pumpkin pie – these are for me. In fact, I have a whole mouth full of sweet teeth which I have carried around the world with me. There is a second answer too. The American South excels at sweetness just as France does at garlickiness.

One reason is the fabulous range of fresh fruit available the year around. Whenever I went South as a child to stay with relatives, we kids would be sent out to pick whatever was needed, blackberries for a cobbler or peaches for an ice cream. We would stay out as long as possible to play and finally trudge home with baskets full and our legs a mess of chigger bites.

Another reason is molasses, which packs a thick rich punch compared to white sugar. When Aunt Ella and my Dad were kids in North Carolina, they used to light a fire under a big old pot, and throw in the sugar cane and boil it down. Then they got the old family donkey to walk around in a circle around the pot all day, turning a machine to grind it down. As he crushed it, the thick juice – molasses – drained off into a trough. They collected it and jarred it up for storage. Then Grandma Maggie would use it to make stacks of pecan pies.

A sure sign of a good soul food dessert is the size of the portion. When we say a slice of apple pie, we don't mean a petite little sliver. You know you're gonna get one big fat healthy hunk of pie filled with fruit piled as high as a mountain and still warm when it's scooped right out of the pan and onto your plate. You're never left wanting for more. Not for a couple of hours. Then – it's time for seconds, if there's ever any left!

AUNT PEACIE'S DOUBLE PIE CRUST

It's confession time, folks! For some reason, pie crusts and I have never gotten along. I mean it! I've had pie crusts stick to my rolling pin and you all know what a real mess that can be. I've had them break up in the pan *after* I'd put in the filling, no less. Once, I even decided to improve on everyone else's pastry and added sugar to the basic recipe. Need I say more?

Anyway, I finally got my hands on Aunt Peacie's recipe. Believe you me, it wasn't easy. She said, 'You add a touch of this and a bit of that, honey, until it feels right in your hands, suga' dumpling.' Well, how the devil was I supposed to know what *it* was supposed to feel like if I had never been able to make *it* successfully in the first place?

One day, determined that pies were no longer going to be my nemesis, I followed Aunt Peacie around her kitchen and wrote down everything she did. I did the measuring for her, she tasted and felt and nodded her approval. So here is Aunt Peacie's recipe.

For two 8–9 in (20–23 cm) crusts:

2 cups (8 oz, 250 g) sifted all-purpose flour

1 teaspoon salt

$\frac{2}{3}$ cup ($5\frac{1}{2}$ oz, 160 g) vegetable shortening or lard

5 tablespoons iced water

Blend the salt into flour with a fork. Using a pastry blender, work the shortening into flour until it resembles little peas. Drop in the water 1 tablespoon at a time, mixing with a fork until all of the flour is moistened and the dough almost cleans the side of the bowl. Up to 2 extra teaspoons of water may be used if necessary.

Divide your dough in half and shape into two mounds. (At this point refrigerate these separately in clear plastic film if the pastry is for use later; bring it back to room temperature before rolling.) On a lightly floured surface, using a floured rolling pin, roll one mound 2 in (5 cm) larger than the pie pan and one into a circle to fit the top.

Fold the larger circle into quarters and unfold gently to cover the bottom of the pan. Pour in the pie filling and cover with the top layer. Seal and flute the edges by pinching them together with your thumb and index finger. Cut small slits into the top to allow steam to escape while baking.

SWEET POTATO PIE

MAKES A 10 IN (25 CM) PIE

Sweet potato pie is my all-time favorite pie – bar none. Each member of my family has his or her own special version. Aunt Peacie follows a tip from the Reverend Jesse Jackson, given in *Ebony* magazine, to replace some of the spices with brandy, and she says that works a treat. To keep from stepping on anyone's toes here, I'll just give you my own personal recipe. But believe you me, one person's version is just as good as the next for this fabulous pie. It's just that some people prefer more cinnamon, less nutmeg, a different kind of cream, etc. So feel free to experiment.

3 cups ($1\frac{1}{2}$ lb, 750 g) warm mashed sweet potatoes

3 large eggs

1–$1\frac{1}{2}$ cups (8–12 oz, 250–375 g) sugar (depending on sweetness of potatoes)

$\frac{3}{4}$ teaspoon salt

$\frac{3}{4}$ teaspoon ground nutmeg

$1\frac{1}{2}$ teaspoons ground cinnamon

$\frac{1}{2}$ teaspoon ground allspice

1 cup (8 fl oz, 250 ml) heavy (double) cream

1 unbaked 10 in (25 cm) pie shell (see below)

In case you need them, instructions on cooking sweet potatoes are given on page 153. Peel them while they're still hot, then mash 'em up. Preheat your oven to 350°F (180°C, gas 4). Beat the eggs, sugar, salt, and spices into the potatoes. Now pour in the cream and stir well. Give one last beating for good measure – about 30 seconds.

Turn your mixture into the unbaked pie shell. Bake in the oven for 1 hour or until the pie is nice and firm. Test by inserting a knife into the center. If it comes out clean your pie is done.

Let it cool down a bit before you cut it. Serve on its own or add a nice dollop of cream, or ice cream, on top.

SINGLE PIE CRUST

I've already given Aunt Peacie's Pie Crust recipe (see page 158). Most times if I'm making a single pie I make it up and freeze one of the dough balls for later use – that way I always have one on hand. But if you've a mind to, here's another recipe which makes the small amount you need for a one crust pie.

For a 9 or 10 in (23 or 25 cm) pie shell:

$1\frac{1}{2}$ cups (6 oz, 175 g) sifted all-purpose flour

$\frac{1}{2}$ teaspoon salt

$\frac{1}{2}$ cup (4 oz, 120 g) lard (or vegetable shortening)

about 3 tablespoons iced water

Put your flour and salt in a bowl and mix lightly with a fork. Use two knives to cut in your shortening until the mixture resembles coarse meal and is very crumbly. Gradually sprinkle on the iced water, stirring lightly with a fork until the dry ingredients hold together but are still dry enough to handle when pressed into a ball. Use your hands to press it into a ball, gathering up any loose bits. Work gently and quickly. Wrap the ball of dough in clear plastic film until ready to roll it out. If you're not rolling it soon, refrigerate it but be sure to let it come back to room temperature before rolling.

On a lightly floured board, roll the dough out to about $\frac{1}{8}$ in (3 mm) thickness, rolling from the center outward and turning your dough as you roll so that you maintain a nice circle as much as possible. Roll about 2 in (5 cm) larger than the pie pan to be used. You can judge this accurately by inverting the pie pan right over the dough. Fold the dough gently into quarters and fit it neatly into the pie pan. Delicately unfold, then trim and flute the edges.

If your recipe calls for a baked pie shell then preheat your oven to 425°F (220°C, gas 7). After crimping the edges of the shell, prick the bottom liberally with a fork. This will eliminate any bubbling. Bake for 12 to 15 minutes or until lightly browned. If a recipe needs a partially baked pie shell, bake it for 10 minutes only.

BLACK BOTTOM PIE

MAKES A 10 IN (25 CM) PIE

Let me tell you a little something about my gorgeous Mom. She has always been the best singer and dancer in our family but the honest-to-goodness worst cook I've ever known. If you have noticed that I have used no recipes attributed to my Mom, you now know the reason why. But when it comes to music and dance, well she has no parallel. She's got a voice like Ella Fitzgerald and she can really cut a rug.

Now, Mom used to tell me tales about Harlem in the Roaring Twenties, when the white world was discovering the black writers, artists, singers, dancers, actors, and musicians who flocked there for a first chance to be free, to be seen, to be heard. At the famous Cotton Club, where all of the performers, cooks, and staff were black, but all the audience was lily-white, one of the most popular dances

My mother, Virginia Cardell Ferguson, one of Grandma Battle's seven children. She worked from her teens to help support the family and never had much time for the domestic events of the kitchen. But when it comes to doing the Black Bottom or crooning out a tune, my Mom has no equal. She used to stand me up on a three-legged stool, put on a Nat King Cole record, and show me how to use my hands gracefully while singing a beautiful ballad.

was the Black Bottom — and that was sometimes the nickname of Harlem itself. I have been told that this pie originated in a Harlem kitchen around the time of the dance. Yet James Beard says in *American Cookery* that recipes for it began appearing at the turn of the century. If he is right, I can only think that it was brought up North by a black Southern cook who baked it up for Harlem audiences.

You've just gotta try it to believe how good it is. Yes, the ingredients list is long and it's a lot of work, but you won't regret it.

20–24 ginger snaps, finely crushed
6 tablespoons melted butter
4 large eggs, separated
2 cups (16 fl oz, 500 ml) scalded milk
1½ tablespoons cornstarch (cornflour)
1 cup (8 oz, 250 ml) sugar
2 oz (60 g) unsweetened chocolate, plus more, grated, for topping (see below)

1 tablespoon pure vanilla extract
1 tablespoon unflavored gelatin
3 tablespoons cool water
½ teaspoon cream of tartar
2 tablespoons bourbon whiskey (or rum)
1 cup (8 fl oz, 250 ml) heavy (double) cream, whipped

Preheat your oven to 350°F (180°C, gas 4).

Mix your crushed ginger snaps and melted butter together to form a nice solid crust, then pat it into a 10 in (25 cm) pie pan, coating the bottom and sides completely. Bake in the oven for 10 minutes, then take it out and set aside.

Meanwhile beat the egg yolks well. Make up a custard in a saucepan using the scalded milk, cornstarch, half of the sugar, and the egg yolks. Cook over low heat, stirring constantly, until the custard coats a spoon, about 7 minutes.

While the custard is cooking, melt the 2 squares of chocolate in a saucepan over very low heat. Remove it from the heat as soon as it melts, and keep it warm if necessary.

Mix half of the hot custard into the melted chocolate. Stir in the vanilla. Let it cool slightly, then pour it into your ginger snap crust. Smooth it around evenly.

Dissolve the gelatin in the 3 spoonfuls of water and stir it into the remaining hot custard, then allow that to cool too.

Beat your egg whites until just foamy, then add in the cream of tartar and remaining sugar. Continue beating until stiff peaks form. Fold this into the cooled custard and stir in your bourbon (I prefer this to rum).

Now, pour all of this goodness onto the layer of chocolate custard in the pie shell. Refrigerate your pie for at least 4 hours, or overnight, if possible. Just before serving, top with whipped cream. Decorate with grated chocolate (in Britain I use crushed chocolate flake, which is great). Now sit back and enjoy the fruits of your labor.

BOBBI-JEAN'S CHEERY CHERRY PIE

MAKES A 9 IN (23 CM) PIE

I think this pie is best when baked with a lattice top crust to allow the ample cherry juice somewhere to go when it starts bubblin'. This recipe was baked deliciously for me by Bobbi-Jean Jackson, a cousin from Martinsville, Virginia, who now teaches and resides in Fort Lauderdale, Florida.

1 recipe Aunt Peacie's Double Pie Crust
   (see page 158)
1½ cups (12 oz, 375 g) sugar
5 tablespoons all-purpose flour
¼ teaspoon salt

2 lb (1 kg) canned, pitted tart cherries,
   drained, or 4 cups (1¾ lb, 800 g) fresh
   sour pitted cherries, washed and
   drained.
4 drops pure almond extract
2 tablespoons butter or margarine

Preheat your oven to 450°F (230°C, gas 8).

Make up your pie dough and roll out 2 circles; but for this recipe make *both*
circles 2 in (5 cm) wider than a 9 in (23 cm) pie pan. Line the bottom of a pie
pan of that size with one circle.

Blend the sugar, flour, and salt, sprinkle this mixture over the cherries, drop
on the almond extract, and gently toss until they are evenly coated. Now pour
the cherry mixture onto the bottom pie crust. Dot with the butter or margarine.

Slice the other circle of pie dough into strips about ½ in (1.5 cm) wide. Moisten
the edges of the bottom crust with a little water. Lay half of the strips equally
spaced across the pie, as far as possible without stretching them, and using shorter
strips at the beginning and end to avoid waste. Then lay the other half across
them at right angles to make a lattice. Press the ends of the strips gently onto
the bottom crust to fix them in place.

Stand your pie pan on a cookie sheet so that if any juice overflows it won't
make a mess of your oven. Bake it for 20 minutes or until the lattice crust is
beginning to turn light brown, then reduce the temperature to 350°F (180°C, gas
4) and continue to cook until the crust is evenly browned and the fruit is cooked
and bubbling gently, another 25 to 35 minutes. Serve warm or cold.

DEEP DISH APPLE PIE

MAKES A 9 IN (23 CM) PIE 2 IN (5 CM) DEEP

The ingredients in an apple pie depend on your own taste. For example, my
children like double the quantity of cinnamon, but my husband doesn't really like
any. The sweetness of apples also depends upon the time of the year as well as
the variety you choose. I have used up to 1½ cups (12 oz) sugar in my own pies;
but then I like a sweet pie, so perhaps you would like to start off with considerably
less and keep adding.

1 recipe Aunt Peacie's Double Pie Crust
   (see page 158)
8–10 tart apples (about 3 lb, 1.5 kg)
1 teaspoon fresh lemon juice
1 cup (8 oz, 250 g) sugar (or to taste)

½ cup (2½ oz, 75 g) all-purpose flour
1 teaspoon ground cinnamon
¼ teaspoon ground nutmeg
¼ teaspoon salt
2 tablespoons butter or margarine

First prepare your pie crust and divide it into two pieces, one about one and a
half times the size of the other. Roll the larger piece out about 5 in (13 cm) wider
than your deep dish pie pan, which should be about 9 in (23 cm) wide and 2 in
(5 cm) deep. (If you don't have a proper pan, use an ovenproof casserole of the
same size.) Roll out the smaller piece to make a top crust, then gently roll it up
like a carpet and refrigerate until ready to use. Line the pan with the larger piece.

Peel and core your apples and thinly slice lengthwise. After slicing each apple, drop the slices into a bowl with the lemon juice, and turn them in it to stop them from going brown. When all are sliced, drain and add the sugar, flour, cinnamon, nutmeg, and salt, and toss the apples in the spicy mixture until evenly coated.

Preheat your oven to 425°F (220°C, gas 7).

Turn the apples into your lined deep dish and dot with butter. Remove the remaining pie crust dough from the refrigerator, unroll, and fold in half. Cut two vents in it near the center to allow the steam to escape. Unfold the circle and lay it gently across the apple filling. Seal and flute the edges.

Bake in the oven for about 50 minutes, or until the crust is evenly browned and the juice begins to bubble through the vents. If your pie appears to be browning too quickly, reduce the temperature to 350°F (180°C, gas 4).

Grandma Maggie Ferguson (left) with her neighbor Pearl. Grandma was born Mary Magaline Lynch and married Granddaddy Ferguson at the age of eighteen. The circumstances surrounding her sudden and early death are still a family mystery. I'm told that she believed she'd been rooted and lost her will to live. Much is the pity; I would have loved to touch her.

GRANDMA MAGGIE'S PECAN PIE
MAKES A 9 IN (23 CM) PIE

There were groves of wild pecan trees down on the back acre on Granddaddy Bert Ferguson's farm in Charlotte, North Carolina. Those tall sweeping old pecan trees were one beautiful sight and the fruits they bore were a real gift to us, as well as a test as to just how much nutcracking the human tooth could endure!

Whenever we went down South to visit our relatives and kinfolk, I could always look forward to Grandma Maggie's pecan pies. She died before I was born, so the pies were made by my Aunt Ella to her recipe. Whenever I look at the only existing picture of Grandma Maggie, I feel strangely as if I know her.

I'm told that Grandma Maggie would stack her pies up, one on top of the other, sometimes up to four or five of them, and when she sliced, she cut straight down through the whole stack. The slices were narrower, of course, but the hunks were bigger and much more fun to eat. I've never known anyone else do this. Here's her recipe, given to me years ago by Granddaddy Bert.

1 unbaked 9 in (23 cm) pie shell (see page 160)
$\frac{3}{4}$ cup (6 oz, 175 g) butter, softened
$\frac{1}{2}$ cup (3$\frac{1}{2}$ oz, 100 g) light brown sugar
$\frac{1}{2}$ cup (4 oz, 120 g) white sugar
3 large eggs, well beaten
$\frac{1}{2}$ cup (4 fl oz, 120 g) dark cane syrup or corn syrup (or 3 fl oz [90 ml] British golden syrup with 1 fl oz [30 ml] black treacle)

2 teaspoons pure vanilla extract
$\frac{1}{2}$ teaspoon salt
1 cup (4 oz, 120 g) broken pecans
pecan halves to decorate (I use about 24, 3 to a slice)

Preheat your oven to 325°F (160°C, gas 3).

Cream your butter with both sugars and blend in the beaten eggs. Stir in your syrup, vanilla, salt, and pecan pieces. Blend well, then pour into the unbaked pie crust. Decorate with the pecan halves and bake in the oven for 1 hour or until your pie resembles a hot rich custard. Serve warm with a big scoop of vanilla ice cream on top or with a dousing of cream. This is Southern soul food eating at its mightiest.

NOTE The beautiful pecan pie featured on pages 170–1 was baked especially for me by cousin Clarissa Johnson, and I thank her.

CHOCOLATE PECAN PIE
MAKES A 9 IN (23 CM) PIE

This recipe was sent to me years ago by my sister, Peaches Hunter Ferguson, who lives in Atlanta, Georgia, where there is no end to her supply of pecan trees and pecans. She tore it out of *Ebony* magazine, the excellent American journal aimed primarily at the black population. It's about the only place one can regularly find decent soul food recipes in print.

1 unbaked 9 in (23 cm) pie shell (see page
160)
1 cup (8 fl oz, 250 ml) light or dark corn
syrup (or cane [golden] syrup)
1 cup (8 oz, 250 g) sugar
3 large eggs, slightly beaten
3 tablespoons melted butter

2 teaspoons pure vanilla extract
5 oz (150 g) melted semisweet chocolate
(if you prefer a less sweet pie, use
unsweetened chocolate)
1 cup chopped pecans
$\frac{1}{2}$ cup pecan halves

This one's as easy as pie! First preheat your oven to 350°F (180°C, gas 4).

Stir everything together except the pecans in one big bowl. When it's all well blended, throw in your chopped pecans and stir to mix. Pour into the unbaked pie shell. Decorate the top with pecan halves. Bake in the oven for about 50 to 55 minutes, or until a knife inserted halfway between the center and the edge comes out clean. Let it cool down a bit before you serve, and when you do, don't forget the whipped cream topping, please!

LEMON MERINGUE PIE

MAKES A 9 IN (23 CM) PIE

No American cookbook would be complete without a lemon meringue pie. But just a word or two to the wise. Do not try to cut corners with one of those old store-bought lemon pie fillings. Who needs to cut corners anyway? You can make this pie in 20 minutes, and probably less if you have a frozen pie crust on hand. So here, my friends, is the real deal just waiting to melt in your mouth and perk up your dinner table.

$1\frac{3}{4}$ cups (14 oz, 430 g) sugar ($\frac{1}{2}$ cup [4 oz,
120 g] of this should be fine [caster]
sugar for meringue)
4 tablespoons cornstarch (cornflour)
$\frac{1}{2}$ teaspoon salt
4 tablespoons all-purpose flour
2 cups (16 fl oz, 500 ml) boiling water

4 large eggs, separated
2 tablespoons butter or margarine
$\frac{1}{3}$ cup ($2\frac{1}{2}$ fl oz, 75 ml) fresh lemon juice
grated rind from 2 lemons
$\frac{1}{4}$ teaspoon cream of tartar
$\frac{1}{2}$ teaspoon pure vanilla extract (optional)
1 baked 9 in (23 cm) pie shell (page 160)

Combine $1\frac{1}{4}$ cups (10 oz, 300 g) sugar, the cornstarch, salt, and flour in a saucepan. Gradually pour in the boiling water, stirring constantly. Place over medium heat and cook for 10 minutes, stirring constantly, until the mixture thickens up and turns clear. No flour lumps, please! If there are, mash 'em out.

Slightly beat the egg yolks and whisk a small amount of the hot mixture into them. Mix thoroughly, then pour the yolk mixture back into the saucepan. Cook over low heat, stirring constantly, for 2 or 3 minutes. Remove the pan from the heat and stir in the butter or margarine, lemon juice, and lemon rind. Set it aside to cool while you concentrate on making the meringue.

Preheat your oven to 425°F (220°C, gas 7).

Beat the egg whites with the cream of tartar until light and frothy. Gradually add the remaining (fine) sugar and the vanilla, beating constantly. The meringue should be as shiny as brand-new Italian tiles. When stiff peaks form, stop beating.

By now your lemon mixture should have cooled down sufficiently for you to spread. Now here comes my special tip. Not a lotta people know this one. Plop about 4 heaping tablespoons of meringue into the lemon mixture. Stir gently, blending until any lumps disappear. This will lighten the filling and make it much fluffier. There's nothing worse than a heavy lemon meringue pie.

Spoon your lemon filling into the baked pie shell. Smooth the top and cover with the remaining meringue. It's best to slap the meringue right smack dab in the middle of the pie and then smooth it outward towards the rim of the pan to ensure that the edges are properly sealed. After smoothing and sealing, make little peaks in the meringue.

Bake in the oven until the delicate peaks of the meringue become a gorgeous dusky brown. This will only take 6 to 8 minutes, depending on the heat of your oven, so watch carefully. Some people prefer to put the pie under their broiler or grill to get the same effect. Let the pie cool down just slightly before serving.

OLD-FASHIONED
PUMPKIN PIE

MAKES A 9 IN (23 CM) PIE

Here is one of the most traditional American holiday pies. As soon as harvest time rolls around, just watch old Jack-o-Lantern's eyes brighten up when you put this on your table. Could be he's a-wonderin' where his innards have gone.

1 unbaked 9 in (23 cm) pie shell (see page 160)
$\frac{3}{4}$ cup (6 oz, 175 g) sugar
$\frac{1}{2}$ cup ($3\frac{1}{2}$ oz, 100 g) dark brown sugar
$\frac{1}{2}$ teaspoon salt
$\frac{1}{2}$ teaspoon ground ginger
$\frac{1}{2}$ teaspoon ground nutmeg

$1\frac{1}{2}$ teaspoons ground cinnamon
$\frac{1}{4}$ teaspoon ground allspice (or cloves)
2 large eggs
1 cup (8 fl oz, 250 ml) evaporated milk (or light [single] cream)
2 cups (16 fl oz, 500 ml) fresh pumpkin purée

The usual way to prepare pumpkin for a pie is to cut a pumpkin in half crosswise, remove the seeds and strings, put the halves cut side down in a pan, and bake in the oven at 325°F (160°C, gas 3) until the flesh is tender and starts to fall apart – the time depends on the size of the pumpkin. If you want the shell to make a lantern, cook the flesh in a casserole with a lid. Meanwhile, make the pie crust.

Mash and strain the pumpkin flesh. Then turn the oven up to 425°F (220°C, gas 7).

Mix all your dry ingredients together, then blend in your eggs, evaporated milk (or cream), and pumpkin (I'm partial to the taste of evaporated milk as opposed to cream in this recipe). Beat until smooth. Pour your pumpkin mixture into the unbaked pie shell and cook in the oven for 15 minutes, then reduce the temperature to 325°F (160°C, gas 3). Continue to bake for another 45 minutes or until a knife inserted into the center comes out clean.

Serve it on its own or with a generous dollop of whipped cream and a sprinkling of nutmeg on each slice.

BLUEBERRY CRUMBLE

SERVES 6

Someone in England said to me quite recently, 'I didn't know you guys had crumbles in the United States,' and I said, 'I didn't know you had 'em in England!' So here, folks, is a truly international dessert. But I have to say that I prefer this richer Stateside version with brown sugar and enough butter to give a crisp but not dry topping.

2 pints (1½ lb, 750 g) fresh or frozen
    blueberries
½ cup (3½ oz, 100 g) light brown sugar
1 teaspoon fresh lemon juice

¾ cup (6 oz, 175 g) sifted all-purpose flour
½ cup (4 oz, 120 g) chilled butter
dash of ground cinnamon (optional)

If using fresh berries, pick them over and discard any bits of stem or leaves. Rinse the berries lightly and gently, then drain on paper towels.

Sprinkle your berries with 2 or 3 tablespoons of the sugar and the lemon juice. Toss them lightly to coat. Now let them stand for about 15 minutes to make a really nice juice, while you preheat your oven to 400°F (200°C, gas 6).

Mix the remaining sugar with the flour, butter, and cinnamon if you're using it. Stir just until crumbly – *do not over-beat.*

Pour your berry mixture into a well buttered 1½ quart (1¼ UK quart, 1.5 l) baking dish – a deep one is best. Spread the brown sugar crumble over the top. Bake in the oven for 25 to 30 minutes, or until the top is golden brown and your blueberries are a-bubblin'. Let it cool down a spell before you serve it up, lavished with generous portions of heavy (double) cream.

COCONUT CUSTARD PIE

MAKES A 9 IN (23 CM) PIE

Oh, you sweet thing you! This is a rich custard pie with just a hint of vanilla and lots of moist delectable coconut. Even kids who won't eat custard seem to love it. I'm a witness, yes sir!

The trick to a really creamy filling is in the timing. The pie should still be slightly soft and shaky in the center because it will finish cooking after it has been removed from the oven.

1 unbaked 9 in (23 cm) pie shell (see page
    160)
4 large eggs
⅔ cup (5½ oz, 160 g) sugar
½ teaspoon salt
2⅔ cups (1 generous pint, 650 ml) milk

1½ teaspoons pure vanilla extract
1 cup (6 oz, 175 g) fresh coconut (canned
    or shredded [desiccated or creamed]
    coconut will do – measure after
    reconstituting)
¼ teaspoon ground nutmeg

Preheat your oven to 425°F (220°C, gas 7).

Beat your eggs just slightly, then add the sugar, salt, milk, and vanilla, and stir until your custard is nice and smooth. Stir in your coconut and pour into the unbaked pie shell. Sprinkle nutmeg over the top.

Bake your pie in the oven for 15 minutes; then lower the heat to 350°F (180°C, gas 4) and bake for 25 to 30 minutes or until a knife inserted into the edge of the custard comes out clean. Even if the center is wobbly, remove the pie from the oven when this stage is reached: it's done.

Put the pie on a wire rack and let it set for at least 30 minutes before cutting.

FRUIT COBBLER

SERVES 6

This marvelous and versatile recipe can be used for apple, peach, cherry, black-berry, blueberry, or any other combination fruit cobbler you care to invent. Cobblers are one of my specialties in view of the trouble I used to have with pie crusts. The dough is more like a soft American biscuit or a shortcake, lighter and flakier than an ordinary pie crust. Remember, when making cobblers, the center of the fruit filling should be piled higher than at the sides to support the dough topping and the edges must be sealed tightly.

3 cups peeled, pitted, or cored fruit –
  apples, peaches, cherries, etc. (1–1¼
  lb, 500–600 g, depending on fruit)
1 cup (8 oz, 250 g) sugar, or to taste (but
  much less for canned fruit in syrup)
2 tablespoons cornstarch (cornflour)
splash of fresh lemon juice

1 tablespoon butter
1 cup (4 oz, 120 g) sifted all-purpose flour
2 teaspoons baking powder
½ teaspoon salt
2 teaspoons vegetable shortening
½ cup (4 fl oz, 120 ml) milk

Thoroughly mix your fruit with the sugar and cornstarch and a splash of lemon juice. Heap this mixture into an 8 or 9 in (20/23 cm) diameter deep dish baking pan (or ovenproof casserole) and dot the top with butter.

Preheat your oven to 375°F (190°C, gas 5).

Make a soft biscuit dough by combining the flour, baking powder, and salt. Cut in the shortening with a fork till the mixture is crumbly, then stir in the milk. Roll out your dough on a lightly floured board, then spread it over the mound of fruit. Cut air vents in the top. Seal and flute the edges.

Bake your cobbler in the oven for about 35 minutes or until it is nicely browned. Serve warm with cream or on its lonesome.

Aunt Peacie's Old-Fashioned Crunchy Cobbler

SERVES 6

Now we're smoking with gas. We're burning, baby, 'cause I've got Aunt Peacie in her kitchen cooking *and* measuring as she goes along. Will wonders never cease? Her recipe is so unusual and original – she puts bits of pie crust right in with the fruit filling – that I know you're gonna love it. Every so often I get to dreaming of these cobblers. You see, Aunt Peacie will now cook and measure for me but she won't mail recipes to me.

6–7 medium-sized tart apples, peeled and cored
4 cups (1¾ pints, 1 l) water
2 cups plus 1 tablespoon (1 lb 0½ oz, 515 g) sugar
½ cup (4 oz, 250 g) butter
1 teaspoon ground mace
1½ teaspoons ground cinnamon

1 teaspoon apple pie seasoning (or ¼ teaspoon allspice and ⅛ teaspoon ground cloves)
1 teaspoon salt
2 cups (8 oz, 250 g) sifted all-purpose flour
½ cup (4 oz, 120 g) margarine
½ cup (4 fl oz, 120 ml) iced water

Cut your apples into thick slices. Place them in a saucepan over medium heat. Stir in the water, all the sugar except 1 tablespoon, the butter, mace, 1 teaspoon cinnamon, and the apple pie seasoning, and bring to a slow boil, then lower the heat and leave to simmer gently while you make the dough. Preheat your oven to 350°F (180°C, gas 4).

Mix the salt into the flour, cut in the margarine until crumbly, and stir in the water. When a dough forms, split it into two balls.

On a lightly floured surface, roll out one ball ⅛ in (3 mm) thick, then cut it into 8 strips. Drop the strips of dough into the simmering apple mixture and simmer for 15 minutes. Pour all this into a well buttered 3 quart (2½ UK quart, 3 l) casserole.

Roll out the remaining dough to fit the top of your casserole and lay it in place. Seal the edges and cut in air vents. Sprinkle with 1 tablespoon sugar mixed with ½ teaspoon cinnamon. Bake in the oven for 45 minutes to 1 hour, or until golden brown.

NOTE For blueberry, peach, or strawberry cobbler you'll need 2 to 3 cups (about 12–18 oz, 375–550 g) of fresh fruit. Go easy on the spices.

Butter-Pecan Prawleens

MAKES 30 TO 40 CANDIES

The name of these Louisiana specialties may be spelt pralines, but it should always be pronounced prawleens. In the South we have praline bars, praline ice cream, praline with almonds, and my favorites, these butter-pecan pralines. This is the closest I've come to duplicating a taste of some beauties I once had down on Bourbon Street in New Orleans. They are truly habit-forming — as a matter of fact I'll betcha you can't eat just one!

Be ready to work very quickly when the candy is ready.

1½ cups (12 oz, 375 g) light brown sugar
1 cup (8 fl oz, 250 ml) evaporated milk
½ cup (4 oz, 120 g) unsalted butter or margarine
2 cups (8 oz, 250 g) pecans, some chopped and some left whole to crunch down on

1½ cups (12 oz, 375 g) white sugar
½ cup (4 fl oz, 120 ml) heavy (double) cream
pinch of salt
2 tablespoons light corn syrup (or golden syrup)
1 tablespoon pure vanilla extract

Combine all the ingredients, except vanilla, in a heavy saucepan. Cook, stirring constantly with a wooden spoon, over medium heat. Keep scraping the sides and bottom of the pan to prevent sticking. Use a candy thermometer if you have one. The temperature must reach 250°F (122°C), which is known as the hard ball stage. If you don't have a thermometer, test by throwing a drop of the candy into ice water. It should form a hard ball. As soon as this point is reached, remove the pan from the heat and stir in your vanilla. Beat rapidly until the candy is very thick and has lost all of its glossy sheen.

Working very quickly, drop the mixture by the tablespoonful onto buttered baking sheets or buttered sheets of wax paper or foil. Let the candy mounds cool down completely before removing them from the buttered surface. When cool, store at room temperature, in airtight containers so that they don't become sticky.

NOTE You can make these candies smaller if you like. I prefer mine bite-size; then again, I like them any way I can get them.

BREAD PUDDING WITH WHISKEY SAUCE

SERVES 6

This is a nice change from plain old bread and butter pudding. I think that bourbon adds a sweeter tang and smoother taste to the sauce than ordinary whiskey does. Do be generous with the sauce.

4 cups (1¾ pints, 1 l) milk
12 thick slices of stale bread from a large loaf, cut into 1 in (2.5 cm) cubes
½ cup (4 oz, 120 g) butter or margarine
1¼ cups (10 oz, 300 g) sugar (¼ cup [2 oz, 60 g] of this should be fine [caster] sugar for meringue)
4 eggs, separated

¼ teaspoon salt
1 teaspoon pure vanilla extract
½ teaspoon ground cinnamon
¼ teaspoon ground nutmeg
1 cup (5½ oz, 160 g) raisins
1 large apple, peeled, cored, and sliced
Whiskey Sauce (see below)

Scald the milk in a large saucepan, remove from the heat, and stir in the bread cubes. Let it soak for 5 minutes.

Meanwhile preheat your oven to 350°F (180°C, gas 4). Cream the butter or margarine and 1 cup (8 oz, 250 g) sugar. Beat in your egg yolks, salt, vanilla, cinnamon, and nutmeg. Combine this mixture with the bread and milk. Generously butter a 3 quart (2½ UK quart, 3 l) casserole and fill with alternate layers of the bread mixture and the apples and raisins, ending with bread on top.

Place your casserole into a larger pan filled with boiling water to reach halfway up the casserole. Bake in the oven for 35 minutes or until a knife inserted in the center comes out clean. Watch the water level and add more boiling water if necessary – *don't let the water pan dry out.*

Meanwhile beat your egg whites with the remaining (fine) sugar until stiff but not dry. When the pudding is done, remove it from the oven and spread this meringue over the top. Lower the oven to 300°F (150°C, gas 2) and bake for 15 minutes or until the meringue is brown. Serve hot or cold, smothered with generous spoonfuls of Whiskey Sauce.

*W*HISKEY SAUCE

½ cup (4 oz, 120 g) butter
1 cup (8 oz, 250 g) sugar
1 egg, well beaten

¼ cup (2 fl oz, 60 ml) bourbon whiskey
1½ cups (12 fl oz, 375 ml) heavy (double) cream

Melt your butter with the sugar in a heavy saucepan, over low heat, stirring constantly until the sugar is dissolved. Add the egg and stir well. Take the pan from the heat and allow it to cool slightly. Then add the whiskey and cream. Pour into an electric blender and blend on high until the sauce is light and frothy (you can do this with a hand whisk but it's hard work). Refrigerate until ready to serve.

*A*UNT PEACIE'S PEACH ICE CREAM

SERVES 12

When I was little, Aunt Peacie and Uncle Thomas took me and the rest of their brood to visit Aunt Peacie's grandparents in Oxford, North Carolina. I'll never forget them because that was the first time, to the best of my recollection, that I'd ever met any sharecroppers. Their names were Naomi and Ed Wilson, and boy, did they work hard from sunup to sundown. While they plowed and sowed the land, they sang.

Our evening meal was always more of a feast than a supper. Aunt Peacie and her sister Frances, a teenybopper heavily into Fats Domino and long fingernails, would do all the cooking because their grandparents couldn't afford to get behind with their summer work. Together those two cooked up a storm: buttermilk biscuits, cracklin' cornbread, fried chicken, greens with salt pork, country ham, baked sweet potatoes, freshly churned butter, and the biggest treat of all, peach ice cream.

We'd happily do anything for peach ice cream. We'd pick the ripest fruit and we'd take turns crankin' that old churner. Aunt Peacie would fill it up with rock salt and ice and we'd sit outside, swatting flies and watching to see when the ice cream got firm so we could start to dip into it. To my mind, peach ice cream remains the ultimate summer dessert.

2 quarts ($1\frac{3}{4}$ UK quarts, 2 l) milk

4 large ($14\frac{1}{2}$ fl oz, 410 ml) cans evaporated milk (total almost $1\frac{1}{2}$ quarts, 1.65 l)

6 large eggs

pinch of salt

2 cups (1 lb, 500 g) sugar

2 tablespoons cornstarch (cornflour)

2–3 tablespoons pure vanilla extract

6 large ripe freestone peaches, peeled, pitted, and chopped

Heat the milk and evaporated milk in a large saucepan over medium heat. While it heats, use a rotary beater to beat in the eggs one at a time. Add the salt, sugar, and cornstarch. As soon as it reaches a simmer turn the heat right down and continue cooking, stirring constantly, until the mixture looks like a rich custard and clings to the spoon, about 15 minutes.

Let it cool slightly, then stir in the vanilla and peaches. Pour into an ice-cream machine and freeze according to the manufacturer's directions.

If you don't have an ice-cream machine, turn the temperature of your freezer as low as it will go and freeze the mixture in shallow metal pie pans. After 45 minutes to 1 hour, depending on the temperature, the mixture will have frozen to the consistency of thick slush. Tip it into a food processor and beat it quickly (or into a bowl and beat it hard with a fork), then return to the pans and the freezer. Repeat every 45 minutes until the ice cream has a good texture, 2 to 4 hours according to the temperature.

If the ice cream is stored in the freezer, transfer it to the refrigerator 1 hour before serving, so that it can soften a bit.

PHILADELPHIA ICE CREAM

SERVES 6

Now this is not strictly a soul food recipe, but since Philadelphia is my home town and my family has eaten its way through mounds of this, I always think of it as Northern soul food.

Philadelphia, of course, is famous as the home of American ice cream. A Frenchman called M. Pierre Bossu started the first ice-cream house in the country there in 1794, near Germantown Road. Alongside various ice creams, he served all kinds of syrups, French cordials, little cakes, and such. We were well ahead here. It was another fifty years before Jacob Fussel, a milk dealer in Baltimore, Maryland, began manufacturing ice cream as a way of using up his surplus cream, wholesaling it for 60¢ a quart.

Nearly a hundred years later we were still ahead. At the Semi-Centennial Exhibition held in Philadelphia during the summer of 1874, a local manufacturer called Robert M. Green demonstrated a new machine which added plain soda water to ice cream. He called it a soda fountain. And where would Lana Turner and millions of American teenagers be today without that?

I also like strawberry ice cream, so my recipe gives you the basic formula plus a strawberry option. After that you're on your own.

4 cups (1¾ pints, 1 l) light (single) cream
(or equal parts heavy and light cream
[or all whipping cream])
1 cup (8 oz, 250 g) sugar

⅛ teaspoon salt
1½ tablespoons pure vanilla extract (or
1 tablespoon vanilla extract and 1
teaspoon finely crushed vanilla beans)

In a medium saucepan over low heat, heat your cream to just lukewarm. *Do not let it boil!* Stir in the sugar, salt and vanilla until the sugar dissolves completely. Let it cool slightly, then freeze in your ice-cream maker according to the manufacturer's directions (or see the previous recipe).

VARIATION Combine 2½ cups (1¼ lb, 600 g) crushed strawberries with ¾ to 1 cup (6–8 oz, 175–250 g) sugar and let them stand at room temperature for at least 1 hour. Stir into your ice cream mixture just before you're about to freeze it. The strawberries will add another 2 or 3 servings of ice cream to the total.

APPLE BROWN BETTY
SERVES 6

I used to eat this everyday after school at a restaurant called Linton's, at Germantown and Chelton Avenues, where all the teenagers used to congregate. We would pool our money and order whatever our allowances would allow. My Mom, getting a little sick and tired of my coming home late, suggested that I make my own Apple Brown Betty. So I've had a lotta practice with this dish.

2 cups (8 oz, 250 g) soft breadcrumbs
¼ teaspoon salt
¼ cup (2 oz, 60 g) melted butter or
margarine
4 cups tart sliced apples (4 medium
apples)

¾ cup (5 oz, 150 g) light brown sugar
1 teaspoon ground cinnamon
2 tablespoons fresh lemon juice
grated rind of 1 lemon
¼ cup (2 fl oz, 60 ml) water at room
temperature

Preheat your oven to 350°F (180°C, gas 4).

Mix the breadcrumbs with the salt and melted butter or margarine, and divide the mixture into three. Place one-third in a greased 1½ quart (1¼ UK quart, 1.5 l) baking dish.

Sprinkle your apples with sugar, cinnamon, lemon juice, and grated rind, and toss to blend. Place one-half of this mixture on top of the crumbs in the baking dish. Add another one-third of the crumbs, then the remaining apples, and a final layer of crumbs. Trickle the water into the side of the dish so as not to moisten the top layer of crumbs.

Cover and bake in the oven for 30 minutes. Remove the cover and continue to bake until the apples are tender and the crumbs a delicious brown, perhaps another 20 or 30 minutes. Serve warm with cream or custard. Sometimes I top mine with a vanilla sauce.

CHERRY FRITTERS

MAKES ABOUT 30 FRITTERS

A fritter – a tiny critter made with a pancake-type batter – can contain almost any kind of fruit. The two important things are a batter which adheres well to fruit, and sufficiently ripe but not mushy fruit. So, whether you're using peaches, apples, apricots, bananas, or cherries, catch 'em before they go over their peak. Fry up a batch of these and you'll soon see them disappear.

2 large eggs, separated
$\frac{2}{3}$ cup ($5\frac{1}{2}$ fl oz, 160 ml) milk or cherry juice
1 tablespoon melted butter
1 cup (4 oz, 120 g) sifted all-purpose flour
1 tablespoon white sugar
$\frac{1}{2}$ teaspoon ground cinnamon

pinch of salt
1 cup (7 oz, 200 g) pitted, cooked, and drained cherries
$\frac{1}{4}$ cup ($1\frac{1}{2}$ oz, 45 g) confectioner's (icing) sugar
3–4 cups ($1\frac{1}{4}$–$1\frac{3}{4}$ pints, 750 ml–1 l) vegetable oil

In a medium-sized bowl, beat your egg yolks until foamy. Then beat in the milk or fruit juice along with the melted butter.

Sift together your flour, sugar, cinnamon, and salt. Add it to the egg mixture and stir with a wooden spoon until well blended. Cover and refrigerate for at least 2 hours, or overnight if you're so inclined.

Stir the batter to remix the ingredients. Beat the egg whites until soft peaks begin to hold their shape. Gently fold them into the batter.

Sprinkle the drained cherries with 1 tablespoon confectioner's sugar. Toss to coat, then stir them into the batter.

Heat your oil in a large skillet or deep-fat fryer. When the oil is hot but not smoking – 380°F (193°C) on a cooking thermometer – spoon in the fritter batter with a tablespoon, with one or two cherries in each spoonful. Fry for 4 or 5 minutes, or until golden brown. As the fritters brown, remove them with a slotted spoon and drain on paper towels.

Dust your fritters with confectioner's sugar and serve warm.

CAKES AND COOKIES

I am a firm believer in scratch cakes — that is, cakes made from scratch without the use of any box mixes. Nothing can duplicate the texture and downright richness of a cake made with fresh ingredients. In the old days we used to call them three-hundred-strokers because that used to be the general rule for beating the batter smooth, but today's mixers and food processors do the hard work.

A few practical tips. All ingredients should be at room temperature before mixing. I use cake flour because I believe it gives a lighter texture. If you prefer, use all-purpose flour and decrease the quantity called for in the recipe by 2 tablespoons per cup (decreasing the weight by one-eighth). Conversely, if a recipe calls for all-purpose flour and you'd prefer to use cake flour, then add 2 tablespoons to each cupful. (In Britain, where special cake flour isn't available everywhere, you can either use this method or lighten British plain flour by replacing up to one-fourth of it with powdered potato starch, which is sometimes sold under its French name of *fécule de pommes de terre*.)

Some recipes really need the flavor of butter and no substitutions should be made. Where I have simply listed shortening, then use whatever you desire: butter, margarine, or white vegetable shortening. My own choice is butter for cakes, but half butter and half vegetable shortening gives the flavor I prefer for some kinds of cookie. The butter gives them flavor, while the shortening gives lightness or crispness.

For baking I use shiny metal pans because they reflect the heat away from the cake. Glass ones will do, but if using glass, reduce the baking temperature by 25°F (roughly 15°C, or one gas mark). As a broad guideline, two standard 8 in (20 cm) round pans are needed for a two-layer cake made with 2 cups (8 oz, 250 g) flour, and two standard 9 in (23 cm) pans for a cake made with $2\frac{1}{2}$ to 3 cups (10–12 oz, 300–375 g) flour. Never fill the pans more than one-half full. A great old-fashioned way of lightly dusting a greased cake pan is to dip a clean powder puff in flour and dust away. Some of the recipes here are for tube cakes, which should be made in a special tube pan (see the note on page 27).

BROWN SUGA' POUND CAKE

MAKES A 10 IN (25 CM) TUBE CAKE

There was a time and not so long ago, when you could be sure that if a good-lookin' man walked down the street, at least one girl could be relied upon to remark, 'Umph, umph, umph, he ain't nothin' but suga'!' Brown sugar, to be precise. Well, I feel that same way about this big bad cake. It ain't nothin' but suga' – brown, rich, sweet, and so élite.

The only ways to eat pound cake of any description are to serve it topped with a large scoop of home-made vanilla ice cream, or with sliced fresh fruits like strawberries, peaches, or blueberries, with heavy cream.

$1\frac{1}{2}$ cups (12 oz, 375 g) butter
2 cups (14 oz, 430 g) light brown sugar
1 cup (8 oz, 250 g) white sugar
5 large eggs
3 cups (12 oz, 375 g) sifted all-purpose
    flour
$\frac{1}{2}$ teaspoon baking powder

$\frac{1}{4}$ teaspoon salt
1 cup (8 fl oz, 250 ml) milk at room
    temperature
1 cup (4 oz, 120 g) chopped walnuts or
    pecans (optional)
1 teaspoon pure vanilla extract

Preheat your oven to 325°F (160°C, gas 3).

Cream your butter until light and fluffy. Slowly add in the brown sugar and beat until well combined. Add the white sugar and keep beating until it becomes as light as butter and sugar could ever possibly be. Now beat in your eggs, one at a time, blending each one thoroughly into the batter.

Sift together your flour, baking powder, and salt. Resift, then beat some of it into your creamed mixture, followed by some milk. Add flour and milk in turn until all are used up, ending with flour. You don't need to break your arm beating this cake, just beat enough to blend after each addition. Finally stir in the nuts and vanilla – no more beating.

Grease and flour a 10 in (25 cm) tube pan – but grease and flour it really well. Pour in your batter and bake in the oven for 45 minutes to 1 hour, or until the sides leave the pan and the top springs back when depressed by two tired fingers.

Let your cake cool down in its pan for 10 minutes or so, then invert the pan onto a wire rack. Turn the cake out and finish cooling.

BLACK WALNUT CAKE

MAKES AN 8 IN (20 CM) 2 LAYER CAKE

$\frac{1}{2}$ cup (4 oz, 120 g) butter
$1\frac{1}{2}$ cups (12 oz, 375 g) dark brown sugar
3 large eggs
2 cups (8 oz, 250 g) sifted cake flour
2 teaspoons baking powder
$\frac{1}{2}$ teaspoon salt
1 teaspoon baking soda

1 cup (8 fl oz, 250 ml) sour milk (see page
    25)
2 teaspoons pure vanilla extract
$\frac{3}{4}$ cup (3 oz, 90 g) coarsely chopped black
    (or English) walnuts
Penuche Frosting (see below)

Preheat your oven to 350°F (180°C, gas 4).

Cream the butter and sugar together until light and fluffy. Add in your eggs and beat well. Sift together the flour, baking powder, and salt and add to the creamed mixture, then dissolve the baking soda in the sour milk and add that. Stir in the vanilla and nuts, and blend well.

Generously grease and flour two 8 in (20 cm) cake pans. Pour equal amounts of batter into each pan and bake in the oven for 30 to 35 minutes, or until a toothpick inserted in the center comes out clean. Allow the layers to cool in their pans for 10 minutes before turning out onto a wire rack to finish cooling.

When cool, cover the top of one layer with Penuche Frosting. Put the other layer on top and coat the entire cake with the rest of the frosting.

PENUCHE FROSTING

$\frac{1}{2}$ cup (4 oz, 120 g) butter

1 tightly packed cup (8 oz, 250 g) dark brown sugar

$\frac{1}{8}$ teaspoon salt

2 tablespoons light corn syrup (or golden syrup)

$\frac{1}{4}$ cup (2 fl oz, 120 ml) milk

2 teaspoons pure vanilla extract

2 cups (9$\frac{1}{2}$ oz, 290 g) confectioner's (icing) sugar

$\frac{1}{4}$ cup (2 fl oz, 60 ml) light (single) cream

In a small saucepan, melt your butter over a very low heat. Slowly stir in the brown sugar, salt, milk, and corn syrup. Raise the heat and bring to a boil, then lower the heat and simmer for 2 minutes. Remove from the heat and let it cool, then stir in the vanilla, confectioner's sugar, and cream and beat until the frosting is thick enough to spread.

ANN CHAMBERS'S STRAWBERRY SHORTCAKE

SERVES 8

Ann Chambers is not really an aunt of mine, but she is the kind of aunt every kid wants to have. To know her is to love her. She is a gifted painter, writer, and cartoonist and makes all of her furniture, clothing, and even some of her own shoes. As you'll see from this, she's also a very creative cook.

1 quart (1$\frac{1}{2}$ lb, 750 g) fresh strawberries

$\frac{1}{4}$ cup (2 oz, 60 g) sugar, or to taste

2 tablespoons water

2 cups (8 oz, 250 g) sifted all-purpose flour

4 teaspoons baking powder

$\frac{1}{2}$ teaspoon salt

2 tablespoons shortening

$\frac{3}{4}$ cup (6 fl oz, 175 ml) milk

about 1 quart (1$\frac{3}{4}$ UK pints, 1 l) peanut oil

Wash, stem, and slice your strawberries. Place them in a bowl and sprinkle with the sugar and water. Cover and refrigerate for at least 1 hour to allow a syrup to develop.

Sift the dry ingredients together and, using your fingertips, work in the shortening until the mixture has an even, grainy consistency. Gradually add the milk, working it into a soft dough. Knead for 3 minutes or until your dough becomes springy. Pinch the dough into walnut-sized balls; then flatten the balls into circles or ovals about $\frac{1}{4}$ in (6 mm) thick with a rolling pin.

Heat about 1 in (2.5 cm) depth of peanut oil in a heavy skillet over medium heat until it is extremely hot but not yet smoking – 390°F (199°C) if you have a cooking thermometer. Drop the circles of dough into the hot oil, using a spatula. Lower the heat and cook the circles on both sides until golden brown, about 5 minutes per side. Lift them out and leave to cool and drain on paper towels.

Cut the circles in half and arrange them on a large serving plate with strawberries between and on top of each half. Top with whipped cream or ice cream. Serve immediately, then sit back, cross your hands, pat your stomach, and smile.

OLD-FASHIONED PINEAPPLE
UPSIDE-DOWN CAKE

MAKES A 10 IN (25 CM) TUBE CAKE

This recipe comes courtesy of Mrs Geri Stowers, a kissin' cousin from Orange, New Jersey. When I tasted Geri's cake, I immediately threw away my Dad's recipe and used hers. This is soul food at its fine-fine-finest, 'cause Geri stepped all in her cake. Guess my Dad only tiptoed in his!

1 small (8 oz, 227 g) can pineapple slices in syrup
2 cups plus 4 tablespoons (1 lb 2 oz, 560 g) butter
2 cups (14 oz, 430 g) brown sugar
4 fresh cherries, halved and pitted
2 cups (9½ oz, 290 g) confectioner's (icing) sugar

6 large eggs
1 teaspoon pure vanilla extract
½ teaspoon pure almond extract
2 cups (8 oz, 250 g) sifted all-purpose flour

Preheat your oven to 325°F (160°C, gas 3).

Drain the pineapple and reserve the syrup.

Melt 4 tablespoons butter in a saucepan over low heat and pour it into the bottom of a 10 in (25 cm) tube pan. Drop the brown sugar and 1 tablespoon pineapple syrup into the melted butter and stir until dissolved.

Cut your pineapple slices in half and arrange them attractively on the bottom of the cake pan. Place a cherry half in the center of each half pineapple slice. Beat the remaining butter and confectioner's sugar until light and fluffy. Beat in the eggs one at a time. Add the vanilla and almond extract.

Resift your flour and gradually add it to the creamed mixture. When it's well blended, spread this batter over the pineapple and sugar mixture in the cake pan.

Bake in the oven for 1 hour and 20 minutes, or until a wooden toothpick inserted into the center comes out clean. Let your cake cool for 10 minutes, then invert it onto a serving platter and turn it out.

CLARISSA'S ZUCCHINI BREAD

MAKES A 10 IN (25 CM) TUBE CAKE

An unusual offering from soulful Cousin Clarissa. This bread is quite delicious, with the light consistency of American coffee cake. The nuts, vanilla, and cinnamon combine with the grated zucchini to give a moist texture and most original flavor. Cousin Clarissa says it's best to use the smaller zucchini since the larger ones give a bitter taste. (British readers: note that zucchini are small courgettes, so you really do have to find little ones.)

3 large eggs
1 cup (8 fl oz, 250 ml) light salad oil
3 teaspoons pure vanilla extract
2 cups (10 oz, 300 g) peeled and grated
   zucchini
1 cup (4 oz, 120 g) chopped walnuts or
   pecans (I prefer walnuts)

$1\frac{1}{2}$ cups (6 oz, 175 g) sifted all-purpose
   flour
1 cup ($4\frac{1}{2}$ oz, 130 g) wholewheat flour
1 teaspoon baking powder
$\frac{1}{2}$ teaspoon baking soda
2 cups (1 lb, 500 g) sugar
3 teaspoons ground cinnamon

Preheat your oven to 325°F (160°C, gas 3).

Beat your eggs until light and foamy. Add in the oil and vanilla, and blend well. Now stir in the zucchini and nuts.

Blend the flours with other dry ingredients and slowly stir into the batter. *Do not beat!* When well blended, pour into a generously greased and floured 10 in (25 cm) tube pan. Bake in the oven for 1 hour and 15 minutes, or until a toothpick inserted in the center comes out clean. Turn your bread out onto a wire cake rack to cool.

RED DEVIL'S FOOD CAKE

MAKES A 9 IN (23 CM) 2 LAYER CAKE

This cake is simply awesome! It looks amazing and the taste comes straight from heaven. You only need 3 oz (90 g) chocolate each for the cake and frosting, but inevitably some gets left in the pan, and chocaholics like me know what happens to that.

$2\frac{1}{2}$ cups (10 oz, 300 g) sifted cake flour
$\frac{1}{2}$ teaspoon salt
$1\frac{1}{4}$ teaspoons baking soda
1 cup (8 oz, 250 g) butter, softened
1 cup (8 oz, 250 g) white sugar
$\frac{1}{2}$ cup ($3\frac{1}{2}$ oz, 100 g) dark brown sugar
4 large eggs
$3\frac{1}{2}$ oz (100 g) unsweetened chocolate,
   melted and slightly cooled

1 cup (8 fl oz, 250 ml) buttermilk, at room
   temperature (or $1\frac{1}{4}$ cups [10 fl oz,
   300 ml] sour cream and reduce butter
   to $\frac{2}{3}$ cup [$5\frac{1}{2}$ oz, 160 g])
2 teaspoons pure vanilla extract
$\frac{1}{2}$ teaspoon red food coloring (optional)
Chocolate Frosting (see below)

Preheat your oven to 350°F (180°C, gas 4).

Sift your flour, salt and baking soda together three times. Set aside.

Great-Uncle Mack and Great-Aunt Fannie (Dad's uncle and aunt), brother and sister but as different as the day is long. They were born in Charlotte, North Carolina, but it didn't hold them for long. He moved to Bessemer, Alabama, and became one of those smart talkin', easy-goin', drinkin'-type preachers, while she moved up to Brooklyn, New York, for the fast life, where she became one mighty hot ticket. She was a bootlegger, operated a juke joint, and lived the life of a notorious woman until she died at the age of seventy-two, scandalously wealthy and surrounded by her feather boas and all those cats.

Cream the butter and both sugars together until light and fluffy. Beat in your eggs one at a time, taking particular care to beat really well between additions. Now stir in your melted chocolate. Beat in one-third of the dry ingredients, followed by one-half of the buttermilk. Repeat until both are used up, ending with dry ingredients. Your cake should be well and truly beaten by now. Stir in the vanilla and food coloring (if used).

Generously grease and flour two 9 in (23 cm) cake pans. Pour equal amounts of batter into each pan and bake in the oven for 35 to 40 minutes, or until a wooden toothpick inserted into the center of the cakes come out clean and the edges are coming away from the sides of the pans. Turn the cakes out immediately onto a wire rack and leave to cool completely.

When cool, coat the bottom layer with Chocolate Frosting. Put on the other layer and generously coat the entire cake with frosting.

CHOCOLATE FROSTING

3½ oz (100 g) unsweetened chocolate
3 tablespoons butter or margarine
2 cups (9½ oz, 290 g) confectioner's (icing) sugar

¼ cup (2 fl oz, 60 ml) milk
2 tablespoons light (single) cream
¼ teaspoon salt
1 teaspoon pure vanilla extract

Combine your chocolate and butter in a saucepan over very low heat. When the chocolate is melted, remove from the heat and stir in the sugar, milk, and cream, a little at a time and in turn. Add the salt and vanilla and beat until smooth.

Let your frosting cool before coating the cake. If you're in a hurry, plunge the pan into a sink full of ice cubes and cold water and continue to beat until cool.

PEANUT BUTTER COOKIES

MAKES ABOUT 2½ DOZEN COOKIES

This recipe is compliments of my two little crumb-crushers. They decided over several Saturday mornings which taste they preferred, and here it is. I've already got them on their way to cooking with a soul cook's instinct.

½ cup (4 oz, 120 g) butter, softened
½ cup (4 oz, 120 g) chunky peanut butter
½ cup (4 oz, 120 g) sugar
½ cup (3½ oz, 100 g) dark brown sugar
1 large egg, well beaten
½ teaspoon pure vanilla extract

1¼ cups (5 oz, 150 g) sifted all-purpose flour
½ teaspoon baking powder
¾ teaspoon baking soda
½ teaspoon salt

Cream the butter and peanut butter together. Beat in the sugars, then stir in the beaten egg and vanilla. Sift together the flour, baking powder, baking soda, and salt and add to the creamed mixture. Mix thoroughly.

Separate your dough into balls the size of large marbles. Place these on an ungreased baking sheet 2 to 3 in (5–8 cm) apart. Using a floured fork, press down on each cookie, making a criss-cross pattern and flattening each cookie to about 2 in (5 cm) diameter. Bake in the oven for 8 to 12 minutes or until light brown. Remove your cookies from the baking sheet as soon as they are set, and cool on wire racks.

DOWN-HOME FRUITCAKE

MAKES ABOUT 14 LB (7 KG)

No Christmas holiday would be complete without a couple of dark rich fruitcakes on hand. Our family bake-up ritual goes something like this. We make the fruitcakes sometime in March when the weather breaks and the mood comes on for some serious cooking. After baking, each one is wrapped in a brandy-soaked cheesecloth, covered tightly with aluminum foil, placed in rustproof lidded cake tins, and stored in a cool dry place for the ageing process to begin.

Every three months the cakes are unwrapped and a few good spoonfuls of brandy, rum, or red wine get poured on each one before resealing. By Christmas, the cakes are richly flavored and downright lethal! Since they are much too rich to gobble up in the holiday season, they usually last almost up until the next March. Now that's my idea of good timing!

Don't worry if you don't have very large baking pans. You can distribute the batter any way you like, according to the size of your pans.

3 lb (1.5 kg) seedless raisins, half of them roughly chopped

1 lb (500 g) sliced candied cherries

$\frac{1}{2}$ lb (250 g) chopped candied orange peel

1 cup (7 oz, 200 g) diced candied pineapple

$1\frac{1}{2}$ lb (750 g) chopped candied citron

1 lb (500 g) currants

1 lb (500 g) almond halves, blanched and toasted

1 lb (500 g) hazelnuts (or pecans), halved

1 cup (8 fl oz, 250 ml) dark Jamaican rum, or equal parts brandy and red wine (optional)

1 lb (500 g) sifted all-purpose flour

1 lb (500 g) butter or margarine

1 lb (500 g) brown sugar

12 large eggs, separated

1 teaspoon baking soda

$\frac{1}{2}$ cup (4 fl oz, 120 ml) fresh lemon juice

$\frac{1}{2}$ cup (4 fl oz, 120 ml) fresh orange juice

1 tablespoon ground cinnamon

1 tablespoon ground cloves

1 teaspoon ground nutmeg

1 teaspoon ground allspice

1 teaspoon ground mace

Start by preparing all of your fruits and nuts. As you finish each ingredient, just throw it into a clean bowl big enough to hold everything. When all are in, add half of the flour and toss until completely mixed and evenly coated. Pour on the rum, or brandy and wine, and set it aside for at least 1 hour.

Meanwhile butter your fruit cake pans thoroughly. Cut pieces of wax (or parchment) paper to line the pans, making sure you fit the corners properly; otherwise the cakes will bake unevenly. Butter the paper too, then set the pans aside.

Cream your butter with the sugar until light and fluffy. Add the egg yolks, yes siree bob, one at a time, beating thoroughly after each addition.

Sift together the remaining flour, baking soda, and spices. Stir this into the creamed mixture a bit at a time, alternating with the fruit juices. When this is well blended, pour it into the soaking fruit mixture and mix well.

Preheat your oven to 250°F (120°C, gas $\frac{1}{2}$).

If you're doing this all by hand, yes, your arms should be about to drop off by now. But you know what's left, don't you? That's right, the beating of the egg whites. Beat them until stiff but not dry, then fold them into the batter.

Fill each cake pan no more than three-fourths full. Bake in the oven for 4 hours. During the last hour of baking, you may want to cover the cakes with aluminum foil to prevent them from getting too brown. When a toothpick inserted in the center comes out clean, the cakes are done.

Allow your cakes to cool in their pans for at least 1 hour. Then remove them from pans and discard the wax paper. Let them go completely cold before wrapping and storing.

THREE-LAYER SOUR CREAM CAKE

MAKES AN 8 IN (20 CM) 3 LAYER CAKE

This is one big bad mammy jammy. It has the texture of old-fashioned pound cake with just a hint of lemon, and when you top it off with Chocolate Cream Cheese Frosting, you'll be delighted. Thank you, Aunt Peacie, for another wonderful concoction.

1 cup (8 oz, 250 g) butter, softened
2 cups (1 lb, 500 g) sugar
3 large eggs
2¼ cups (9 oz, 275 g) sifted cake flour
¼ teaspoon salt
½ teaspoon baking soda

1 cup (8 fl oz, 250 ml) sour cream
½ teaspoon pure vanilla extract
½ teaspoon pure lemon extract
Chocolate Cream Cheese Frosting (see
  below)

Preheat your oven to 350°F (180°C, gas 4).

Cream your butter and sugar together until light and fluffy. Beat in your eggs, one at a time, until well blended.

Sift together the flour, salt, and baking soda, then gradually stir it into your creamed mixture. Pour in your sour cream, a little at a time, beating all the while. Stir in your flavorings.

Grease and flour three 8 in (20 cm) cake pans. Pour equal amounts of batter into each pan and bake in the oven for 30 minutes, or until the cakes spring back when depressed by your fingers. Turn them out onto a wire cake rack.

Cool completely, then ice with Chocolate Cream Cheese Frosting. Coat the tops of two of the layers. Place one on top of the other, then top with the final layer. Coat the entire cake with the remaining frosting.

CHOCOLATE CREAM CHEESE FROSTING

8 oz (250 g) semisweet chocolate
1 tablespoon butter
3 cups (14 oz, 430 g) confectioner's
  (icing) sugar

1 cup (8 fl oz, 150 ml) evaporated milk
  or light (single) cream
1 teaspoon pure vanilla extract
1 cup (8 oz, 250 g) cream cheese, softened

Melt the chocolate and butter over low heat, stirring constantly. Stir in the confectioner's sugar and cream. Remove the saucepan from the heat and add the vanilla. Using an electric mixer, beat in your cream cheese until very smooth. Let it cool slightly before using.

BLUE COCONUT CAKE

MAKES AN 8 IN (20 CM) 3 LAYER CAKE

After much practice, this cake has become a real humdinger. It's the kind that makes everyone keep coming back for 'just another little sliver.' I always tint my fresh coconut a delectable sky blue, and that color atop the snow-white marshmallowy Seven-Minute Frosting gives a magnificent effect. I won't pretend it's not a lot of work, but the end result is well worth the effort. I also prefer baking each of the layers individually to guarantee that the heat is evenly distributed. It makes for a longer ordeal, but it never fails me.

1 ripe coconut
3 cups (12 oz, 375 g) sifted cake flour
$\frac{1}{2}$ teaspoon salt
3 teaspoons baking powder
3 large eggs, separated
1$\frac{3}{4}$ cups (14 oz, 430 g) sugar
1 cup (8 oz, 250 g) butter, softened
$\frac{1}{4}$ cup (2 fl oz, 60 ml) milk

$\frac{3}{4}$ cup (6 fl oz, 175 g) coconut milk (see note below)
2 teaspoons pure vanilla extract
few drops of blue food coloring
1 cup (8$\frac{1}{2}$ oz, 260 g) pineapple or lemon-lime marmalade
Seven-Minute Frosting (see below)

Hammer or drill a hole into the eye of the coconut. Drain off the fluid and discard it – it isn't coconut milk, and it's tasteless. Keep hammering to break the coconut into pieces. If you get frustrated, throwing it down hard on the outside pavement works too. After getting the beast open, peel the brown skin from the white meat. Finely grate the white meat, reserving $\frac{1}{4}$ cup (1$\frac{1}{2}$ oz, 45 g) for the cake batter and the rest for the topping.

Preheat your oven to 350°F (180°C, gas 4).

Sift your cake flour, salt, and baking powder together twice and set aside.

Beat the egg whites until stiff. Stir $\frac{1}{4}$ cup (2 oz, 60 g) sugar into the egg whites and set aside.

Cream your butter while slowly adding the remaining sugar. Throw in the egg yolks and continue to beat until smooth. (I prefer to use a wooden spoon to cream my cakes so that I can be sure that the sugar doesn't remain grainy.)

Combine the milk and coconut milk. Alternately blend some of the flour and some of the milks into your creamed mixture, beginning and ending with flour. Beat until really smooth – no lumps please! Now gently fold $\frac{1}{4}$ cup (1$\frac{1}{2}$ oz, 45 g) grated coconut and the vanilla into the batter. Lastly, fold the stiffly beaten egg whites into batter by hand. Do not beat!

Divide your cake batter evenly into 3 generously greased and floured 8 in (20 cm) cake pans. Bake in the oven for 30 minutes or until a wooden toothpick comes out clean when inserted into the center of the cakes. Turn them out onto a wire rack and leave to cool completely while you color the coconut and make the Seven Minute Frosting.

Put your grated coconut in a plastic bag and add a few drops of blue food coloring. Shake the bag until the coconut is tinted pale blue. This also gives an uneven color which I think is very effective. Remember, you can always add color but you can't take it away. So do be careful when adding the food coloring – just add a drop or two at a time is my advice!

Generously cover the top of each of two layers with marmalade. Lay one on top of the other and then add the third layer. Coat the entire cake with Seven-Minute Frosting. (A word to the wise: be certain that the frosting is really stiff and the cake is completely cool, otherwise the icing will run down the sides of the plate. I know, I've done it! It would be such a shame to get this far and then to mess it up.) After frosting the cake, sprinkle or throw on the blue coconut. Be sure to cover the top and sides thickly and lavishly. See the glorious result on pages 178–9.

SEVEN-MINUTE FROSTING

I don't know for the life of me why Betty Crocker and everyone else insist upon calling this Seven-Minute Frosting, because it has never taken me just 7 minutes to cook it. In my humble kitchen it takes me about 15 minutes to get it to thicken up properly. However, who am I to argue with the experts? Maybe I'm just slow, huh?

2 large egg whites
1½ cups (7 oz, 200 g) confectioner's (icing) sugar
¼ teaspoon salt
⅓ cup (2½ fl oz, 75 ml) cold water

¼ teaspoon cream of tartar (or 1 tablespoon light corn syrup [or golden syrup])
2 teaspoons pure vanilla extract

Put all of your ingredients except the vanilla into the top half of a double boiler over rapidly boiling water, taking care that the water does not touch the bottom of the upper pan or the frosting will stick.

Beat ferociously, as though a demon has taken possession of you, for 7 minutes or until the frosting begins to make stiff peaks. Remove from the heat and stir in vanilla. Continue beating off the heat until your frosting is very thick and spreadable.

NOTE As I've said, the liquid inside a ripe coconut is not coconut milk – a lotta folks don't know that. Canned coconut milk is available in specialty food shops. If you can't find it, place ¾ cup (2½ oz, 75 g) sweetened shredded (desiccated or creamed) coconut in ¾ cup (6 fl oz, 175 ml) scalded milk. Leave it for about 20 minutes and then strain through cheesecloth.

You can also shred the white meat of a fresh coconut and bring it to a boil with ½ cup (4 fl oz, 120 ml) milk. Remove it from the heat and leave for 30 minutes, then strain it through cheesecloth or by wringing through a kitchen towel. For this recipe you will need two fresh coconuts, as an average coconut will yield just about ¾ cup (6 fl oz, 175 ml) of coconut milk.

COUSIN BEVERLY'S CHOCOLATE CHIP COOKIES

MAKES 3–4 DOZEN COOKIES

Cousin Beverly is one mean cook. And, I might add, it is just as hard getting a recipe out of her as it is from Aunt Peacie. My sister Linda had to telephone her three times to get all of the details and ingredients straight for this recipe. It must have been tough work 'cause Linda wrote, 'Boy, these people aren't accustomed to giving up their recipes. This is harder than going to the dentist!'

⅓ cup (2½ oz, 75 g) butter, softened
⅓ cup (2½ oz, 75 g) shortening (I use a
   solid vegetable one)
½ cup (4 oz, 120 g) sugar
½ cup (3½ oz, 100 g) light brown sugar
1 large egg, well beaten
1 teaspoon pure vanilla extract
1½ cups (6 oz, 175 g) sifted all-purpose
   flour

½ teaspoon salt
½ teaspoon baking soda
1 cup (6 oz, 175 g) semisweet chocolate
   bits
½ cup (2 oz, 60 g) chopped walnuts
   (Beverly doesn't use them, but I do)

Preheat your oven to 375°F (190°C, gas 5).

Cream the butter and shortening with the sugars. Add in your beaten egg and beat until nice and fluffy. Stir in the vanilla extract.

Sift together your flour, salt, and baking soda, then slowly add this to the creamed mixture. Stir in the chocolate bits. If your batter seems too firm, stir in 1 tablespoon milk. But if it is too firm you didn't sift the flour before measuring, there's just too much flour in the batter. Start again!

Drop by the tablespoonful onto an ungreased cookie sheet and bake in the oven for 8 to 10 minutes or until light brown.

*S*PICE SHEET CAKE

MAKES AN 8 × 12 IN (20 × 30 CM) CAKE

In my mind, sheet cakes go with social gatherings like church suppers − which inevitably last all day long down South − baby or bridal showers, or children's theme parties. But they're also fine any old time, especially when you wanna begin Monday with something sweet to pick on all week long.

1 cup (8 oz, 250 g) butter or margarine,
   softened
1 cup (8 oz, 250 g) white sugar
1 generous cup (8 oz, 250 g) dark brown
   sugar
4 large eggs
3 cups (12 oz, 375 g) sifted all-purpose
   flour
2 teaspoons baking soda
1 teaspoon salt

4 teaspoons powdered cocoa
2 teaspoons ground cinnamon
pinch of cayenne pepper
¼ teaspoon ground cloves
1 teaspoon ground allspice
¼ teaspoon ground nutmeg
2 cups (16 fl oz, 500 ml) buttermilk or
   sour milk (see page 23)
Brown Sugar Frosting (see below)

Preheat your oven to 350°F (180°C, gas 4).

Cream your butter or margarine until light, then gradually add the sugars and continue to beat until light and fluffy. Add your eggs, one at a time, and beat really thoroughly. Sift together your dry ingredients and spices and add to the creamed mixture. Add in buttermilk and beat just to blend − do not over-beat.

Pour your batter into a generously greased and floured 8 × 12 in (20 × 30 cm) sheet pan. Bake in the oven for 45 to 50 minutes, or until a toothpick inserted in the center comes out clean.

Allow your cake to cool in the pan for 5 minutes before turning it out onto a wire rack to finish cooling. Try to keep from picking at it. Then cover it with Brown Sugar Frosting.

BROWN SUGAR FROSTING

6 tablespoons butter or margarine
$\frac{1}{2}$ cup ($3\frac{1}{2}$ oz, 100 g) light brown sugar
$\frac{1}{4}$ cup (2 fl oz, 60 ml) milk
$1\frac{1}{2}$ cups (7 oz, 200 g) confectioner's sugar

$\frac{1}{4}$ teaspoon salt
1 teaspoon pure vanilla extract
2 tablespoons light (single) cream

Slowly melt the butter in a small saucepan over low heat, then stir in your brown sugar and milk. Raise the heat and bring it to a rapid boil. Cook for 3 minutes. Remove the saucepan from the heat and beat in your confectioner's sugar, salt, vanilla, and cream. Continue beating until your icing is thick and cool enough to spread, then — go for it in a big way!

CARROT CAKE
MAKES A 10 IN (25 CM) TUBE CAKE

This cake is so moist that you don't really need a frosting, but it can only be enhanced by coating it with cream cheese.

3 large eggs, separated
1 cup (8 fl oz, 250 ml) vegetable oil
$1\frac{1}{2}$ cups (12 oz, 375 g) sugar
1 teaspoon pure vanilla extract
2 tablespoons boiling water
$1\frac{1}{2}$ cups (6 oz, 175 g) sifted all-purpose flour
$\frac{3}{4}$ teaspoon salt
2 teaspoons ground cinnamon

$\frac{1}{2}$ teaspoon ground nutmeg
$1\frac{1}{4}$ teaspoons baking soda
1 cup (4 oz, 120 g) chopped pecans (or walnuts)
$1\frac{1}{2}$ cups (8 oz, 250 g) finely grated raw carrots
Cream Cheese Frosting (optional — see below)

Preheat your oven to 375°F (190°C, gas 5).

Combine your egg yolks, oil, sugar, vanilla, and boiling water in a large bowl and beat until well blended.

Sift together the flour, salt, cinnamon, nutmeg, and baking soda, then blend it into the eggs. Throw in your nuts and carrots and blend. Beat your egg whites until they can make stiff peaks, then fold them in as well.

Pour your batter into a generously greased and floured 10 in (25 cm) tube pan. Bake in the oven for 50 minutes to 1 hour, or until the cake springs back when you press your fingers into it.

Run a blunt knife around the inside edges of the pan to loosen the cake, but don't remove it for 15 minutes. Then turn it out onto a wire cake rack to cool down thoroughly.

When cool, frost with Cream Cheese Frosting if you like.

CREAM CHEESE FROSTING

This is one of those frostings that seems to disappear on its way to the cake, simply because it's so darn hard to keep from tasting it to death. It's very creamy and deliriously delicious.

$1\frac{1}{2}$ cups (7 oz, 200 g) confectioner's (icing)
  sugar
$\frac{1}{2}$ teaspoon pure vanilla extract

$\frac{1}{8}$ teaspoon salt
4 tablespoons cream cheese, softened
$1\frac{1}{2}$ tablespoons butter, softened

Blend all the ingredients together and beat until smooth. You can either frost the cooled cake as usual or you can warm up the frosting a wee bit and pour it over the cake like a glaze.

ANGEL FOOD CAKE
MAKES A 10 IN (25 CM) TUBE CAKE

While reading Maya Angelou's gripping autobiographical series, I came across a remark that jolted me back to a tender reminiscence of my own childhood. She wrote that one could always tell when there'd been a death, because somebody would be in the kitchen, baking, in the middle of the day. This is so true. It has always been our custom to bestow foods, and various articles of necessity upon a bereaved family during their time of sorrow.

This habit dates back directly to African tribal customs and is still a common practice amongst our people today. A wide variety of gifts are given, and there is always an outstanding array of cakes and pies on hand. Perhaps this natural sweetening helps to soften the emotional turmoil of a time of mourning. Angel food cakes are particular favorites for post funeral feasting.

$1\frac{1}{2}$ cups egg whites (from about 12 large
  eggs)
$\frac{1}{4}$ teaspoon salt
$1\frac{1}{2}$ teaspoons cream of tartar
1 cup (4 oz, 120 g) sifted cake flour

2 cups (8 oz, 250 g) fine white (caster)
  sugar
2 teaspoons pure vanilla extract
1 teaspoon almond extract
Rum-Butter Glaze (optional – see below)

Preheat your oven to 300°F (150°C, gas 2).

Beat your egg whites along with the salt until they are nice and frothy, then add in the cream of tartar and continue to beat until stiff peaks form but the egg whites are still moist.

Now sift your flour and sugar together four times, then carefully fold them into the egg whites, about $\frac{1}{4}$ cup (3 oz, 90 g) at a time, until completely absorbed. Gently and carefully fold in your flavorings with easy slow movements. Then gently cut down through your cake batter with several strokes of a knife. This eliminates any nasty air pockets.

Turn the batter out into an ungreased 10 in (25 cm) tube pan and bake in the oven for 50 minutes, then turn off the heat and leave your cake in the oven for 10 minutes longer. The cake is done if it springs back when you press it lightly with your fingers; if it isn't ready, turn the oven back on at 300°F (150°C, gas 2) and give it a few minutes longer.

Invert the pan on a wire cooling rack, but don't shake the cake out yet. Let it cool completely. Then and only then, remove the pan very carefully – with the touch of an angel.

This cake is so feather-light that you may want to eat it just as it is; but the following light glaze is perfect for it.

Rum-Butter Glaze

The quantities given here are for glazing the top only. If you want to cover the complete cake as in the picture on pages 130–1, make double quantities and glaze the top when the mixture is hot, then let the glaze cool slightly until it is thick enough to spread on the sides.

$\frac{1}{3}$ cup ($2\frac{1}{2}$ oz, 75 g) butter
2 cups ($9\frac{1}{2}$ oz, 290 g) confectioner's (icing) sugar

1 tablespoon rum (or 1 teaspoon rum flavoring)
2–3 tablespoons boiling water

Melt your butter in a saucepan over low heat and let it brown slightly – not too dark, just a hint of color. Use a wooden spoon to blend in the sugar and rum until smooth. Stir in the water just 1 teaspoon at a time, stopping when you reach a smooth pouring consistency. Immediately but gently spread the hot glaze over the cake, smoothing it out quickly with a knife dipped in hot water. Some glaze will trickle down the sides but don't worry, the effect is quite decorative.

The All-American Brownie

MAKES 12–18 SQUARES

Brownies are uniquely American and original in their texture and taste: rich and moist, chocolaty and chewy, nutty and fudgy, falling deliciously somewhere between a cookie, a cake, and a candy. Beware if you've only had store-bought brownies, because real home-made ones are very much richer. So don't pig out. And never over-bake.

4 oz (120 g) unsweetened or semisweet chocolate
$\frac{1}{3}$ cup ($2\frac{1}{2}$ oz, 75 g) butter
2 large eggs
1 cup (8 oz, 250 g) sugar

1 teaspoon pure vanilla extract
$\frac{3}{4}$ cup (3 oz, 90 g) sifted all-purpose flour
$\frac{1}{4}$ teaspoon salt
1 cup (4 oz, 120 g) coarsely chopped walnuts

Preheat your oven to 350°F (180°C, gas 4).

Melt the chocolate and butter in the top half of a double boiler over hot water.

Allow it to cool down a spell while you beat the eggs. Now add the sugar, chocolate and butter mixture, and vanilla to the eggs. Blend well.

Sift your flour and salt together, add to the batter and blend again. Throw in the nuts and stir well.

Butter a 9 × 9 in (23 × 23 cm) square or an oblong 8 × 12 in (20 × 30 cm) pan and spread your batter evenly in it. Bake in the oven for about 25 minutes.

When done, the slab will feel dry to the touch and almost but not completely firm. It will also begin to come away from the sides of the pan. Remove it from the oven at once and leave to cool in the pan on a wire rack for about 15 minutes. Cut into 2 in (5 cm) squares. Just watch the faces around your table light up at the taste.

Rich CHRISTMAS COOKIES

MAKES ABOUT 5 DOZEN COOKIES

My late Uncle Mozie used to love it when I got out the flour and the cookie gun. He loved my Christmas cookies as much as I loved baking them.

1 cup (8 oz, 250 g) butter
$\frac{2}{3}$ cup ($5\frac{1}{2}$ oz, 160 g) sugar
2 large eggs, well beaten

$1\frac{1}{2}$ cups (6 oz, 175 g) sifted all-purpose flour
1 teaspoon pure vanilla extract

Preheat your oven to 375°F (190°C, gas 5).

Cream your butter until light, then slowly add the sugar, beating until very light and fluffy. Add the well beaten eggs and vanilla. Pour on your flour and blend well.

Drop the mixture by the teaspoonful onto a well greased baking sheet and spread thinly with a knife dipped in cold water, or put it into a cookie gun (or forcing bag) and shoot different shapes onto the baking sheet.

Bake in the oven until the edges are brown, about 8 minutes for each batch. Remove the cookies from the baking sheet as soon as they are done, and cool on wire racks.

You can decorate your cookies with blanched raisins, nuts, or different colored sugars or sprinkles before they go into the oven.

PICKLES AND DRINKS

*T*hese few recipes are the icing on the cake, so to speak. They are just those little extras that the soul food cook puts on the table to show that she knows a thing or two about settin' a mean scene.

LILLIE-MAE JOHNSON'S WATERMELON RIND PICKLES

MAKES ABOUT 2 QUARTS (1¾ UK QUARTS, 2 L)

Lillie-Mae is one of my pinochle-playing partners over in East Orange, New Jersey. She is not only an accomplished card player, but quite a formidable cook as well. One of her specialties is pickling, a skill she learned while growing up in Richmond, Virginia. Here is her sweet and spicy recipe for watermelon rind pickles.

8 cups (3 lb, 1.5 kg) firm watermelon rind, trimmed and cubed (see below)
2 quarts (1¾ UK quarts, 2l) limewater (2 teaspoons calcium hydroxide or calcium oxide dissolved in cold water – but see note)
2½ cups (1 pint, 600 ml) cider vinegar
1 cup (8 fl oz, 250 ml) water, more only if necessary

4 cups (2 lb, 1 kg) sugar
2 tablespoons ground allspice
6 in (15 cm) cinnamon stick, broken into pieces
1 tablespoon whole cloves
Mason (Kilner) jars

Scoop out or cut away all of the red flesh of the watermelon. Slice off all the dark green outer skin, leaving only the white rind. Cut the rind into 1 in (2.5 cm) cubes until you have 8 cups (3 lb, 1.5 kg).

Throw the cubed rind into the limewater in a large enamel or nonstick (not bare metal) pot and let it stand at room temperature for 4 hours.

Drain off the limewater and rinse the rind in fresh cold water. Leave it to soak for 20 minutes, then rinse again with fresh cold water. Do this at least 3 times, then cover with fresh cold water and bring to a boil. Turn down the heat and simmer until the rinds are fork tender, about 10 minutes. When done, remove them from the pot and leave to drain.

Mix the vinegar, water, sugar, allspice, cinnamon stick, and cloves together in the pot and bring to a boil. Lower the heat and simmer until the sugar is dissolved. Add the rinds and bring back to boiling, with additional water if there is not enough liquid to cover the rinds. Simmer the rinds for 10 or 15 minutes, or until they are clear and tender. Meanwhile sterilize the jars and seals with boiling water.

Pack the rinds into hot sterilized jars, using a slotted spoon so that you don't get any of the spices into the jar (unless you want them in). After packing the jars, pour syrup almost to the top, leaving just under $\frac{1}{4}$ in (5 mm) at the top of each jar. Seal tightly and store in a dark cool place.

NOTE   Use calcium hydroxide (slaked lime) if possible. Calcium oxide (quicklime) is corrosive until thoroughly wetted. If using this, wear rubber gloves and a plastic apron, and stand well back when adding it to the water. If you get the dry powder on your skin, rinse at once with plenty of water.

C.J.'S PICKLED PEACHES

MAKES ABOUT $1\frac{1}{2}$ QUARTS ($1\frac{1}{4}$ UK QUARTS, 1.5 L)

Clarissa's pickled peaches are just plain fabulous. Cousin C.J. says they are a must beside a bowl of pinto beans or collard greens. She peels the peaches first, but you can leave the skin on if you prefer.

1 generous cup (8 oz, 250 g) light brown sugar
1 cup (8 oz, 250 g) white sugar
4 cups ($1\frac{3}{4}$ pints, 1 l) cider vinegar

1 tablespoon pickling spices
2 lb (1 kg) firm ripe peaches, peeled, pitted, and halved or thickly sliced
Mason (Kilner) jars

Dissolve the sugars in the vinegar in a large enamel or nonstick (not bare metal) pot. Bring to a boil, then add the spices and peaches. Simmer for 30 minutes or until the peaches are tender. Meanwhile, sterilize the jars with boiling water.

Put the peaches in the jars, cover with syrup, and seal tightly. Store in a cool dark place. If you intend to serve them immediately, cool to room temperature, then cover and refrigerate for at least 2 hours.

PICKLED BEANS

MAKES ABOUT $1\frac{1}{2}$ QUARTS ($1\frac{1}{4}$ UK QUARTS, 1.5 L)

This versatile recipe may be used for pickling fresh or dried beans. You can also make a luxurious and delectable salad with these pickled beans.

2 lb (1 kg) fresh string or wax beans, or 1 lb (500 g) dried kidney or pinto beans
about 1 quart ($1\frac{3}{4}$ UK pints, 1 l) cider vinegar (you may need more)

$\frac{1}{2}$ cup (4 oz, 120 g) sugar (for above amount of vinegar)
1 teaspoon salt (ditto)
Mason (Kilner) jars

If you are using dried beans, wash them thoroughly and discard any discolored or damaged ones. Put them in a pot, pour boiling water over them to cover, put the lid on the pot, and leave for 3 hours. Then drain the beans, cover with fresh water, and cook them until tender but not mushy – test by piercing them with a toothpick.

If using fresh beans, trim them as necessary, wash them, break them into pieces about 1 in (2.5 cm) long, and boil until tender but still firm.

While your beans are cooking, sterilize the jars and seals with boiling water. Add the sugar and salt to your cider vinegar and heat this in another pan so that it is just boiling by the time the beans are done. Pack the beans into the jars. Cover them completely with your hot vinegar – if necessary, boil up some more with added sugar and salt in the same proportions. Seal the jars tightly and store in a dark cool place.

*F*RUIT PUNCH

MAKES ABOUT 50 SMALL CUPFULS

This is a refreshing cold non-alcoholic punch. It was much too hot to use sherbet in the photo on pages 130–1. We couldn't even find any ice left in all of East Orange, New Jersey, on that blistering August day in the searing summer of 1988.

2 cups (16 fl oz, 500 ml) water for syrup, plus another 3 quarts (2½ UK quarts, 2 l), some of which can be sparkling if you like

2 cups (1 lb, 500 g) sugar

2 cups (16 fl oz, 500 ml) strong tea, made with about 3 teabags

2 cups (16 fl oz, 500 ml) fresh orange juice

1 cup (8 fl oz, 250 ml) fresh lemon juice

2 cups (16 fl oz, 500 ml) other fruit juice (white grape, pineapple, cranberry, or whatever you like)

1–2 quarts (1¾–3½ UK pints, 1–2 l) ginger ale

1 pint (16 fl oz, 500 ml) lemon-lime sherbet (sorbet) (optional)

Use 2 cups (16 fl oz, 500 ml) water and the sugar to make a syrup. Boil it until it thickens, then leave to cool. Make up your tea. Remove the teabags after 5 minutes and leave the tea to cool.

When ready to serve, pour all your ingredients into a large punchbowl containing plenty of ice. Pour in the sparkling water (if used) and the ginger ale last. At the final moment, if you like, add the sherbet. Spoon it in with an ice-cream scoop to make decorative islands of color, or just plop it in the center.

*I*CED TEA

Iced tea is a real favorite of my Uncle Frankie, who now lives with Uncle Thomas in Germantown, Pennsylvania. When we were home visiting last summer, Uncle Frankie asked the twins and me if we would like some iced tea. Well, I forgot myself for a moment and said quite casually but with much dignified British aplomb, 'Yes, we'd love a spot of tea.' Uncle Frankie said, 'We ain't got no spots here, but you can have some tea if you like.' Everyone roared with laughter at my foolishness, while the twins looked on in amazement because a spot of tea sounded absolutely normal to them. My American family! They sure know how to nuke a body and in one fell swoop. That was the last time I dared to use a British accent in America, at least around my family, that is.

1 teabag for every 2 persons (no one in my family uses loose tea leaves but I suppose if you use a compact container for the leaves, it could be possible)

cold water
sugar to taste
lemon wedges (optional, but I use them everytime)

Uncle Frankie puts his teabags in a pitcher or pot with the tags hanging over the side and pours boiling water over them. The tea needs to be two or three times the normal strength, so figure on about 1 cup (8 fl oz, 250 ml) water to each two or three bags used. Let the bags steep for about 5 minutes.

Remove the teabags, fill with cold water, and slowly add sugar to taste until it's just the right sweetness for you. Some like it tart and some like it really sweet. Serve over ice cubes in tall glasses, with lemon wedges. Remember that when the ice melts, it will weaken the tea considerably.

NOTE I usually add the juice of a freshly squeezed lemon to each pitcher as well as a few ice cubes, and sometimes I garnish each glass with an orange wedge instead of lemon. It depends on my mood or, more honestly, what's in the fridge. Some people prefer to use mint leaves.

FRESH LEMONADE
MAKES ABOUT 2 QUARTS (1¾ UK QUARTS, 2 L)

When the humidity's killing you and it's one hundred degrees in the shade with not a piece of shade in sight, the tart sweet taste of ice-cold lemonade is as refreshing a treat as you could ever wish to find. I remember many a night when I lay beside a big old window fan with a tall glass at my side, all the while trying in vain to keep the mosquitoes from devouring me. Down South, even in cool weather, there would be a big pot filled with lemonade and covered with muslin. We would dip in with the ladle from the well. For some reason, it always tasted better that way.

6 large thin-skinned lemons
1 cup (8 oz, 250 g) sugar

about 8 cups (1¾ quarts, 2 l) cold water

Roll the lemons on a hard surface to loosen the juice. Cut them in half and squeeze out the juice. Strain it into a large pitcher. Add the sugar and 1 cup (8 fl oz, 250 ml) water. Use a wooden spoon to mix until all of the lemon pulp is crushed. Add the remaining water and stir until the sugar is dissolved.

Taste, and adjust the sugar or water. You may also need more lemon juice – it all depends on your individual tastebuds. Some people like tart lemonade and some people prefer it really sweet. I usually throw in a few slices of lemon for color. Serve in tall glasses over ice cubes.

C·J.'S FOX GRAPE WINE

MAKES 12 QUARTS (9½ UK QUARTS, 12 L) WINE

Here's Cousin Clarissa Johnson's recipe for fox grape wine. I hear she won a bottle of pink champagne at the county fair for her efforts.

(Readers outside the States won't be able to get fox grapes. You can use any tart grapes, though the taste will be different. They must be fresh, because fermentation is carried out by the yeast which forms a bloom on the skin.)

1 gallon (7 lb, 3.5 kg) stemmed ripe fox grapes
12 lb (6 kg) sugar

4 × 1 gallon (3½ UK quarts, 4 l) wide-mouth jugs

Sterilize the jugs with boiling water. Wash the grapes, leaving skins on. Divide equally between the jugs. Dissolve the sugar in 4 quarts (3½ UK quarts, 4 l) cold water. Divide the sugar water equally among the jugs. Fill to within 6 or 8 in (15–20 cm) of the top with more water. Cover the tops of the jugs with cheesecloth, tie with string, and leave them in a cool dark place for 6 weeks.

Strain your wine through cheesecloth two or three times. Then pour it into 12 sterilized quart containers, filling them right to the top, seal tightly, and store in a dark cool place until needed.

EGGNOG PUNCH

MAKES 24–30 SMALL CUPFULS

Eggnog has been a traditional Christmas to New Year's celebratory drink for as long as I can remember. Whenever family or friends stop by to say hello, or to exchange presents, they're always greeted at the door with a cup of fresh eggnog from the big punchbowl. People inevitably remark on how potent it is compared to someone else's up the road.

Don't worry about the kids – I always make an alcohol-free children's batch so that they can enjoy it as much as the grown-ups do.

12 large egg yolks
2 cups (1 lb, 500 g) sugar
1 cup (8 fl oz, 250 ml) dark rum
1 cup (8 fl oz, 250 ml) bourbon (or other) whiskey
8 large egg whites
½ teaspoon salt
6 cups (1¼ quarts, 1.5 l) heavy (double) cream

2 tablespoons pure vanilla extract
freshly grated nutmeg
2–4 cups (16 fl oz–1½ pints, 500 ml–1 l) liquor of your choice (optional, but powerful)
2 cups (16 fl oz, 500 ml) milk (optional and only for thinning)

Beat your egg yolks together with the sugar until thick and lemon-colored. Continue beating while you pour in the rum and whiskey. This is the basic nog. Cover and refrigerate for several hours or until well chilled. The chilling will get rid of the eggy taste.

My Dad (with the pipe) and his best childhood buddy, Charlie Sifford. As boys they taught themselves to play golf, using sticks and marbles. In spite of many adversities, they both became professional golfers as adults, regularly touring the major circuits. My Dad has enough trophies around the house to sink a bad biscuit and still plays golf every single day after a 5 am country breakfast, and he gets together with Charlie at least once a year to reminisce about the old days and share a glass or two of home-made brew.

Beat the egg whites and salt until soft peaks form. In another bowl, beat the cream until stiff, then stir in the vanilla. Pour the nog into a large punchbowl. Fold in the whipped cream, then the egg whites. Chill for another hour.

Now the eggnog is ready for tasting. Ah ha! Now you know why it's called eggnog punch — as it warms up your innards it packs a walloping punch. You can throw in up to 4 cups additional liquor or you can add 2 cups milk if you want to thin the eggnog. Just before serving, top with a sprinkling of freshly ground nutmeg. Happy holidays!

MINT JULEP

Now, if I was speakin' the gospel truth, I'd have to be admittin' that never in all my born days have I seen a person of color delicately sippin' on a mint julep. We folks stuck to the makin' of these drinks in the back kitchens of the old plantations while the white folks were a-doin' their Southern hospitality bit.

Howessenever, I reckon mint juleps deserve a small place in dis here book so we can drink together to the passin' of the old plantation South — may it lay to rest forever.

For each glass

3 sprigs fresh mint
1 tablespoon confectioner's (icing) sugar
1 teaspoon white sugar
1 tablespoon very warm water

4 fl oz (120 ml) bourbon whiskey
dash of Angostura bitters
crushed ice

Wash the mint sprigs. Set one aside for decoration. Shake the water from the others and coat them with confectioner's sugar. Put these in a chilled julep mug (or a tall glass) and crush them with a muddler or a spoon. Let it stand for a few minutes, then discard the mint leaves.

Stir the white sugar into very warm water until dissolved, then pour this into the mug. Pack the mug with finely crushed ice. Slowly pour on the bourbon and Angostura. Stir until the glass is frosty. Garnish with a large sprig of fresh mint hanging decoratively over the side, and serve immediately.

*F*URTHER READING

BEARD, James, *James Beard's American Cookery*, Little, Brown, 1972

DARDEN, Norma Jean and Carole, *Spoonbread and Strawberry Wine*, Doubleday, 1978

DUPUY, Chachie, *New Orleans Home Cooking*, Macmillan, 1985

Ebony: Pictorial History of Black America, Johnson Publishing, 1971

EGERTON, John, *Southern Food*, Alfred A. Knopf, 1987

FOGEL, Robert William and Engermann, Stanley L., *Time on the Cross: The Economics of American Negro Slavery*, Wildwood House, 1974

GENOVESE, Eugene D., *Roll, Jordan, Roll: The World the Slaves Made*, Pantheon Books, 1974

GROSVENOR, Vertamae Smart, *Vibration Cooking, or The Travel Notes of a Geechee Girl*, Doubleday, 1970

HUGHES, Langston and Meltzer, Milton, *Black Magic: A Pictorial History of the Negro in American Entertainment*, Prentice-Hall International, 1967

JEFFRIES, Bob, *Soul Food Cookbook*, Bobbs, 1970 (quoted in Egerton)

JONES, Evan, *American Food: The Gastronomic Story*, E.P. Dutton, 1975; second edition, Random House, 1981

JOYNER, Charles, *Down by the Riverside: A South Carolina Slave Community*, University of Illinois, 1984

KANE, Joseph Nathan, *Famous Facts*, H.W. Wilson, 4th edition, 1981

LITTLEFIELD, Daniel C., *Rice and Slaves*, Louisiana State University, 1981

MENDES, Helen, *The African Heritage Cookbook*, Macmillan, 1971

MICKLER, Ernest Matthew, *White Trash Cooking*, Jargon Society, Winston-Salem, North Carolina, 1986

PRUDHOMME, Paul, *Chef Paul Prudhomme's Louisiana Kitchen*, William Morrow, 1984

RANDOLPH, Mrs Mary, *The Virginia House-Wife*, Plaskitt & Cugle, 1824; reprinted with commentaries by Karen Hess, University of South Carolina Press, 1984

ROBERTS, Leonard E., *The Negro Chef Cookbook*, 1960

SOKOLOV, Raymond, *Fading Feast*, Farrar, Straus, & Giroux, 1982

THOMPSON, Terry, *Cajun-Creole Cooking*, HP Books, 1986

THORNE, John, *Beans & Rice*, Jackdaw Press, 1981

TURNBLOW, Grover Dean and Raffet, Lloyd Andrew, *Ice Cream*

USHERWOOD, Stephen, *Food, Drink and History*, David & Charles, 1972

WHITCOMB, Ian, *After the Ball*, Allen Lane, 1972

INDEX